# THE southwest COOKBOOK

SOUTHERN LIVING
PROGRESSIVE FARMER

Favorite Recipes Press © MCMLXXII
Library of Congress Catalog
Card Number 73-186662

# contents

# preface

The Southwest has always had an aura of drama. People love to dream of the heroic taming of this territory and the romance of cowboy life on the range. Even today regional natives are regarded as a unique breed of people with a strong love for adventure and a special gusto for active outdoor life.

The cookery of the Southwest is part of this concept. There is something rousing about the Old Southwestern call of "Come and get it!" and the image of rugged, sun-burned cowboys clustering around the chuck wagon for steaming coffee and chunky stew. The many Mexican dishes adopted by Southwesterners have made the cookery even more exciting. They lend fiery hot zest to a ranch hand's diet of beef and biscuits. And the bustle of a barbecue finds a natural home in the Southwest among these outdoor lovers.

*The Southwest Cookbook* captures and presents to you the spirit of this regional cuisine. You'll find recipes for cowboy favorites like stews and breads, for Mexican dishes, and for barbecued foods. There are also recipes for appetizers, salads, casseroles, beverages, and desserts with all the lively flavor unique to Southwestern cookery.

This cookbook brings you *all* the excitement of the Southwest and its cuisine. From our kitchens to yours, welcome to the wonderful world of cooking — Southwestern style!

From the South has come one of America's richest and most varied regional cuisines, Southwestern cookery. Southwestern cookery is a lively hodge-podge of chuck wagon fare, Mexican-style cooking, and barbecued foods. The natural bounty and yield of the land — wild game, fish and shellfish, fruits and vegetables — also contribute to the richness of Southwestern cookery. Unlike all of America's other regional cuisines, here is one that cannot be neatly defined. Perhaps it is the most diverse regional cookery of which America can boast.

## CHUCK WAGON FARE

Since the 1830's the cattle industry has dominated the Southwest, and probably beef has contributed more to shaping Southwestern cookery than

# DEVELOPMENT OF THE

# southwest cuisine

any other food. The Texas Longhorn played the most important part in the development of the cattle industry and the substantial chuck wagon fare associated with it.

The Texas Longhorn was the descendent of Spanish steers brought to the New World in the sixteenth century. After the American Civil War, more than six million Longhorns roamed the Texas plains. These animals were lean, sturdy, and disease resistant. They required little water during the long, hot, dry, months and on the seemingly endless drives to the railroad cattle yards. Later, meatier breeds of cattle like the Black Angus, Shorthorn, and Hereford replaced the Longhorn.

The chuck wagon was an animal-drawn vehicle that carried the cowboys' food and cooking utensils on the cattle drives to the railroad yards. Predictably, chuck wagon fare was founded on beef, of which there was plenty. From chuck wagon cookery emerged famous Cowboy Stew, variously known as Son-of-a-Gun, Boss Man, or Supervisor Stew. Beef was slaughtered young in the Southwest, and ranch hands were reluctant to discard any parts of the slain animal. Tasty and hearty Cowboy Stew included the tongue, liver, heart, sweetbreads, and marrow gut of calves. The marrow gut, or tube connecting the two stomachs of the animal, was the essential ingredient that provided the distinctive flavor of the dish.

Today Cowboy Stew remains a regional specialty. And the influence of early ranch hands is still evident in the Southwest, for you'll find many other Southwestern stews that are made from various parts of steer.
In the cattleman's West, biscuits were the favorite accompaniment to beef. In fact, the earliest cowboy cook probably created the forerunner of the modern biscuit. When he traveled alone, he liked to go light and fast; he also

liked to eat well. So before bedding down the night of a journey, he would toss flour, salt, and baking powder into a sack and fasten the sack onto his horse's saddle. To prepare hot and filling biscuits the next day, he simply added water to the mixture, heated grease in a skillet over his fire, and dropped the batter into the sputtering grease. Sometimes "lick" or syrup was poured over the biscuits to satisfy any hunger for sweets.

Later spoon bread and corn bread was introduced to the Southwestern cowboy by settlers moving westward from the East. Soon these breads were being cooked in the heavy Dutch ovens of the chuck wagon. The cowboy learned to love them as much as he did his own original biscuits.

Ranch hands always demanded steaming hot coffee with beef and biscuits. Legend has it that the coffee had to be strong; usually black; and, if a horseshoe, railroad spike, or iron wedge wouldn't float on top, the coffee was hardly fit to drink! Many modern Southwesterners still claim to apply this test to coffee before drinking it.

## MEXICAN INFLUENCE

It didn't take long for alert, old-time ranch hands to sniff the aroma of spicy Mexican food from south of the border. Once exposed to it, Southwesterners quickly inherited from their Mexican neighbors a love for the tang of hot food. Many Mexican dishes became firmly established in Southwestern cookery and today help define this cuisine.

Most of these dishes developed from the fusion of Mexican Indian with Spanish food customs. When the Spanish explorer Cortez landed in Mexico in the sixteenth century, he discovered a sophisticated Indian cuisine. It consisted of savory meat dishes, seasonings, confections, and pastries. The Indians used herbs, onions, garlic, fruit, and honey in their cookery, and they relied on the region's abundant game and fish as mainstays of their diet. Indian cooking styles were influenced by the Spanish conquerors, and from the union emerged the characteristic dishes that later became so much a part of Southwestern cookery.

Today Mexican *frijoles* are standard daily food in the Southwest and appear on many dining tables as regularly as bread. Frijoles mean pinto beans to Southwesterners. The name "pinto" is derived from the spots of brown which characterize the bean. When cooked, the pinto bean loses its spots and the whole surface turns a faded brown. This little bean is tough and requires boiling, simmering, mashing, and frying before it is edible. The favorite version is *frijoles refritos*, or refried beans. Frijoles not eaten at one meal are simply recooked for the next meal. Some Southwesterners claim that the beans taste better with each frying!

Regional cooks also prepare *tortillas*, round, flat thin bread made from ground corn and water and baked on a griddle until soft and tender; *enchiladas*, tortillas rolled around a meat or cheese filling and served hot with a sauce; *empanadas*, consisting of dough wrapped around a ground meat or chopped fruit filling; *tacos*, tortillas folded over a filling, usually one of ground beef, grated cheese, and shredded lettuce; *tamales*, steamed corn husks wrapped around a meat, cheese, or sweet filling; *guacamole*, highly seasoned mashed avocado served as a dip or used as a salad dressing; *sopapillas*, pastry-light bread fried in hot fat and served with butter, honey, confectioners' sugar, or syrup; and many other dishes of Mexican origin.

Tortillas, used in some of the foods mentioned above and in many other Mexican dishes, are an important part of the Mexican cookery that Southwesterners have inherited. Tortillas are called the bread of Mexico. They are prepared from *masa*, or flour which is made from ground corn. Mexican Indians prepared tortillas over 3000 years ago from native corn growing in their country. Today, tortilla factories mass produce these corn cakes, using the same ingredients as the early Indians: corn, powered lime, and water.

Because of its Spanish name, chili or chili con carne is believed to be Mexican in origin. Actually, chili con carne was first made in the Southwest from local ingredients: coarse red peppers, wild marjoram, and beef. The fiery zest of chili, however, shows strong Mexican influence. There are many popular versions of chili con carne, and some recipes call for beans. But many Southwestern natives violently object to having beans in their chili. They don't need beans to enjoy chili as a satisfying main course!


## THE BARBECUE

The origin of barbecuing as a method of cooking is uncertain. The word "barbecue" is probably derived from the Spanish "barbacoa," which refers to the raised frame or platform on which meats are roasted in parts of Central and South America. Certainly barbecuing goes back as far as the early American Indians. In seventeenth century Virginia, barbecuing was a favorite method of meat preparation. Virginians gathered together socially to roast hogs outdoors over the coals. With increased westward expansion the custom spread throughout the South and eventually into the Southwest.

Today barbecuing is a specialty of the Southwest. Some outsiders claim that Southwesterners will barbecue any food. This may or may not be true, but beef and poultry roasted outdoors over an open fire are two regional favorites. The Southwest is especially famous for its barbecued spareribs.

Southwesterners will also find in almost any event a chance to hold a barbecue. Whether it's the first day of spring or an important political victory, you'll see them grilling their favorite foods outdoors.


## GAME AND FISH

In addition to chuck wagon fare, Mexican cookery, and the barbecue, Southwestern cuisine has been influenced by the natural bounty and yield of the land. This regional cookery boasts recipes for the wild game that animate Southwestern woods, valleys, and mountains; freshwater fish that swim in lakes, rivers, and streams; and saltwater fish and shellfish that abound in the Gulf of Mexico.

The Southwest is one of the nation's best hunting grounds for large game animals like deer, elk, and antelope. Small game animals are found here, too, especially squirrel, rabbit, raccoon, and porcupine. Game birds — quail, dove, duck, goose, pheasant, pigeon — are plentiful. Wild turkey from Rio Grande country is particularly favored in the Southwest.

Favorite freshwater fish include trout, bass, perch, crappie, and catfish. Accessible from Gulf waters are king mackerel, flounder, red snapper, and many more kinds of fish. Shellfish such as crabs, shrimp, oysters, and lobsters are available, too. With Louisiana next door, many Creole recipes for seafood, especially gumbo recipes, have become part of Southwestern cookery. With bread and salad, seafood gumbos make a much welcomed full-coarse meal in the Southwest. And, of course, barbecued fish always wins a brand of approval.

### FRUITS AND VEGETABLES

The Rio Grande Valley produces some of the nation's biggest and choicest avocados, grapefruits, watermelons, cantaloupes, figs, and oranges. Plums, strawberries, and dewberries ripen in other parts of the Southwest. In western Colorado, peaches and pears are especially abundant from late August to early September. As expected, fresh fruit recipes, especially those for desserts, are popular all other the Southwest. Nuts are also used in Southwestern cookery. Pecans, walnuts, and hickory nuts are native favorites.

Southwesterners also grow and enjoy many vegetables, including turnip, collard, and mustard greens; radishes; onions; tomatoes; potatoes; peas; celery; squash; cabbage; cucumbers; okra; spinach; yams; beans; and corn. Some of these vegetables were cultivated by the American Indians of the Southwest long before colonization. Their productive field and garden crops consisted of yams, beans, squash, tomatoes, potatoes, onions, and corn. Like the Indians before them, Southwesterners today especially love husked ears of corn roasted until tender over hot coals. Cooked black-eyed peas, fresh in spring and summer months, are also Texas specialties. Texans eat them on New Year's Day for good luck, and all the rest of the year for good dining! Texans say that their gardens grow the best black-eyed peas in the nation.

The richness and variety of Southwestern cookery can best be understood by the many recipes in the following pages. These recipes are representative of every facet of this regional cuisine. There are recipes for the "man's fare" of the Old Southwest, characteristic Mexican dishes, barbecued foods, and the natural yield of the land.

# MEASURES, SUBSTITUTIONS AND EQUIVALENTS

## MEASURES

3 tsp. = 1 tbsp.
2 tbsp. = 1/8 c.
4 tbsp. = 1/4 c.
8 tbsp. = 1/2 c.
16 tbsp. = 1 c.
5 tbsp. + 1 tsp. = 1/3 c.
12 tbsp. = 3/4 c.
4 oz. = 1/2 c.
8 oz. = 1 c.
16 oz. = 1 lb.
1 oz. = 2 tbsp. fat or liquid
2 c. fat = 1 lb.

2 c. = 1 pt.
2 c. sugar = 1 lb.
5/8 c. = 1/2 c. + 2 tbsp.
7/8 c. = 3/4 c. + 2 tbsp.
1 oz. butter = 2 tbsp.
1 lb. butter = 2 c. or 4 sticks
2 pt. = 1 qt.
1 qt. = 4 c.
A few grains = less than 1/8 tsp.
Pinch = as much as can be taken
   between tip of finger and thumb
Speck = less than 1/8 tsp.

## SUBSTITUTIONS

Try 1 cup minus 2 tablespoons all-purpose flour as a substitute for 1 cup cake flour.

Add 1/4 teaspoon baking soda and 1/2 cup buttermilk to equal 1 teaspoon baking powder. The buttermilk will replace 1/2 cup of the liquid indicated in the recipe.

Use 3 tablespoons dry cocoa plus 1 tablespoon butter or margarine instead of 1 square (1 ounce) unsweetened chocolate.

Make 1 cup of sour milk by letting stand for 5 minutes 1 tablespoon lemon juice or vinegar plus sweet milk to make 1 cup.

Substitute 1 package (2 teaspoons) active dry yeast for 1 cake compressed yeast.

Mix 1/2 cup evaporated milk with 1/2 cup water (or 1 cup reconstituted nonfat dry milk with 1 tablespoon butter) to replace 1 cup whole milk.

Substitute 1 tablespoon prepared mustard for 1 teaspoon dry mustard.

Use 1/8 teaspoon garlic powder instead of 1 small pressed clove of garlic.

Substitute 2 tablespoons of flour for 1 tablespoon of cornstarch to use as a thickening agent.

Make catsup or chili with 1 cup tomato sauce plus 1/2 cup sugar and 2 tablespoons vinegar.

## EQUIVALENTS

1 lemon makes 3 tablespoons juice
1 lemon makes 1 teaspoon grated peel
1 chopped onion, medium, makes 1/2 cup pieces
1 pound unshelled walnuts makes 1 1/2 to 1 3/4 cups shelled
1 pound unshelled almonds makes 3/4 to 1 cup shelled
8 to 10 egg whites make 1 cup
12 to 14 egg yolks make 1 cup
1 pound shredded American cheese makes 4 cups
1 cup unwhipped cream makes 2 cups whipped

**Arroz con pollo** (ah ROS kawn pool yo) — A dish of Mexican origin made with chicken, rice, seasonings, and often tomatoes; Spanish for "rice with chicken."

**Chile or chili** (CHIL ee) — A hot pungent pepper used to flavor many Mexican and Southwestern foods; also, the shortened name for chili con carne.

**Chiles rellenos** (CHIL eez ray YAH noz) — A dish of Mexican origin usually consisting of strips of green pepper wrapped around cheese, dipped in batter, and fried; Spanish for "stuffed peppers."

**Chili con carne** (CHIL ee kon KAHR nee) — A dish of Southwestern origin usually made from ground beef, minced chilies or chili powder, tomatoes, and sometimes kidney beans; Spanish for "chili with meat."

**Chili con queso** (CHIL ee kon KAY so) — Chili made with grated cheese; Spanish for "chili with cheese."

# glossary

**Enchilada** (en chee LAH dah) — A food of Mexican origin consisting of a tortilla rolled around a highly seasoned meat or cheese filling and usually served hot with a zesty sauce.

**Frijoles** (free HOH lays) — Beans, especially pinto beans, a staple of Southwestern cookery.

**Frijoles refritos** (free HOH lays ray FREE toz) — Beans usually cooked with tomatoes and seasonings, then fried, mashed, and fried again; Spanish for "refried beans."

**Gazpacho** (gahz PAH cho) — A soup of Spanish origin usually made with tomatoes, peppers, garlic, olive oil, vinegar or lemon juice, and spices; it can be garnished with cucumber slices and bread crumbs and is served cold.

**Guacamole** (gwah kah MO lay) — Hotly seasoned mashed avocado served as a cocktail dip or used as a salad dressing.

**Jalapeno** (ha la PEEN yo) — A species of hot pepper or chili.

**Pinto beans** — Dull brownish-white beans covered with brown spots, from which they derive their name; they are native to the Southwest and used extensively in Southwestern cookery.

**Sopapillas** (so pa PEE yahz) — A light fat-fried bread of Mexican origin served as a hot bread with butter or as a sweet with honey, syrup, or confectioners' sugar.

**Taco** (TAH ko) — A food of Mexican origin consisting of a fried tortilla folded over any one of a variety of fillings, especially a ground beef filling with a lettuce and grated cheese garnish.

**Tamale** (tah MAH leh) — A food of Mexican origin consisting of steamed corn husks filled with a seasoned meat, cheese, or sweet stuffing.

**Tortilla** (taw TEE ah) — A flat, thin round bread made of ground corn and water and baked on a griddle until soft and tender.

The cookery of the Southwest is so varied that nearly every herb and spice on your shelf is important in the characteristic recipes of the region. Listed below are some of the most often used seasonings and the foods they complement. Herbs, spices, blends, and seeds that are especially associated with Southwestern cuisine are starred (*).

*Allspice* — Flavors beef, especially pot roasts, meat loaves, and beef stews; lamb and ham; fish and shellfish; tomatoes, squash, turnips, and spinach; pea soup; fruits; baked goods; mincemeat; relishes; preserves, gravies, tomato sauces, pickling liquids; puddings.

*Anise Seed* — Used in many foods of Mexican origin; beef stew and veal stew; chicken and duck dishes; fruit compotes and fillings; cookies, coffee cakes, sweet rolls; candies; beverages.

# seasonings

## USED IN SOUTHWEST COOKERY

**Barbecue Spice* — Sprinkled on steaks, spareribs, hamburgers, chicken, and other meats while grilling.

*Basil* (Sweet Basil) — Added to meat pies; lamb chops; beef soups and stews; shellfish; peas, beans, cucumbers; squash, spinach, and potatoes; vegetable soups; tomato dishes.

*Bay Leaves* — Flavor meat, poultry, game, and fish stews; tomatoes, onions, green beans, squash, potatoes; vegetable soups; chili con carne; sauces.

**Chili Powder* — Seasons many Mexican-style foods, including chili con carne, tamale pie, arroz con pollo, enchilada sauce; ground meats; vegetable or meat soups; barbecue sauce and seafood cocktail sauce; gravies.

*Cinnamon* — Added to squash; stewed fruits and broiled grapefruit; baked goods; sopapillas; sweet tamale fillings; chocolate desserts and drinks; spiced beverages; custards and puddings; pickles; mincemeat.

*Cloves* — Flavor meat stews, beef soups, meat gravies; squash and beans; vegetable soups; fruit desserts; baked goods; hot beverages; puddings; mincemeat.

*Coriander Seed* — Added to rice and meat dishes of Mexican origin; roasted pork; frankfurters; mixed green salads; buns, biscuits, cookies, cakes, pastries.

**Cumin Seed* (Cominos) — Used in meat loaves and hamburgers; chili con carne and hot tamales; beans; soups and stews; rice; breads; tomato sauces.

*Dill Seed* — Enhances lamb chops and lamb stew; broiled mackerel, salmon, and halibut; peas, beans; turnips; vegetable soups; potato salads and cole slaw; canapes; sauces.

**Garlic* (Salt, Powder, Flakes, Minced) — Seasons roasts; chili con carne; soups; salads and salad dressings; gravies; barbecue sauce.

*Ginger* — Highlights meats, especially beef, lamb, and veal; poultry; fish; glazed squash; bean, onion, or potato soups; pears and other fruits; baked goods such as cakes, cookies, and pies; puddings; conserves.

*Mace* – Added to fish and fish sauces; cream sauces for vegetables; fruit cobblers and pie fillings; all chocolate dishes; stuffings; pickles; preserves.

*Marjoram* — Seasons roast beef, lamb, veal, mutton, pork, chicken, duck, and goose; baked and broiled fish; lima beans, green beans, peas, and spinach; soups and stews; stuffings.

*Mustard* (Dry) — Flavors meats; poultry; fish; lima beans; soups; gravies; barbecue sauce and other sauces.

*Nutmeg* — Added to beef and chicken dishes; fish cakes and casseroles; squash, green beans, boiled potatoes, spinach, corn on the cob; berries with cream; pears; baked goods; doughnuts; beverages; puddings and custards.

**Onion* (Salt, Powder, Flakes, Minced) — Highlights meats, especially steaks, roasts, and hamburgers; vegetables; soups and stews; salads; gravies; barbecue sauce.

**Oregano* — Used in dishes of Mexican origin, including hot tamales, enchiladas, chili con carne; all beef dishes; roast lamb; tomato dishes; onions, potatoes, string beans; fish and shellfish salads; soups; omelets and boiled eggs; sauces and gravies.

*Paprika* — Garnishes and flavors meats; chicken; fish and shellfish; vegetables, including baked potatoes; salads and salad dressings; eggs; canapes.

*Parsley* — Highlights meats; fish; vegetable dishes; salads; soups; sauces.

*Pepper, Black and White* — Seasons any food.

**Pepper, Red* (Cayenne) — Added to very hot, fiery dishes such as chili con carne; barbecued meats; hot sauces; deviled eggs; canapes; pickles; relishes.

**Saffron* — Famous in arroz con pollo and other rice dishes; baked goods.

*Sesame Seeds* — Sprinkled over green beans and asparagus and baked on rolls, breads, and buns.

*Tarragon* — Flavors meats, especially veal and lamb; chicken; seafood; egg dishes; tomato dishes; salads; sauces; pickles.

*Thyme* — Enhances creamed chipped beef; lamb, veal, and chicken stews; fish soups and chowders; beans, peas, spinach; vegetable soups; salad dressings; sauces.

# salads and appetizers

Long tall Texans probably scowled when their women first served them salads and appetizers. Their idea of right eating meant more substantial man-sized fare like beef and potatoes, and they hardly considered these two new food versions worthwhile. But the region's vegetables, fruits, and fish just lent themselves to salads and appetizers. Even the most robust and stubborn Southwesterner couldn't resist them for long!

One of the first salads to win its way into Southwestern hearts was cole slaw. The first settlers in this region grew cabbage, and crisp crunchy slaws were natural developments. And what cowboy could turn his broad back on a salad made from native pinto beans? Other Southwestern vegetables were converted into salads, too, and today regional favorites include corn, spinach, and green bean salads.

Salads were also made from abundant native fruits like grapefruit and peaches, and from Gulf shellfish such as crab and shrimp. The same kinds of vegetables, fruits, and fish used in salads went just as naturally into appetizers. Avocado dip, made from locally grown fruit and fiery hot seasonings, immediately won the Southwestern brand of approval, as did pickled shrimp and crab meat dip.

You'll find recipes for these and other salads and appetizers in the following pages. If they could please skeptical six-footers, they're sure to win you over, too!

## SPRING SALMON SALAD

| | |
|---|---|
| 1/2 c. sour cream | 8 cherry tomatoes, sliced |
| 1/3 c. mayonnaise | 1 avocado |
| 1/3 c. milk | Lemon juice |
| 1 tbsp. vinegar | 4 hard-cooked eggs, sliced |
| 1/2 tsp. curry powder | 1   1-lb. can salmon, drained |
| 1/4 tsp. hot sauce |      and flaked |
| Salad greens | |

Blend the sour cream, mayonnaise, milk, vinegar, curry powder and hot sauce in a small bowl. Refrigerate for about 1 hour to blend flavors. Tear the salad greens into pieces and toss with sliced tomatoes in a bowl. Spoon half of the salad dressing over tomato mixture and toss thoroughly. Peel the avocado and slice in wedges. Sprinkle with lemon juice. Arrange the avocado and eggs on greens mixture and mound salmon in middle of salad. Spoon remaining dressing over salmon. Garnish with additional cherry tomato slices. 4-6 servings.

## CRAB SALAD DELUXE

| | |
|---|---|
| 3 c. shredded lettuce | 1/2 c. grated hard-cooked egg yolks |
| 6 cooked artichoke hearts | 1 c. Thousand Island  dressing |
| 3 c. flaked crab meat | |

Place the lettuce on 6 plates. Place an artichoke heart, cup side up, on lettuce on each plate and fill with crab meat. Sprinkle with egg yolks and top with the Thousand Island dressing.

*Mrs. Dick De Bray, Mobile, Alabama*

## OLIVE-SHRIMP MOLD

| | |
|---|---|
| 4 env. unflavored gelatin | 1/3 c. mayonnaise |
| 1 lge. can tomato juice | 1 1/2 lb. cleaned cooked |
| 1/4 tsp. hot sauce | shrimp |
| 1/2 tsp. chili powder | 1 c. finely chopped stuffed |
| 1/2 tsp. paprika | olives |
| 1/2 c. lemon juice | 1 c. finely chopped celery |
| 1  8-oz. package cream | Sliced stuffed olives |
| cheese, softened | |

Sprinkle the gelatin over 2 cups tomato juice in top of a double boiler. Add remaining tomato juice, hot sauce, chili powder and paprika and cook over boiling water until gelatin dissolves, stirring constantly. Add the lemon juice and cool. Combine the cream cheese and mayonnaise in a bowl and beat until smooth. Add tomato juice mixture gradually and mix well. Chill until slightly thickened. Chop the shrimp and fold into the cream cheese mixture. Fold in the chopped olives and celery and turn into a 2 1/2-quart mold. Chill until firm. Unmold and garnish with sliced olives. 6-8 servings.

*Mrs. Evelyn V. Taylor, Atlanta, Georgia*

## SHRIMP SALAD

| | |
|---|---|
| 1/2 c. mayonnaise | 2 tbsp. chopped dill pickle |
| 1/4 c. catsup | 1 tsp. garlic salt |
| 4 hard-cooked eggs, grated | 1/4 tsp. hot sauce |
| 1/2 c. chopped celery | Salt and pepper to taste |
| 2 tbsp. chopped onion | 4 lb. cleaned cooked shrimp |
| 2 tbsp. chopped green pepper | Paprika |

Combine the mayonnaise and catsup in a bowl and stir in eggs. Add remaining ingredients except shrimp and paprika and mix well. Stir in the shrimp and refrigerate for at least 4 hours. Serve on lettuce and sprinkle with paprika. 6 servings.

*Mrs. Joseph J. Finley, New Orleans, Louisiana*

## MACARONI-TUNA SALAD

| | |
|---|---|
| 3 tsp. salt | 1 c. diced cucumber |
| 2 qt. boiling water | 2 tbsp. pickle relish |
| 1  4-oz. package elbow | 1 tbsp. chopped parsley |
| macaroni | 1/4 c. mayonnaise |
| 1  7-oz. can grated tuna, | 1/8 tsp. pepper |
| drained | |

Add 2 teaspoons salt to boiling water in a saucepan and add macaroni gradually. Cook, stirring occasionally, until macaroni is tender, then drain. Rinse with cold water and drain. Place in a bowl. Add the tuna, cucumber, pickle relish, parsley, mayonnaise, remaining salt and pepper and toss lightly. Chill. Serve on lettuce or watercress. 4-6 servings.

*Mrs. Simon L. Bean, Clifton, Texas*

### JACKSTRAW TUNA SALAD

| | |
|---|---|
| 1 c. grated carrots | 1/2 c. salad dressing |
| 1 c. sliced celery | 1 tbsp. prepared mustard |
| 1/4 c. minced onion | 1 c. canned shoestring |
| 1 c. tuna | potatoes |

Combine the carrots, celery, onion, tuna, salad dressing and mustard in a bowl and chill. Stir in potatoes just before serving. 6 servings.

*Fern McCraw, Waurika, Oklahoma*

### APRICOT SALAD

| | |
|---|---|
| 1  1-lb. 1-oz. can apricots | Juice of 1 orange |
| 1 sm. package lemon gelatin | 3/4 c. chopped nuts |
| Juice of 1 lemon | 1 sm. package cream cheese |

Drain the apricots and reserve juice. Place 1 cup reserved juice in a saucepan and bring to a boil. Add the gelatin and stir until dissolved. Mix the lemon juice and orange juice and add enough remaining apricot juice to make 1 cup liquid. Stir into gelatin mixture. Mash the apricots through a sieve and add to gelatin mixture. Chill until slightly thickened. Add the nuts. Shape cream cheese into small balls and place in individual molds. Fill molds with gelatin mixture and chill until firm.

*Mrs. Elizabeth Temple, Gulfport, Mississippi*

### COTTAGE WALDORF SALAD

| | |
|---|---|
| 4 med. tart apples | 1 tbsp. lemon juice |
| 1/2 c. raisins | 1/2 c. cottage cheese |
| 1/4 c. chopped walnuts | 1/2 c. sour cream |
| 1 tbsp. sugar | |

Quarter and core the apples, then cut into cubes. Combine the apples, raisins and walnuts in a bowl. Sprinkle with the sugar and lemon juice and toss lightly. Blend the cottage cheese and sour cream in a bowl and pour over the apple mixture. Toss lightly until all ingredients are well coated.

*Mrs. E. R. Bobo, Ft. Payne, Alabama*

### FRESH GRAPE SALAD

| | |
|---|---|
| 2 tbsp. butter | 2 lb. fresh green grapes |
| 1 tbsp. flour | 1 sm. can pineapple |
| 1 1/2 c. milk | 1 c. chopped pecans |
| 1 c. miniature marshmallows | |

Melt the butter in a saucepan and blend in the flour. Add the milk gradually and cook, stirring constantly, until thickened. Add the marshmallows and stir until melted. Pour the sauce over the grapes in a bowl. Stir in the pineapple and pecans and chill.

*Mrs. W. B. Harvey, Bryan, Texas*

## CHILLED FRUIT PLATTER

| | |
|---|---|
| 1 fresh pineapple | 1 fresh lime |
| 1 fresh cantaloupe | 1 fresh banana |
| 1 lge. fresh orange | Fresh strawberries |
| 1 fresh honeydew melon | 1 fresh pomegranate, halved |
| 1 fresh avocado | 1 fresh papaya, halved |
| Juice of 1 fresh lemon | |

Cut the top and bottom from the pineapple. Remove pulp of pineapple in 1 piece with a sharp knife, leaving pineapple shell. Cut the pulp lengthwise into strips. Place the pineapple shell in center of a platter and place pineapple strips in the shell. Peel the cantaloupe and cut in wedges. Peel and slice the orange. Peel the honeydew melon and cut in wedges. Cut the avocado in half, remove seed and sprinkle avocado with half the lemon juice. Cut the lime in half and slice the cut side in serrated design. Peel and slice the banana and sprinkle with remaining lemon juice. Arrange all the fruits around the pineapple and garnish with sprigs of fresh mint.

*Photograph for this recipe on page 14.*

## MOLDED MANDARIN ORANGE SALAD

| | |
|---|---|
| 2 sm. packages lemon gelatin | 2  11-oz. cans mandarin oranges |
| 1 c. boiling water | 1 pt. whipped cream |
| 1 c. cold water | 2 bananas, diced |
| 1  12-oz. can frozen orange juice | 1/2 pt. mayonnaise |
| | 1 sm. can crushed pineapple |

Dissolve the gelatin in boiling water in a bowl. Add cold water and orange juice and stir until orange juice is thawed. Drain the oranges and stir into gelatin mixture. Pour into a ring mold and refrigerate until set. Mix the whipped cream, bananas and mayonnaise. Drain the pineapple and fold into banana mixture. Place in center of salad. Garnish with maraschino cherries and mint, if desired, and serve at once.

*Mrs. Joe Henery Nuckols, Dumas, Arkansas*

## SPICED PEACH SALAD

| | |
|---|---|
| 1 env. unflavored gelatin | 6 whole cloves |
| 1 tbsp. sugar | 1 stick cinnamon |
| 1/4 tsp. salt | 1/4 c. vinegar |
| 1  1-lb. can sliced peaches | |

Mix the gelatin, sugar and salt in a saucepan. Drain the peaches, reserving the syrup. Add enough water to the reserved syrup to make 1 1/4 cups liquid. Add to the gelatin mixture, then add the cloves and cinnamon and simmer for about 10 minutes. Strain, then stir in vinegar. Chill until thickened, then fold in the peaches. Pour into a 2-cup mold or individual molds and chill until firm. Unmold on lettuce leaves.

*Thelma Farmer, Summers, Arkansas*

## WALNUT JEWEL SALAD

1 sm. can crushed pineapple
1 pkg. pineapple gelatin
1 c. hot water
1/2 tsp. salt
1 c. chopped cranberries

1/2 c. diced celery
1/2 c. chopped California
　walnuts
Walnut halves

Drain the pineapple and reserve syrup. Add enough water to reserved syrup to make 1 cup liquid. Dissolve the gelatin in hot water in a bowl. Add the salt and pineapple syrup mixture and mix well. Chill until slightly thickened. Fold in remaining ingredients except walnut halves. Turn into a 1-quart mold and chill until firm. Unmold onto a bed of lettuce and decorate with walnut halves.

### Honey Creme Salad Dressing

1　3-oz. package cream cheese
1/4 tsp. salt

2 tbsp. honey
1/4 c. sour cream

Place the cream cheese, salt, honey and sour cream in a small bowl and whip with electric mixer until smooth.

## GRAPEFRUIT SALAD

1 grapefruit
1 sm. package lemon gelatin

1/2 c. hot water
1/2 c. cold water

Cut the grapefruit in half crosswise, then remove the pulp and juice from the rinds. Strain and reserve 1/2 cup juice and all of the pulp. Dissolve the gelatin in hot water in a large bowl, then add the cold water and grapefruit juice. Add sugar to taste, if desired. Chill until partially set. Add the grapefruit pulp, then pour into the grapefruit shells. Place the shells in a pan and chill until firm. Cut the grapefruit halves in half lengthwise.

Dressing

| | |
|---|---|
| 1  3-oz. package cream<br>     cheese | Juice of 1 lime |
| 1 tbsp. honey | 1/2 c. whipped cream |

Soften the cream cheese at room temperature, then combine the cream cheese, honey and lime juice in a bowl until smooth. Fold in the whipped cream and refrigerate for 4 hours. Serve with grapefruit.

*Ruth Averitt, Lexington, Kentucky*


## BEET SALAD RING

| | |
|---|---|
| 1  1-qt. can diced beets | 2 tbsp. horseradish |
| 2 sm. packages lemon gelatin | 1 tsp. grated onion |
| 1/3 c. vinegar | 1 c. chopped celery |

Drain the beets, reserving the liquid. Add enough water to the reserved liquid to make 3 cups liquid. Pour into a saucepan and bring to a boil. Pour over the gelatin in a large bowl and stir until dissolved. Add the vinegar, horseradish and onion and chill until slightly thickened. Add the beets and celery and pour into a 9-inch ring mold. Chill until firm.

*Mrs. Noah Elam, Index, Kentucky*


## CABBAGE SLAW

| | |
|---|---|
| 1 lge. head cabbage | 2 tbsp. brown sugar |
| 6 green onions with tops | 2 tbsp. vinegar |
| Salt and pepper to taste | 1/2 tsp. celery seed |
| 3/4 c. mayonnaise | 6 slices bacon |
| 3/4 c. sour cream | |

Shred the cabbage and chop the green onions, then combine in a large bowl. Add the salt, pepper, mayonnaise, sour cream, brown sugar, vinegar and celery seed and mix well. Fry the bacon until crisp, then drain and crumble. Stir into the slaw just before serving. 12 servings.

*Mrs. O. F. Crider, Leander, Texas*


## CORN SALAD

| | |
|---|---|
| 1 No. 2 can whole kernel<br>     corn | 1 sm. green pepper, chopped |
| 1 pimento, chopped | 1 sm. cucumber, chopped |
| 1 sm. onion, chopped | 1/2 c. French dressing |

Drain the corn. Combine all the ingredients in a bowl and toss to mix well. Serve in lettuce cups. 4 servings.

*Mrs. Judy Brumley, Kyle, Texas*

## FRESH SPINACH SALAD

| | |
|---|---|
| 1 lb. fresh spinach | 1/2 c. Italian salad |
| 8 slices bacon |    dressing |
| 4 hard-cooked eggs, chopped | Salt to taste |
| 1/4 c. chopped green onions | |

Remove the large stems from the spinach and tear into small pieces. Fry the bacon until crisp, then drain and crumble. Combine the spinach, eggs and bacon. Add the onions and toss lightly. Add the dressing and salt just before serving.

*Mrs. Jane Davis, Corpus Christi, Texas*

## GREEN BEAN SALAD

| | |
|---|---|
| 1 can cut green beans | 1/4 c. sliced green pepper |
| 1 can cut wax beans | 1/2 c. vinegar |
| 1 can kidney beans | 1/2 c. sugar |
| 1/2 c. diced onions | 1/3 c. oil |
| 1/2 c. diced celery | Salt and pepper to taste |
| 1/2 c. chopped pimento | |

Drain the beans. Combine all ingredients in a bowl and chill overnight to blend flavors.

*Ida F. Simerick, Morgantown, West Virginia*

## PINTO PATIO SALAD

| | |
|---|---|
| 2 1/2 c. cooked pinto beans | 1 tsp. chili sauce |
| 4 hard-cooked eggs, chopped | 1 tsp. mustard |
| 1 c. cubed American cheese | 1/4 tsp. salt |
| 1/4 c. chopped onion | 1 tsp. pepper |
| 2 tsp. salad dressing | |

Combine the beans, eggs, cheese and onion in a large bowl and chill. Mix remaining ingredients and stir into the bean mixture. Garnish with crumbled crisp bacon and minced parsley. 4-6 servings.

*Mrs. Jessie Barton, Belen, New Mexico*

## INDIAN SUMMER SALAD

| | |
|---|---|
| 4 c. cooked whole kernel | 2 sprigs of fresh dill |
|    corn, drained | Avery Island Dressing |
| 1 c. sliced celery | Salad greens (opt.) |
| 1 c. diced tomatoes | Onion rings |
| 1/4 c. chopped green pepper | |

Combine the corn, celery, tomatoes, green pepper and 1 sprig of dill in a bowl. Pour the Avery Island Dressing over top and marinate in refrigerator for about 1 hour, stirring occasionally. Place in a bowl lined with salad greens, if desired. Garnish with onion rings and remaining dill. 4-6 servings.

## Avery Island Dressing

3/4 c. salad oil
1/4 c. vinegar
1 tsp. sugar
1/2 tsp. salt

1/2 tsp. paprika
1/2 tsp. dry mustard
1/4 tsp. hot sauce

Combine all ingredients in a bowl and beat with rotary beater until blended.

*Photograph for this recipe on page 121.*

## OLIVE AND VEGETABLE SALAD

Whole pimento-stuffed olives
1 lge. cucumber
2 tomatoes
1 lge. onion
2 hard-boiled eggs
1 lge. green pepper

6 slices bacon
1 c. bread cubes
Olive oil
1 c. slivered toasted almonds
Vinegar and oil dressing

Slice 1 cup olives. Dice the cucumber and tomatoes and drain. Chop the onion, eggs and green pepper. Cook the bacon in a skillet over low heat until crisp. Drain and crumble. Cook the bread cubes in small amount of oil in a saucepan until brown, stirring constantly. Place the sliced olives, cucumber, tomatoes, onion, eggs, green pepper, bacon, bread cubes and almonds in a salad bowl. Serve topped with the vinegar and oil dressing and whole olives.

## BEEF SALAD

1 lb. boneless stew meat
6 hard-boiled eggs
1 stalk celery
Pickles to taste

Green onions to taste
1/2 c. mayonnaise
Salt and pepper to taste

Cook the stew meat in boiling, salted water until tender, then drain. Grind in a food chopper with the eggs, celery, pickles and onions. Place in a bowl. Add the mayonnaise, salt and pepper and mix well.

*Mrs. Delia G. Sanson, Wildsville, Louisiana*

## HOT BEEF SALAD

1 sm. head lettuce
1 tomato, diced
1 onion, chopped
1 lb. ground beef

1  8-oz. can tomato sauce
2 tbsp. chili powder
Salt and pepper to taste
1 med. package corn chips

Tear the lettuce into small pieces, then combine with the tomato and onion in a bowl. Cook the ground beef in a frypan until brown. Add the tomato sauce, chili powder, salt and pepper and cook until blended. Pour the ground beef mixture over the lettuce mixture and toss until well mixed. Add the corn chips and toss lightly. Serve immediately. 6 servings.

*Mrs. Allen Daggett, Houston, Texas*

## JELLIED BEEF LOAF

1 env. unflavored gelatin
1/4 c. cold water
3/4 c. boiling tomato juice
1/4 c. vinegar
1/2 tsp. salt
1/2 c. mayonnaise

2 c. diced cooked beef
1/4 c. diced celery
1/4 c. chopped pimento
1/4 c. chopped green pepper
1/4 c. minced onion
2 hard-cooked eggs, sliced

Soften the gelatin in the cold water in a cup, then stir into the hot tomato juice until dissolved. Stir in the vinegar and salt and chill until thickened. Combine remaining ingredients except eggs. Arrange the egg slices along bottom and sides of a loaf pan. Combine the gelatin and beef mixtures and mix thoroughly. Turn into the loaf pan and chill until firm. Serve on lettuce. 6 servings.

*Mrs. Miles Nelson, Bryson, Texas*

## BUFFET HAM RING

1 can tomato soup
2 tbsp. unflavored gelatin
1  3-oz. package cream cheese
2 tbsp. lemon juice

1 tbsp. grated onion
1/2 c. mayonnaise
2 tbsp. prepared mustard
2 c. ground cooked ham

Combine the soup and 3/4 cup water in a saucepan and heat through. Remove from heat. Soften the gelatin in 1/2 cup water. Add to soup mixture with cream cheese and beat with rotary beater until smooth. Cool. Add lemon juice, onion, mayonnaise, mustard and ham and mix well. Pour into ring mold rinsed with cold water and chill until firm. Unmold on lettuce leaves and garnish with hard-cooked eggs and stuffed olives. 8-10 servings.

*Mrs. Burt Decker, Cumberland, Maryland*

## BUFFET LAMB SUPREME WITH CURRIED MAYONNAISE

| | |
|---|---|
| **3 apples** | **Curried Mayonnaise** |
| **Lemon juice** | **Golden seedless raisins,** |
| **2 c. cherry tomatoes** | **plumped in dry sherry** |
| **6 c. julienne-style cooked lamb** | **Shredded coconut** |
| **2 c. diagonally sliced celery** | **Chopped avocado, sprinkled** |
| **2 lge. green peppers, cubed** | **with lemon juice** |
| **2 Spanish onions, sliced** | **Chopped hard-cooked eggs** |
| **Salad greens** | **Cooked crisp bacon, crumbled** |

Core and slice the apples and sprinkle with lemon juice. Stem the tomatoes and cut in halves. Arrange the lamb, apple slices, celery, tomatoes, green peppers and onions in a bowl lined with salad greens. Serve topped with Curried Mayonnaise, raisins, coconut, avocado, eggs and bacon.

### Curried Mayonnaise

| | |
|---|---|
| **3 c. mayonnaise** | **1 tbsp. curry powder** |
| **2 sm. cloves of garlic,** | **6 tbsp. lemon juice** |
| **crushed** | |

Blend the mayonnaise with the garlic, curry powder and lemon juice and chill well.

### MOLDED LAMB SALAD

| | |
|---|---|
| 2 sm. packages lemon gelatin | 1/2 c. vinegar |
| 2 c. hot water | 1/4 c. prepared horseradish |
| 2 c. cold water | 1 tbsp. salt |
| 1/2 c. sliced olives | 1/2 tsp. Worcestershire |
| 4 c. diced cooked lamb | sauce |
| 1/2 c. chopped green pepper | |

Dissolve the gelatin in the hot water, then add the cold water. Make a design with some of the olives in a 5 x 9-inch pan and cover with a thin layer of gelatin. Chill until firm. Chill remaining gelatin until partially set. Add the lamb, green pepper, vinegar, horseradish, salt, Worcestershire sauce and remaining olives and mix well. Pour over design in loaf pan and chill until firm. Garnish with tomato slices. 10 servings.

*Mrs. J. J. Brackin, Simmesport, Louisiana*

### PORK SALAD DELIGHT

| | |
|---|---|
| 2 c. diced cooked pork | 1/2 tsp. pepper |
| 1/2 c. diced cucumbers | 2 tbsp. mustard |
| 1/4 c. diced green pepper | 2 tbsp. evaporated milk |
| 1/4 c. diced red pepper | Pimento strips |
| 1/2 c. diced celery | 2 hard-cooked eggs, sliced |
| 1/2 tsp. salt | Sliced stuffed olives |

Combine the pork with the vegetables in a bowl and add salt and pepper. Blend the mustard and milk and add to the pork mixture. Toss to mix well. Serve on lettuce. Garnish with pimento, eggs and olives. 8 servings.

*Mrs. Mabel Watson, Bradenton, Florida*

### VEAL SALAD SUPREME

| | |
|---|---|
| 2 c. diced cooked veal | 1/2 c. cooked green peas |
| 1 c. French dressing | 1 pimento, minced |
| 1 c. chopped celery | 1/2 c. chopped pecans |
| 1/2 c. diced pineapple | 2 tbsp. mayonnaise |

Marinate the veal in the French dressing in a bowl for 30 minutes, then drain. Stir in remaining ingredients and chill. Serve on lettuce. 4 servings.

*Mrs. J. A. Satterfield, Fort Worth, Texas*

### EXOTIC LUNCHEON SALAD

| | |
|---|---|
| 3 c. mayonnaise | 2 lb. seedless grapes |
| 1 tsp. curry powder | 2 c. sliced celery |
| 2 tbsp. soy sauce | 2 c. slivered almonds |
| 2 qt. chopped cooked chicken | 1 lge. can pineapple chunks |
| 1  20-oz. can water chestnuts | 2 cans mandarin oranges |

Mix the mayonnaise with curry powder and soy sauce in a large bowl. Add the chicken and mix. Drain and slice the water chestnuts and add to chicken mixture. Add the grapes, celery and almonds. Drain the pineapple and oranges and add to chicken mixture. Mix well and chill for several hours. Serve on lettuce. 12 servings.

*Mrs. Paul B. MacMichael, Lubbock, Texas*

## CRUNCHY CHICKEN SALAD

| | |
|---|---|
| 2 c. green grapes | 1/2 c. mayonnaise |
| 3 c. diced cooked chicken | 1 tbsp. tarragon vinegar |
| 1 c. chopped cashews | 1 tbsp. sugar |
| 2/3 c. sesame seed | 1 tsp. salt |
| 1 tbsp. butter | White pepper to taste |
| 1 c. sour cream | |

Mix the grapes, chicken and cashews in a bowl. Saute the sesame seed in butter in a saucepan until brown, then cool. Add remaining ingredients and mix well. Pour over chicken mixture and toss well. 10 servings.

*Mrs. Howard Boydstun, Hot Springs, Arkansas*

## PICKLE-CHICKEN SALAD

| | |
|---|---|
| 2 c. diced cooked chicken | 1 tbsp. sweet pickle liquid |
| 1/2 c. chopped sweet mixed | 1/4 tsp. salt |
|    pickles | 1/8 tsp. pepper |
| 1/2 c. diced celery | 1/8 tsp. tarragon leaves |
| 2 tbsp. chopped onion | Crisp salad greens |
| 1 tbsp. chopped pimento | Tomato slices |
| 1/3 c. mayonnaise | |

Combine all ingredients except the salad greens and tomato slices and toss lightly. Chill. Serve on salad greens in a bowl and garnish with tomato slices. 3-4 servings.

## OVEN CHICKEN SALAD

| | |
|---|---|
| 4 c. chopped cooked chicken | 1 tbsp. instant minced onion |
| 2 c. thinly sliced celery | 1 tsp. salt |
| 2 c. toasted bread cubes | 1 tbsp. lemon juice |
| 1 c. mayonnaise or salad dressing | 3 drops of hot sauce |
| 1/3 c. evaporated milk | 1/4 lb. grated American cheese |
| 1/4 c. drained pickle relish | 1/4 c. whole blanched almonds |

Mix all ingredients except cheese and almonds and place in 6 individual greased baking dishes. Place on a large cookie sheet and sprinkle cheese and almonds on top. Bake at 450 degrees for 10 to 12 minutes or until cheese is melted and almonds are toasted. 6 servings.

*Mrs. Earl L. Faulkenberry, Lancaster, South Carolina*

## CANNED CORNED BEEF PATE

| | |
|---|---|
| 1 sm. onion, coarsely chopped | 1/2 tsp. salt |
| 1   5-oz. package fresh mushrooms, sliced | 1/2 tsp. rosemary |
| | 1/2 tsp. monosodium glutamate |
| 1/4 c. dry red wine | 1/2 tsp. dry mustard |
| 1/2 c. sour cream | 1/2 tsp. tarragon |
| 1   12-oz. can corned beef, coarsely chopped | 1/4 tsp. pepper |
| | 1 tbsp. horseradish |

Place the onion, mushrooms and wine in an electric blender container and blend until smooth. Add remaining ingredients and blend until smooth. Chill for several hours. Onion, mushrooms and corned beef may be ground fine and mixed with remaining ingredients, if desired. 1 1/2 cups.

## CHILES RELLENOS CON QUESO

| | |
|---|---|
| 1  4-oz. can whole green chilies | 2 eggs, separated |
| 1/2 lb. Monterey Jack cheese | 2 tbsp. flour |
| | Shortening |

Rinse the green chilies in cold water and cut each green chili in half lengthwise. Cut the cheese into 2 x 1/2 x 1/2-inch strips. Wrap each chili strip around a cheese strip. Beat the egg whites until stiff peaks form and fold in lightly beaten egg yolks. Fold in the flour. Dip the chilies into the egg mixture. Place in 1/2 inch hot shortening in a large skillet and cook until brown on both sides. Drain. Place on a platter.

### Spanish Sauce

| | |
|---|---|
| 1 tbsp. butter or margarine | 1 c. chicken broth |
| 1 tbsp. cornstarch | 1/8 tsp. leaf oregano |
| 1  4-oz. can taco sauce | |

Melt the butter in a small saucepan over medium heat and stir in the cornstarch. Stir in remaining ingredients gradually and cook, stirring, until mixture is thickened. Spoon over chiles rellenos.

*Photograph for this recipe on page 1.*

## CHAFING DISH MEATBALLS

| | |
|---|---|
| 2 lb. ground beef | 1 bottle chili sauce |
| 1 egg, slightly beaten | 1/2 lge. jar grape jelly |
| 1 lge. onion, grated | Juice of 1 lemon |
| Salt to taste | |

Combine the beef, egg, onion and salt in a bowl and mix well. Shape into tiny balls. Brown in a skillet. Combine remaining ingredients in a saucepan. Add the meatballs and simmer until meatballs are tender. Reheat in a chafing dish to serve.

*Mrs. Charles A. Haden, Nashville, Tennessee*

## SOMBRERO SPREAD

| | |
|---|---|
| 1 lb. ground beef | 2  8-oz. cans kidney beans |
| 1 c. chopped onion | 1 c. shredded sharp American cheese |
| 1/2 c. hot catsup | 1/2 c. sliced stuffed olives |
| 3 tsp. chili powder | |
| 3 tsp. salt | |

Brown the beef and 1/2 cup onion in a skillet and stir in the catsup, chili powder and salt. Mash the beans with liquid in a bowl, then stir into the beef mixture. Stir in the cheese. Place in a chafing dish and sprinkle with remaining onion and olives. Serve with corn chips.

*Mrs. Barbara Gravelle, Lexington, Kentucky*

## CHEESE BALL PICK-ME-UPS

| | |
|---|---|
| 1  8-oz. package cream cheese | 1/4 tsp. garlic powder |
| 1  4-oz. package bleu cheese | 1 tbsp. Worcestershire sauce |
| 1  5-oz. jar Old English | 1/8 tsp. hot sauce |
|    cheese | 1 c. parsley flakes |
| 1  6-oz. roll smoked cheese | 1 c. finely chopped pecans |
| 1 tsp. monosodium glutamate | Pretzel sticks |
| Dash of salt | |

Have the cheeses at room temperature. Place in a bowl and stir in the monosodium glutamate, salt, garlic powder and sauces. Add 1/3 cup parsley and 1/2 cup pecans and blend. Chill until easy to handle. Shape into 1-inch balls. Mix remaining parsley and pecans. Roll the cheese balls in parsley mixture and chill. Insert a pretzel stick in each cheese ball just before serving.

*Mrs. Lura Lee Davis, Sweetwater, Texas*

## CHEESE STRAWS

| | |
|---|---|
| 1/2 lb. sharp Cheddar | 1 tsp. salt |
|    cheese, grated | 1/2 tsp. red pepper |
| 1 c. butter, softened | 1 tsp. hot sauce |
| 1 3/4 c. flour, sifted | |

Blend the cheese and butter in a bowl. Stir in the flour and seasonings and mix well. Squeeze through a pastry tube in 3 1/2-inch strips onto an ungreased cookie sheet. Bake at 375 degrees until done. May be rolled out and cut in strips instead of placing in a pastry tube. 6 dozen.

*Mrs. C. R. Kamerer, Fort Worth, Texas*

## CHILI-CHEESE LOG

| | |
|---|---|
| 3/4 lb. Cheddar cheese, | 1/8 tsp. garlic salt |
|    grated | 1 1/2 tsp. Worcestershire |
| 1  3-oz. package cream |    sauce |
|    cheese, softened | 1/2 c. chopped nuts |
| 1/4 tsp. salt | Chili powder |
| 1/8 tsp. pepper | |

Mix the cheeses, salt, pepper, garlic salt and Worcestershire sauce in a bowl with an electric mixer until smooth. Stir in the nuts and shape into 2 logs. Sprinkle a heavy layer of chili powder on a sheet of waxed paper. Roll each cheese log in chili powder until coated. Wrap in waxed paper and refrigerate for 3 to 4 days to ripen.

*Mrs. Joy Noel, Farmington, New Mexico*

## AVOCADO DIP

| | |
|---|---|
| 1 lge. ripe avocado | Dash of pepper |
| 1/4 tsp. onion juice | Dash of curry powder |

Dash of cayenne pepper        1/4 tsp. salt
1 tbsp. white wine vinegar

Peel avocado and remove seed. Place in a bowl and mash until smooth. Stir in remaining ingredients. Serve with potato chips, cauliflowerets, carrot slices or cheese crackers. 1 cup.

*Mrs. Homer E. Melton, Woodlawn, Virginia*

## DEVILED EGGS

6 hard-cooked eggs, chilled      1/2 c. mayonnaise
1 tsp. prepared mustard      1/2 c. round cheese cracker
1 tbsp. chopped parsley        crumbs
1/4 tsp. salt      Paprika
1/8 tsp. pepper

Slice the eggs in half lengthwise and remove yolks. Place egg yolks in a bowl and mash. Add the mustard, parsley, salt, pepper, 1/4 cup mayonnaise and half the crumbs and blend. Fill egg whites with yolk mixture and press halves together. Dip both ends of each egg in remaining mayonnaise, then in remaining crumbs. Sprinkle with paprika.

*Mrs. Jack J. Durham, Amhurst, Texas*

## JALAPENO CHEESE DIP

2 lb. Velveeta cheese      1 garlic pod, finely
2 tbsp. flour        chopped
3/4 c. cream      1 med. green pepper, finely
2 tbsp. margarine        chopped
1 pt. cottage cheese      1 med. onion, finely
4 jalapeno peppers, chopped        chopped

Cut the Velveeta cheese into small cubes. Mix the flour and cream in a double boiler. Stir in the margarine and cheeses and cook until the cheeses melt, stirring frequently. Add remaining ingredients and cook for 10 to 15 minutes or until thick, stirring occasionally. 2 pints.

*Mrs. Stanley Horst, Houston, Texas*

## SAUSAGE BALLS

2 lb. hot country sausage      1/2 c. (packed) brown sugar
1/2 c. catsup      1 tbsp. soy sauce
1/2 c. wine vinegar      1/2 tsp. ginger

Shape the sausage into small balls. Fry in a skillet over low heat until well done, then drain on paper towels. Combine remaining ingredients in a saucepan and heat through. Add meatballs, making certain all are completely covered. Cool, then refrigerate for at least 24 hours. Reheat to serve. May be refrigerated for 4 to 5 days or frozen. 40-50 meatballs.

*Mrs. L. G. Sheets, Brunswick, Georgia*

## CRAB MEAT DIP

| | |
|---|---|
| 2  3-oz. packages cream cheese | 1/2 c. finely chopped celery |
| 3 tbsp. milk | 1 tsp. Worcestershire sauce |
| 1 tbsp. mayonnaise | 2 tsp. lemon juice |
| | 1  6-oz. can crab meat |

Soften the cream cheese in a bowl, then stir in the milk and mayonnaise. Add remaining ingredients and mix well. Refrigerate for 1 hour to blend flavors.

*Mrs. Donald C. Johnson, College Park, Maryland*

## PICKLED SHRIMP

| | |
|---|---|
| 1 lb. cleaned cooked shrimp | 1/2 tsp. dry mustard |
| 2 med. onions, cut in rings | 1/3 c. catsup |
| 3 bay leaves, broken in pieces | 1/3 c. vinegar |
| 1 c. salad oil | 1 tsp. salt |
| 2 tsp. sugar | Dash of red pepper |
| 2 tbsp. Worcestershire sauce | Dash of hot sauce |
| | 1 clove of garlic, chopped |

Place alternate layers of the shrimp, onions and bay leaves in a container. Mix remaining ingredients and pour over shrimp mixture, making certain that the sauce covers shrimp mixture. Refrigerate for 24 hours.

*Mrs. John Sawyer Barr, III, Oak Ridge, Louisiana*

## LIVER SPREAD

| | |
|---|---|
| 1 lb. sliced liver | 1/2 tsp. salt |
| 1  2-oz. jar pimentos | 1/2 pkg. onion salad dressing mix |
| 4 stalks celery | |
| 5 leeks | 2  3-oz. packages cream cheese, softened |
| 4 hard-cooked eggs | |
| 1/4 tsp. garlic salt | 1/2 c. mayonnaise |
| 1/4 tsp. pepper | Paprika |
| 1/4 tsp. celery salt | |

Place the liver in a baking pan. Bake at 375 degrees for 10 minutes. Drain and chop the pimentos. Grind the liver, celery, leeks and egg whites and place in a bowl. Add seasonings, salad dressing mix, cream cheese, mayonnaise and pimentos and mix well. Sprinkle with grated egg yolks, then paprika. 2 cups.

*Jackie Downs, Boulder, Colorado*

## CHILI CON QUESO DIP

| | |
|---|---|
| 2 cans green chilies | 1 garlic clove, pressed |
| 2 onions, chopped | 2 tbsp. cooking oil |

2 No. 2 cans tomatoes, well
   drained
1/2 tsp. salt

1/2 tsp. oregano
1 lb. Velveeta cheese,
   grated

Drain and chop the green chilies. Saute the onions and garlic in oil in a saucepan until onion is tender. Add the tomatoes, green chilies, salt and oregano and cook over low heat for about 30 minutes. Remove from heat. Add the cheese and stir until melted. Place in a chafing dish and keep warm. Serve with corn chips or crackers. 25 servings.

*Mary L. Harris, Patagonia, Arizona*

## COCKTAIL TACOS WITH STUFFED OLIVES

2  11-oz. packages frozen
   heat-and-serve cocktail
   beef tacos
2 c. red pepper relish

1 green pepper, chopped
2  4 3/4-oz. jars pimento-
   stuffed olives

Prepare the beef tacos according to package directions for crisp tacos. Open the beef tacos gently and fill with relish and chopped pepper. Arrange on a platter and garnish with olives.

# meats

When a Southwesterner thinks food, he thinks *meat*. Meat makes a hearty, solid meal and fills up the hungriest cowboy on the range. On many ranches, a big meat meal is served at midday. This is the time that four o'clock risers most need substantial fare.

Southwesterners naturally prefer thick, juicy beef steaks and roasts, but they'll admit that pork and lamb taste mighty good to a hungry man. True to their heritage of Cowboy Stew, they appreciate variety meats fixed almost any way. And there's something satisfying about eating game animals they've bagged themselves.

Number one choice of meat preparation is barbecuing. That's why you'll find this section chock full of recipes for barbecued meats, like barbecued round steak and lamb chops . . . even barbecued rabbit! But the open-minded range natives have also adopted recipes for boiling, braising, and frying meats, all of which are included right here.

Mexican influence is obvious, too, when you come to recipes for tamales and tongue-tingling enchiladas. Southwesterners seem to favor hotly seasoned ground beef wrapped in corn husks or soft baked tortillas.

But whatever the meat, whatever the method, every recipe in the following pages is guaranteed to fill up a man!

## BOILED BEEF INTERNATIONAL

| | |
|---|---|
| 2 env. beef broth mix | 1 bay leaf |
| 6 c. boiling water | 1 tsp. oregano |
| 3 sprigs of parsley | 1 tbsp. salt |
| 2 tsp. celery flakes | 1 tsp. sugar |
| Dash of hot sauce | 6 lb. boned and rolled beef |
| 4 peppercorns | 6 tbsp. butter or margarine |
| 3 med. onions, halved | 6 tbsp. flour |
| 1 tsp. monosodium glutamate | 1 c. sour cream |
| 2 garlic cloves | 1/4 c. prepared horseradish |

Dissolve the beef broth mix in boiling water in a kettle. Add the parsley, celery flakes, hot sauce, peppercorns, onions, monosodium glutamate, garlic, bay leaf, oregano, salt and sugar and bring to a boil. Add the beef and reduce heat. Simmer for about 3 hours or until beef is tender. Chill the beef in broth overnight. Remove fat from surface. Heat until beef is heated through. Remove beef to a platter and keep warm. Strain the broth and reserve 3 cups. Melt the butter in a saucepan and blend in flour. Add the reserved broth and cook over medium heat, stirring constantly, until smooth and thickened. Stir in sour cream slowly and add horseradish. Serve with beef.

*Wanda M. Argo, Knoxville, Tennessee*

## SPANISH ROAST

| | |
|---|---|
| 1   5-lb. rump roast | 1 lge. can tomatoes |
| 2 cans pimento strips, drained | 1 can tomato soup |
| 12 sm. onions | 3 soup cans water |
| 3 green peppers, cut into strips | 2 bay leaves |
| 2 stalks celery, sliced | 4 whole cloves |
| 6 sm. carrots, sliced | 2 tsp. salt |
| | 18 sm. potatoes |

Place the roast in a large roaster. Bake at 400 degrees for 30 minutes or until brown, then reduce temperature to 350 degrees. Add remaining ingredients except potatoes and cover. Bake for 1 hour and 30 minutes or until roast is almost done. Place the potatoes around roast and bake for 30 minutes longer or until roast and potatoes are tender.

*Mrs. G. Harmon English, Hickory, North Carolina*

## PATIO ROAST DELUXE

| | |
|---|---|
| 1   3 1/2-lb. rump or round roast | 1 tsp. Worcestershire sauce |
| Meat tenderizer | 1/4 c. brown sugar |
| 1   3-oz. bottle soy sauce | 1/4 c. bourbon |
| 1 tbsp. lemon juice | 1 1/2 c. water |

Sprinkle the roast with tenderizer according to package directions and let set for 30 to 45 minutes. Combine remaining ingredients and pour over roast in a bowl. Cover bowl and marinate for 3 hours. Turn the roast and marinate for 3 hours longer. Let charcoal burn for 45 minutes. Place roast on grill 5 inches from coals and cook for 30 minutes on each side, basting frequently with marinade. Slice across grain to serve. 6-10 servings.

*Anne Jolley, Columbus, Georgia*

## PARSLIED OVEN POT ROAST

| | |
|---|---|
| 2 1/2 tsp. salt | 1 bay leaf |
| 1/4 tsp. pepper | 1/2 tsp. instant minced |
| 1   4 1/2 to 5-lb. bottom |    garlic |
|    round of beef | 6 med. peeled carrots, |
| 1   1-lb. 12-oz. can tomatoes |    sliced |
| 3/4 c. dry red wine | 1 1/2 lb. zucchini, sliced |
| 1/4 c. instant minced onion | 2 c. cherry tomatoes |
| 2 tbsp. parsley flakes | |

Preheat oven to 450 degrees. Rub 1 1/2 teaspoons salt and the pepper over the beef. Place the beef, fat side down, in a Dutch oven. Bake for 50 to 60 minutes or until well browned. Drain off fat. Break up the canned tomatoes with a spoon, then mix with wine, onion, parsley, bay leaf, garlic and remaining salt. Pour over the beef and cover. Reduce temperature to 350 degrees and bake for 2 hours. Add the carrots and cover. Bake for 20 minutes. Add the zucchini and cover. Bake for 10 minutes. Prick the cherry tomatoes with a fork and add to the carrot mixture. Cover and bake for 10 minutes longer or until beef is tender. Slice the beef and serve with the vegetables. 8-10 servings.

## CHATEAUBRIAND

| | |
|---|---|
| 1  8-lb. beef tenderloin | Juice and grated rind of |
| Salt and pepper to taste |    1/2 lemon |
| Monosodium glutamate | Dash of hot sauce |
| 1 c. butter | 3 cans mushrooms, drained |

Sprinkle the tenderloin with salt, pepper and desired amount of monosodium glutamate. Cook on a grill over medium coals for 1 hour and 15 minutes, turning twice. Cook over low coals for 30 minutes longer, turning once. Melt the butter in a saucepan and stir in the lemon juice, rind and hot sauce. Let stand for 30 minutes. Add the mushrooms and heat through. Serve with the tenderloin.

*Mrs. Jack M. Campbell, Santa Fe, New Mexico*

## BEEF SHORT RIBS

| | |
|---|---|
| 4 lb. beef short ribs | 1 c. water |
| 2 tbsp. shortening | 6 carrots, quartered |
| Salt and pepper to taste | 8 sm. white onions |
| 1 onion, sliced | 1 box frozen lima beans |

Cut the beef ribs into serving pieces. Brown in shortening in a Dutch oven and sprinkle with salt and pepper. Add sliced onion and water and cover. Bake at 375 degrees for 2 hours. Add the carrots and whole onions and sprinkle with salt. Cover and bake for 30 minutes. Add the beans. Cover and bake for 30 minutes longer.

*Ethel Mae Blending, Alcolu, South Carolina*

## FOIL STEAK SUPPER

| | |
|---|---|
| 1 chuck steak, 1 in. thick | 1/2 green pepper, sliced |
| 1 env. onion soup mix | 1 med. onion, sliced |
| 2 med. potatoes, halved lengthwise | Butter or margarine |
| 3 carrots, sliced | Salt and pepper to taste |
| 2 stalks celery, sliced | |

Place the steak in center of piece of foil and sprinkle with onion soup mix. Cover with the potatoes, carrots, celery, green pepper and onion and dot with butter. Sprinkle with salt and pepper. Fold foil over, leaving a space for steam, and seal edges. Place in baking pan. Bake in 350-degree oven for about 1 hour and 30 minutes.

*Mrs. Charles Redfield, Riverdale, Georgia*

## SPANISH SWISS STEAK

| | |
|---|---|
| 1 tsp. salt | 1  2 1/2-lb. round steak, |
| 1/4 tsp. pepper |    1 in. thick |
| 1/2 c. flour | 2 tbsp. shortening |

**2 c. canned tomatoes**　　　**1/2 c. chopped green pepper**
**1/3 c. chopped onion**

Mix the salt, pepper and flour and pound into the steak. Brown in hot shortening in a skillet. Add the tomatoes, onion and green pepper and cover tightly. Bake at 350 degrees for 2 hours and 30 minutes to 3 hours. 6 servings.

*Mrs. Beryl Ingle, Dover, Oklahoma*

## MIXED GRILL

| | |
|---|---|
| **3 tsp. soy sauce** | **8 sm. sausages** |
| **1/4 c. salad oil** | **8 sm. onions** |
| **Pepper to taste** | **4 slices bacon** |
| **Grated rind of 1/2 lemon** | **2 firm tomatoes** |
| **1  1/2-lb. beef tenderloin** | **1 green pepper** |
| **1/2 lb. calf liver** | **Salt to taste** |

Mix the soy sauce, oil, pepper and lemon rind in a bowl. Cut the tenderloin into 4 slices. Cut the calf liver into 8 pieces. Place the beef, liver and sausages in soy sauce mixture and refrigerate for several hours. Parboil the onions. Roll up the bacon slices. Cut the tomatoes in thick slices and cut the green pepper in large pieces. Drain the meats and reserve marinade. Thread the meats and vegetables on 4 skewers and brush with the reserved marinade. Grill over hot coals for 4 to 5 minutes on each side, then sprinkle with salt.

## BARBECUED ROUND STEAK

| | |
|---|---|
| 1 1/2 lb. round steak, 1 1/2 in. thick | 1 tsp. paprika |
| 2 tbsp. oil or shortening | 2 tbsp. Worcestershire sauce |
| 1 clove of garlic, minced | 1/2 c. catsup |
| 3/4 c. vinegar | 1 tsp. salt |
| 1 tbsp. sugar | 1 tsp. powdered mustard |
| | 1/2 tsp. pepper |

Cut the steak across the grain into 1-inch slices. Heat the oil in a skillet and brown steak in the oil. Place steak in a casserole. Pour off oil and place remaining ingredients in the skillet. Simmer for 3 minutes and pour over the steak. Cover. Bake at 350 degrees for 1 hour. Uncover and bake for 30 minutes longer. 4 servings.

*Mrs. O. W. Schaeffer, Knoxville, Tennessee*

## CABBAGE TAMALES

| | |
|---|---|
| 1 head cabbage | 1 can tomato paste |
| 1 lb. hamburger | 1 egg |
| 1 c. rice | 1 tsp. chili powder |
| 1 sm. onion, minced | Salt and pepper to taste |
| 1 clove of garlic, minced | |

Wilt the cabbage in boiling salted water, then cool enough to separate the leaves. Combine the hamburger with the remaining ingredients and mix well. Place a small amount of the hamburger mixture in each cabbage leaf, then roll up and secure with wooden pick. Place in a skillet in a small amount of water. Cover and cook over low heat for 45 minutes.

*Mrs. L. J. Blazek, Houston, Texas*

## DO-YOUR-OWN-THING TOSTADOS

| | |
|---|---|
| 3 soft California avocados | 1 pkg. taco seasoning mix |
| 3/4 tsp. seasoned salt | 8 corn tortillas |
| 1 tbsp. lemon or lime juice | Oil |
| 1/2 c. diced green chilies | Lemon juice |
| 1/4 tsp. Worcestershire sauce | 1 c. shredded Jack cheese |
| 6 tbsp. grated onion | 1 c. shredded Cheddar cheese |
| 2 canned tomatoes, drained | 1 20-oz. can refried beans, heated |
| 2 tbsp. minced green pepper | 2 c. thinly sliced chicken |
| 1 c. vinegar | 1 sm. head lettuce, shredded |
| 1 tsp. salt | 2 tomatoes, sliced |
| 1/4 tsp. garlic powder | 1 pt. sour cream |
| 1/8 tsp. oregano | 1 sm. can ripe pitted olives |
| 1/8 tsp. cumin | Red or green pickled chilies |
| 1 lb. ground beef | |

Peel 2 avocados and mash in a bowl for guacamole. Add the seasoned salt, lemon juice, 1/4 cup green chilies, Worcestershire sauce and 2 tablespoons grated onion and mix well. Cover and chill. Place the canned tomatoes in a bowl and mash for taco sauce. Add remaining green chilies and grated onion, green pepper, vinegar, salt, garlic powder, oregano and cumin and mix well. Let stand at room temperature for 1 hour, then chill. Brown the ground beef in a skillet, stirring until crumbly, then drain off fat. Add the seasoning mix. Add the water and simmer according to seasoning mix directions. Keep warm. Fry the tortillas in small amount of hot oil until crisp. Drain on paper towels. Place in 200-degree oven to keep warm. Peel and slice the remaining avocado and sprinkle with lemon juice. Mix the cheeses and place in a bowl. Place the guacamole, taco sauce, ground beef mixture, tortillas, cheese, beans, chicken, lettuce, sliced tomatoes, sour cream, olives, pickled chilies and sliced avocado on a buffet table. Let guests assemble the tostados as desired. 8 servings.

*Photograph for this recipe on page 5.*

## OLD EL PASO TAMALES AND BEANS

| | |
|---|---|
| 1   15-oz. can tamales | Lettuce leaves |
| 1   15-oz. can refried beans | Jalapeno peppers |
| 1/2 c. shredded Cheddar | 1 pkg. tortillas |
|    cheese (opt.) | Shortening |
| Tomato wedges | Salt to taste |

Empty the tamales into a saucepan and cover. Cook over low heat for 15 minutes. Remove corn husks from tamales and place in a serving dish. Pour the sauce in the saucepan over the tamales. Place the refried beans in a small saucepan and heat through, stirring occasionally. Place in the serving dish and top with cheese. Garnish the dish with tomato wedges, lettuce and jalapeno peppers. Cut each tortilla into 6 wedge-shaped pieces and fry in small amount of hot shortening until crisp. Drain and sprinkle with salt. Serve with the tamales and beans.

## CARNE ASADA

| | |
|---|---|
| 1 c. rice | 1 red bell pepper |
| 1 onion, chopped | 1 green bell pepper |
| 1 tbsp. butter | Salad oil |
| 1 can tomatoes | 1 1/2 lb. ground chuck |
| 1 tsp. chili powder | 2 onions, sliced |
| 1/4 tsp. garlic powder | 1 head lettuce, shredded |
| Salt and pepper to taste | 2 tbsp. grated Parmesan |
| Hot sauce to taste | cheese |

Cook the rice according to package directions. Cook the chopped onion in the butter in a saucepan until soft. Add the tomatoes and cook until thickened, breaking up tomatoes with a spoon. Season with the chili powder, garlic powder, salt, pepper and hot sauce and mix well. Cut the red and green peppers in strips and saute in small amount of oil until tender-crisp. Shape the ground chuck into steaks and sprinkle with salt and pepper. Cook in a small amount of oil in a skillet to desired doneness. Place the ground chuck steaks on 4 plates and spoon the tomato mixture over the steaks. Arrange the sliced onions, pepper strips, rice and lettuce around the steaks and sprinkle the cheese on the lettuce.

*Photograph for this recipe on cover.*

## HAMBURGER WITH GUACAMOLE TOPPING

| | |
|---|---|
| 2 soft California avocados, pureed | 1 sm. peeled tomato, chopped |
| 1 tbsp. fresh lemon or lime juice | 1 tsp. seasoned salt |
| | Hot sauce to taste |
| 1 1/2 tbsp. finely grated onion | 8 thick hamburger patties |
| | 8 hamburger buns, heated |

Mix the avocados with remaining ingredients except hamburger patties and buns. Chill. Grill the hamburger patties over hot coals to desired doneness. Place on buns and top with avocado mixture. Taco sauce or diced chili pepper may be substituted for hot sauce.

*Photograph for this recipe on page 34.*

## RIO GRANDE MEAT LOAF

| | |
|---|---|
| 1   1-lb. can red kidney beans | 1/4 tsp. pepper |
| 2 lb. ground beef | 1 tsp. garlic powder |
| 3 tbsp. minced onion | 2 eggs, beaten |
| 2 tsp. salt | 1/2 c. cracker crumbs |
| 1 tsp. chili pepper | 1 c. canned tomatoes |

Drain and mash the kidney beans. Combine all ingredients thoroughly. Line a 9 x 5 x 3-inch loaf pan with foil and pack beef mixture into foil. Bake at 350 degrees for 1 hour and 30 minutes. 10-12 servings.

*Doris Sanders, Weir, Mississippi*

## ENCHILADAS

| | |
|---|---|
| 2 lb. ground beef | 1 tsp. chili powder |
| 1 can enchilada sauce | 1 pkg. flat tortillas |
| 1/2 sm. bottle catsup | Grated Cheddar cheese |
| 2 tsp. pickle relish | Chopped onion |
| 2 tsp. salt | |

Brown the ground beef in a skillet, then drain. Add 1/2 can enchilada sauce, catsup, relish, salt and chili powder and simmer for 30 minutes. Dip tortillas in remaining enchilada sauce and place in a cookie pan. Spread beef sauce 1/2 inch deep on each tortilla and cover with cheese. Place 2 teaspoons chopped onion on each enchilada. Bake in 350-degree oven until cheese melts.

*Mrs. Ronald L. Hudson, Dublin, Texas*

## BARBECUED SPARERIBS

| | |
|---|---|
| 1 fresh onion, chopped | 3 tbsp. Worcestershire sauce |
| 2 tbsp. brown sugar | 1/4 c. vinegar |
| 1 tsp. paprika | 1 c. tomato juice |
| 1 tsp. salt | 1/4 c. catsup |
| 1 tsp. dry mustard | 1/2 c. water |
| 1 tsp. chili powder | 3 lb. spareribs |
| 2 dashes of hot sauce | 1 fresh lemon, thinly sliced |

Mix the onion, brown sugar, paprika, salt, mustard, chili powder, hot sauce, Worcestershire sauce, vinegar, tomato juice, catsup and water in a saucepan and simmer for 15 minutes. Cover and set aside. Cut the spareribs into serving pieces and place on rack in a shallow baking pan. Place a lemon slice on each serving piece. Bake at 450 degrees for 30 minutes. Pour the sauce over the spareribs. Reduce temperature to 350 degrees and cover. Bake for 1 hour and 30 minutes longer, basting frequently. 6 servings.

## COMIDA MEXICANA

| | |
|---|---|
| 2 lb. bulk pork sausage | 2 c. vermicelli |
| 1 c. diced onion | 1 tbsp. chili powder |
| 1 c. diced green pepper | 1/8 tsp. comino seed |
| 2 c. tomatoes | 1 tsp. salt |
| 2 c. cream or buttermilk | |

Brown the sausage, onion and green pepper in a skillet. Add the tomatoes, cream, vermicelli, chili powder, comino seed and salt and cover. Simmer for 20 minutes.

*Paul Beeson, Cacht, Oklahoma*

## MEXICAN-STYLE PORK RIBS

| | |
|---|---|
| 3 lb. spareribs | 1 c. tomato sauce |
| 1 lge. onion, sliced | 1 tbsp. chili powder |
| Salt and pepper | 1 c. hot water |
| 1 lge. green pepper, chopped | 1/2 tsp. nutmeg |
| 1/2 tsp. oregano | 2 tbsp. flour |
| 1 clove of garlic, minced | 2/3 c. cold water |
| 1 tbsp. cider vinegar | |

Cut the spareribs in serving pieces and brown in a heavy skillet in a small amount of bacon drippings. Add the onion and cook until transparent. Place spareribs and onion in a large casserole and add salt and pepper to taste, green pepper, oregano and garlic. Mix the vinegar and tomato sauce and stir in the chili powder. Pour over spareribs and add hot water. Bake for 40 minutes at 325 degrees. Mix the nutmeg, flour and cold water and add 1/2 teaspoon salt. Stir into liquid in casserole and bake for 20 minutes longer. 4 servings.

*Mrs. J. C. Key, Charleston, South Carolina*

## PORK LOIN SUPREME

| | |
|---|---|
| 2 cloves of garlic | 2 onions |
| 2 tsp. salt | 2 carrots |
| 1 tsp. sage | 1 c. water |
| 1/2 tsp. pepper | 1/4 c. currant jelly |
| 1/2 tsp. nutmeg | 1 tsp. dry mustard |
| 1  4-lb. pork loin roast | Whole cloves |

Mash the garlic in a bowl with salt, sage, pepper and nutmeg. Rub into roast. Slice the onions and carrots and place in a shallow roasting pan. Place the roast, fat side up, on vegetables and pour water into pan. Roast in 325-degree oven for 1 hour and 30 minutes. Remove roast from oven and score the fat in crisscross pattern. Combine the jelly and mustard and spread over roast. Stud with cloves and roast for 1 hour longer. 6 servings.

*Mrs. Russell Bean, Lubbock, Texas*

## UPSIDE-DOWN HAM LOAF

| | |
|---|---|
| 1/3 c. (firmly packed) brown sugar | 2 eggs, beaten |
| 1 c. crushed pineapple, drained | 1 c. milk |
| 1 lb. ground ham | 1 c. chopped celery |
| 1 lb. ground pork | 1/4 tsp. pepper |
| 1 c. fine dry bread crumbs | Maraschino cherries |
| | Parsley sprigs |

Sprinkle the brown sugar over bottom of a greased 9 x 5 x 3-inch loaf pan and spread the pineapple over sugar. Combine remaining ingredients except cherries and parsley in a bowl, then pack into loaf pan. Bake at 350 degrees for 1 hour and 15 minutes. Unmold onto a heated platter and garnish with cherries and parsley sprigs.

*Mrs. B. D. Hunt, El Reno, Oklahoma*

## MINT-BARBECUED LEG OF LAMB

| | |
|---|---|
| 1/2 c. butter | 1/4 c. dried mint leaves |
| 1/2 c. vinegar | 1 leg of lamb |
| 1/2 c. sugar | Salt and pepper to taste |
| 1 tbsp. Worcestershire sauce | |

Combine the butter, vinegar, sugar, Worcestershire sauce and mint in a small saucepan and heat, stirring, until sugar dissolves. Set aside. Place the leg of lamb on spit of rotisserie and insert a meat thermometer. Cook for 2 hours and 30 minutes to 3 hours or to 180 degrees on meat thermometer, basting frequently with the mint mixture during last 30 minutes of cooking. Season with salt and pepper. Spoon any remaining mint mixture over the lamb when served. 8 servings.

## LAMB BALLS EN BROCHETTE

| | |
|---|---|
| 1/2 c. lemon juice | 1/2 tsp. salt |
| 1/2 c. salad oil | 1/2 tsp. garlic salt |
| 1/4 c. water | 1/4 tsp. pepper |
| 2 tbsp. dark brown sugar | 1/4 tsp. tarragon leaves |
| 1 tbsp. soy sauce | 1/4 tsp. savory |
| 1/4 tsp. ginger | 1 1/2 lb. ground lamb |
| 2 cucumbers | 12 lge. fresh pineapple wedges |
| 1  6-oz. can evaporated milk | 6 plum tomatoes |
| 1 egg, beaten | 2 cucumbers |
| 1 c. soft bread crumbs | Cooked rice |

Mix the lemon juice, salad oil, water, brown sugar, soy sauce and ginger in a bowl and set aside. Cut the cucumbers in 1/2-inch slices. Mix the undiluted milk and egg in a bowl. Add the crumbs and seasonings and let stand to soften crumbs. Add the lamb and mix well. Shape into 18 balls about 1 1/2 inches in diameter and chill for several hours or overnight. Place the lamb balls on skewers. Place on a grill 4 to 5 inches from heat and cook for 5 to 7 minutes on each side or to desired doneness, brushing frequently with the lemon sauce. Place the pineapple, tomatoes and cucumber slices on skewers and cook on the grill for 4 to 5 minutes on each side, brushing frequently with lemon sauce. Serve on rice with remaining sauce.

*Photograph for this recipe on page 2.*

## CROWN LAMB ROAST WITH APPLE STUFFING

| | |
|---|---|
| 1 crown lamb roast | 6 tbsp. butter |
| Salt and pepper | 1/2 c. pignolia nuts |
| 2 tsp. instant minced onion | 1/2 tsp. ground ginger |
| 1 c. chopped celery | 1 tsp. ground marjoram |
| 3 c. dry bread crumbs | Sliced bacon |
| 3 c. chopped apple | |

Preheat oven to 350 degrees. Rub roast with salt and pepper to taste. Saute the onion, celery, bread crumbs and apple in butter until celery is tender. Add the nuts, 1/2 teaspoon salt, 1/8 teaspoon pepper, ginger and marjoram and mix lightly. Place roast in a baking pan. Fill the roast with apple mixture and wrap bacon around rib ends to prevent charring. Roast for 30 to 35 minutes per pound. Remove bacon and replace with paper frills.

*Mrs. Merle M. Blackburn, Montgomery, Alabama*

## SAVORY LAMB ROLL

| | |
|---|---|
| 1  3 to 4-lb. lamb shoulder | Dash of pepper |
| 1 clove of garlic, minced | 1 tbsp. lemon juice |
| 4 tbsp. all-purpose flour | Dash of Kitchen Bouquet |
| 2 tsp. salt | |

Bone the lamb shoulder, roll and tie with string. Combine the garlic, 1 tablespoon flour, salt, pepper and lemon juice and rub over the lamb. Place lamb on a large sheet of heavy-duty foil and wrap securely. Place in a shallow baking pan. Roast at 425 degrees for 2 hours and 30 minutes. Open foil and bake for 30 minutes longer. Remove lamb to a platter. Pour juices into 2 cup measure and add enough water to make 1 3/4 cups liquid. Pour into a saucepan. Mix remaining flour with 1/2 cup cold water and stir into liquid in saucepan. Cook and stir till thickened. Add Kitchen Bouquet and season to taste with additional salt and pepper. Serve with lamb. Garnish lamb with pears and mint jelly, if desired.

*Mrs. J. W. Howell, Bentonia, Mississippi*

## RIBS OF LAMB

| | |
|---|---|
| 1   2 1/2-lb. strip lamb ribs | 1 tbsp. soy sauce |
| Salt and pepper to taste | 1 tbsp. tomato puree |
| 2 tbsp. salad oil | 1 clove of garlic, crushed |

Have the thick, bony side of the lamb ribs cut through in several places when bought. Sprinkle the ribs with salt and pepper and place on a rack in a roasting pan, meat side down. Bake at 350 degrees for 30 minutes. Turn and bake for 30 minutes. Mix the oil, soy sauce, tomato puree, garlic, salt and pepper and brush on the ribs. Bake for 30 minutes longer. Cut the ribs in serving pieces before serving.

## STUFFED SHOULDER OF LAMB

| | |
|---|---|
| 1 c. bread crumbs | 1 egg, beaten |
| 1 tbsp. chopped parsley | 1   3 to 3 1/2-lb. boned shoulder |
| Grated rind of 1/2 lemon |     of lamb |
| 3 tbsp. bacon drippings | 1 1/2 tbsp. flour |
| Salt and pepper | 1 1/2 c. water or stock |

Combine the bread crumbs, parsley, lemon rind, 1 tablespoon bacon drippings, salt and pepper to taste and egg and mix well. Stuff cavity of the lamb and sew up opening. Place in a roasting pan. Roast at 300 degrees for 30 to 35 minutes per pound. Melt remaining bacon drippings in a saucepan and stir in the flour. Cook until brown. Add the water gradually and bring to a boil, stirring constantly. Add salt and pepper to taste and simmer for 5 minutes. Serve with the lamb.

*Mrs. Sidney G. Ingram, Statesville, North Carolina*

## LAMB RIBLETS AND KIDNEY BEANS

| | |
|---|---|
| 3 lb. lamb riblets | 1/2 c. diced celery |
| Salt | 1/4 c. chopped parsley |
| 1   1 1/2-oz. package | 1   1-lb. 4-oz. can white |
|     spaghetti sauce mix |     kidney beans, drained |
| 1   8-oz. can tomato sauce | |

Combine the riblets, 1 teaspoon salt and enough water to cover in a large saucepan. Bring to a boil and reduce heat. Cover and simmer for 45 minutes. Drain the riblets and trim off excess fat. Blend the sauce mix, tomato sauce and 2 tomato sauce cans water in the same saucepan and heat to simmering. Add the

riblets and celery and cover. Simmer for 25 minutes, stirring occasionally. Add the parsley, beans and salt to taste and cook for 10 minutes longer. Garnish with parsley sprigs. 4 servings.

## BARBECUED LAMB CHOPS

6 lamb chops
1 med. onion, sliced
1 1/2 tsp. ground ginger
1 1/2 tsp. dry mustard
1 tsp. salt
1/4 tsp. pepper
1/4 tsp. garlic salt

3 tbsp. chili sauce
3 tbsp. salad oil
1 1/2 tbsp. vinegar
1 tbsp. Worcestershire
    sauce
1/4 c. water

Place the lamb chops and onion slices in a shallow baking pan. Combine remaining ingredients and pour over chops mixture. Bake at 350 degrees for 40 minutes or until done, basting occasionally.

*Mrs. Harry P. Leber, Jr., Deerfield Beach, Florida*

## LAMB CHOP DINNER

4 lamb chops
Salt and pepper to taste
1/4 c. salad oil
1 clove of garlic, halved
1 c. boiling water

1 bouillon cube
1 lge. white onion, chopped
8 pared carrots, cubed
3 med. potatoes, cubed

Trim fat from the lamb chops. Sprinkle chops on both sides with salt and pepper. Heat the oil with garlic in a large skillet. Add the chops and brown on both sides. Remove garlic. Add the boiling water and bouillon cube and stir until bouillon is dissolved. Cover. Simmer for about 35 minutes or until chops are partially done. Place the onion, carrots and potatoes around chops and sprinkle with salt and pepper. Cover and simmer for about 30 minutes longer or until vegetables are tender.

*Mrs. R. D. Smallwood, Worthington, West Virginia*

## LAMB PILAF

2 lb. shoulder lamb, cubed
1 tsp. salt
4 tbsp. butter
1 med. onion, chopped fine

1 c. tomato sauce
2 c. water
1 1/2 c. long grain rice

Season the lamb with salt and place in a deep saucepan with the butter and onion. Saute until brown and add tomato sauce and water. Bring to boiling point, decrease heat and simmer for 1 hour and 30 minutes or until the lamb is tender. Drain liquid from the saucepan and add enough water to make 3 cups liquid. Pour back into the saucepan and bring to boiling point. Stir in the rice slowly, then cover. Decrease heat and simmer for 10 minutes or until the rice is cooked and liquid absorbed. Cover and let stand for 10 minutes.

*Mrs. James Winning, Greenville, South Carolina*

## TEXAS STEAK

| | |
|---|---|
| 2 lb. round veal steak | 1  3-oz. can mushrooms |
| 2 tbsp. fat | 1/2 c. chopped celery |
| 1 lge. onion, chopped | 1  8-oz. can tomato sauce |
| 1 clove of garlic, chopped | 1 tsp. salt |
| 2 tbsp. flour | 1 tbsp. Worcestershire sauce |
| 1 c. sour cream | |

Cut the steak in small cubes. Brown in hot fat in a skillet, then remove from skillet. Add the onion and garlic to the skillet and cook until onion is golden. Blend in flour. Add sour cream and cook, stirring constantly, until thickened. Return veal to skillet and add remaining ingredients. Mix well and turn into a greased 3-quart casserole. Bake at 350 degrees for 1 hour and 30 minutes or until veal is tender and serve over noodles or rice. 6 servings.

*Mrs. W. B. McDowell, Kaufman, Texas*

## VEAL BIRDS

| | |
|---|---|
| 1 1/2 lb. thinly sliced veal steak | 1/8 tbsp. pepper |
| | 1 egg, beaten |
| 2 tbsp. finely chopped onions | 2 c. soft bread crumbs |
| | 1/4 c. flour |
| 2 tbsp. butter | 3 tbsp. shortening |
| 1 tbsp. salt | 1 c. boiling water |

Cut the veal into 6 portions. Cook the onions in butter in a saucepan for 1 minute. Stir in the salt, pepper, egg and bread crumbs. Place on each veal portion. Fold over and fasten with small skewers. Roll in flour, then brown in shortening in a skillet. Add the water and cover. Cook over low heat for 50 minutes.

*Ruby Faye Criswell, Springfield, Arkansas*

## VEAL PARMESAN

| | |
|---|---|
| 2 tsp. margarine or oil | 1/2 tsp. salt |
| 2/3 c. evaporated milk | Dash of pepper |
| 5/8 c. grated Parmesan cheese | 4 slices veal, 1/2 in. thick |
| 1/4 c. flour | 1  8-oz. can tomato sauce |

Preheat oven to 350 degrees. Melt the margarine in a 12 x 8-inch pan. Pour 1/2 of the milk into a bowl. Mix 2 tablespoons Parmesan cheese, flour, salt and pepper. Dip the veal in milk, then in flour mixture. Place in the margarine in the pan. Bake for 30 minutes. Mix remaining milk and Parmesan cheese. Pour tomato sauce over veal and spoon cheese mixture over sauce on the veal. Bake for 20 to 25 minutes longer or until veal is tender.

*Mrs. Hilda Coufal, Hungerford, Texas*

## ANTELOPE IN CREAM

| | |
|---|---|
| 1 antelope steak | 1 c. half and half |
| 1/4 tsp. salt | Pinch of thyme |
| 1/2 tsp. pepper | Pinch of oregano |
| Flour | Celery flakes to taste |
| Juice of 1/2 lemon | |

Season steak with salt and pepper and dredge with flour. Brown on both sides in small amount of fat in a skillet. Place in a greased baking pan. Combine remaining ingredients and pour over steak. Bake at 325 degrees for 1 hour or until tender.

*Mrs. Warren Blass, Houston, Texas*

## WESTERN MEAT LOAF

| | |
|---|---|
| 2 slices rye bread | 1 egg, beaten |
| 2 slices bread | 1 tsp. salt |
| 1  8-oz. can tomato sauce | 1/4 tsp. pepper |
| 1 1/2 lb. ground antelope | 1 tbsp. oregano |
| 1 onion, finely chopped | 2 tbsp. butter |
| 3 tbsp. grated Parmesan cheese | |

Soak bread slices in 1 cup water and 1/2 can tomato sauce in a bowl. Add the ground antelope, onion, cheese, egg, salt, pepper and oregano and mix well. Shape into a loaf. Place in a baking pan and dot with butter. Bake at 375 degrees for 30 minutes. Pour remaining tomato sauce over the loaf and bake for 30 minutes longer. 4-6 servings.

*Mrs. Chester L. Bynum, Farmington, New Mexico*

## WILD GAME RAGOUT

| | |
|---|---|
| 3 tbsp. olive oil | 1 can tomato soup |
| 3 lb. antelope | 1 1/2 qt. water |
| 3 lge. onions, chopped | 2 tbsp. bourbon |
| 5 garlic cloves, crushed | 1/4 c. beer |
| 1/2 lb. bacon, chopped | 1 tbsp. salt |
| 1 tsp. curry powder | 1/2 lb. fresh mushrooms, sliced |

Heat the olive oil in an electric skillet. Cut the antelope into 1 1/2-inch cubes and add to the olive oil. Add the onions, garlic and bacon and cook until browned, stirring frequently. Add remaining ingredients except mushrooms and cover. Simmer for 50 minutes. Add the mushrooms and simmer for 10 minutes longer. Serve over rice. 8 servings.

*Mrs. David E. Chadwick, Albuquerque, New Mexico*

## BARBECUED RABBIT

| | |
|---|---|
| 2 wild rabbits | 1 c. vinegar |
| 1 lge. onion, minced | 1/2 c. catsup |
| 1 clove of garlic, minced | 1/2 c. Worcestershire sauce |
| 2 green peppers, minced | 1/4 c. butter |
| 1 can tomato juice | 1 tsp. salt |
| 1 c. water | 1/2 tsp. cayenne pepper |

Cut the rabbits into serving pieces. Combine remaining ingredients in a saucepan and cook for 5 minutes. Place the rabbits in a baking pan in a single layer and pour the sauce over rabbits. Bake at 300 degrees for 3 hours or until tender, turning occasionally.

*Mrs. Maurine E. Patton, Cookeville, Tennessee*

## HASENPFEFFER

| | |
|---|---|
| 1 rabbit, cleaned | 2 tsp. salt |
| 2 c. wine vinegar | 1/4 tsp. allspice |
| 1 c. water | 1/2 tsp. pepper |
| 1 lge. onion, sliced | Flour |
| 1 bay leaf | 1 c. sour cream |

Cut the rabbit into serving pieces. Combine remaining ingredients except flour and sour cream in a bowl. Add the rabbit and refrigerate for 12 to 24 hours. Remove the rabbit and strain the marinade. Brown the rabbit in small amount of fat in a heavy skillet. Add 1 cup marinade and simmer for 1 hour or until rabbit is tender. Place the rabbit on a platter. Thicken gravy with a small amount of flour mixed with water, then stir in sour cream. Serve with rabbit.

*Mrs. Lillie Handrick, Albany, Texas*

## FRIED SQUIRREL

| | |
|---|---|
| 1 squirrel | Salt and pepper to taste |
| 1 clove of garlic, chopped | Flour |
| 1/2 c. olive oil | |

Cut the squirrel in serving pieces and place in a bowl. Cover with salted water and refrigerate overnight. Drain. Saute the garlic in olive oil in a skillet for several minutes. Sprinkle the squirrel with salt and pepper and dredge with flour. Fry in the oil until well browned, turning once.

*Mrs. Allie W. Baugh, Groves, Texas*

## BARBECUED VENISON STEAK

| | |
|---|---|
| 1   2 1/2-lb. venison steak | 1/2 tsp. garlic salt |
| 1 c. flour | 1/4 tsp. pepper |
| 1 1/2 tsp. salt | 1/2 c. catsup |

| | |
|---|---|
| **3 tbsp. vinegar** | **1 tbsp. Worcestershire** |
| **1/4 c. chopped onion** | **sauce** |
| **3 tbsp. brown sugar** | **1/2 c. water** |

Cut the steak in serving portions. Mix the flour, salt, garlic salt and pepper and dredge venison in seasoned flour. Brown in small amount of fat in a skillet over high heat, then place in a casserole. Combine remaining ingredients in a saucepan and cook for 5 minutes. Pour over venison and cover. Bake at 300 degrees for 2 hours and 30 minutes, adding water, if needed.

*Mrs. Keith Ethridge, Stroud, Oklahoma*

## VENISON ROYAL

| | |
|---|---|
| **1/2 c. flour** | **1 lge. onion, thinly sliced** |
| **Salt and pepper to taste** | **Juice of 1 orange** |
| **1/2 tsp. cayenne pepper** | **2 tbsp. Worcestershire** |
| **1/4 tsp. nutmeg** | **sauce** |
| **1/4 tsp. cloves** | **1 1/2 c. Burgundy** |
| **1/4 tsp. thyme** | **1 whole clove** |
| **1 venison rump steak,** | **1/2 garlic clove, minced** |
| **3/4 in. thick** | **1 c. mushrooms, sauteed** |
| **3 tbsp. cooking oil** | |

Mix the flour, seasonings and spices and pound into steak. Cut the steak into serving pieces and cook in hot oil in a heavy skillet until lightly browned. Add onion and cook until brown. Add the orange juice and simmer for 3 minutes. Add the Worcestershire sauce, Burgundy, clove, garlic, salt and pepper and cover tightly. Bake at 300 degrees for 2 hours or until steak is tender. Remove from oven. Add mushrooms and simmer for 5 minutes. 4 servings.

*Mrs. John D. Clark, Rising Star, Texas*

## VENISON PARMIGIANA

| | |
|---|---|
| **1 1/2 lb. venison, 1 1/2 in.** | **1/4 tsp. pepper** |
| **thick** | **1/2 tsp. sugar** |
| **1 egg, beaten** | **1/2 tsp. marjoram** |
| **1/3 c. fine dry bread crumbs** | **1   6-oz. can tomato paste** |
| **1/3 c. grated Parmesan cheese** | **2 c. hot water** |
| **1/3 c. cooking oil** | **1/2 lb. mozzarella cheese,** |
| **1 med. onion, minced** | **sliced** |
| **1 tsp. salt** | |

Pound the venison thin and cut in serving pieces. Dip into egg and roll in mixture of crumbs and Parmesan cheese. Brown in oil in a skillet and place in a shallow baking dish. Cook onion in remaining oil in skillet until soft and add salt, pepper, sugar, marjoram and tomato paste. Add water gradually and cook for 5 minutes. Pour half the sauce over venison and top with cheese slices. Add remaining sauce. Bake at 350 degrees for 1 hour. 4-6 servings.

*Mrs. Carl H. Panzer, Sweetwater, Texas*

## STUFFED LEG OF VENISON

| | |
|---|---|
| 1 leg of venison, boned | 3 cloves of garlic, chopped |
| 2 1/2 lb. chopped pork | 1 c. chopped parsley |
| 1/2 lb. grated mozzarella cheese | 2 tsp. pepper |
| 1 c. chopped shallots | 1 qt. Chianti |

Place the venison in a baking pan. Mix the pork, cheese, shallots, garlic, parsley and pepper and place on the venison. Roll as for jelly roll and tie with heavy string. Pour the Chianti over venison and marinate in refrigerator overnight. Drain and reserve Chianti. Bake at 350 degrees for 3 hours and 30 minutes or until done, basting every 30 minutes with reserved Chianti. Make a gravy with remaining Chianti and drippings, if desired.

*Mrs. Richard D. Moers, Smithville, Texas*

## BRAINS A LA KING

| | |
|---|---|
| 1 lb. brains | 2 tbsp. chopped pimento |
| 4 c. water | 1/4 c. melted butter |
| 1 tbsp. vinegar | 1/4 c. flour |
| 1 tsp. salt | 2 c. milk |
| 1/2 c. minced celery | 1/2 tsp. salt |
| 1/4 c. minced green pepper | Dash of pepper |
| 2 tsp. grated onion | 6 slices toast |

Wash the brains. Combine the water, vinegar and salt in a skillet and bring to a boil. Add the brains and simmer for 20 minutes. Drain and cool. Separate the brains into small pieces. Cook the celery, green pepper, onion and pimento in the butter in a saucepan until celery is tender. Stir in the flour. Add the milk and cook until thickened, stirring constantly. Add the salt, pepper and brains and heat through. Serve on toast and garnish with parsley.

*Mrs. Adrienne King, Dallas, Texas*

## BRAIN LOAF

| | |
|---|---|
| 2 lb. beef or pork brains | 7 eggs |
| 1 env. unflavored gelatin | 1 1/4 c. bread crumbs |
| 2 tbsp. cold water | 1 c. heavy cream |
| 2 tbsp. butter | 5 hard-boiled eggs, chopped |

Cook the brains in salted, boiling water until tender, then drain. Soften the gelatin in water. Melt the butter in a saucepan and remove from heat. Beat 4 eggs and 4 egg yolks in a bowl. Cut the brains in cubes and add to the eggs. Stir in the bread crumbs. Stir into the butter and place over low heat. Add the heavy cream, hard-boiled eggs and gelatin and stir until thickened. Remove from heat. Beat the egg whites until stiff and fold into the brains mixture. Place in a casserole. Bake at 350 degrees for 30 minutes or until brown.

*Mrs. Meredith J. Cox, Richmond, Kentucky*

## CREAMED EGGS IN CORNED BEEF CRUST

1   12-oz. can corned beef
1 slice bread
1 egg, slightly beaten
1 can mushroom soup
1/4 c. milk or water

1   3-oz. can sliced
    mushrooms
1 tsp. Worcestershire sauce
6 hard-cooked eggs, sliced

Flake the corned beef with a fork and place in a bowl. Tear the bread into small pieces and add to the corned beef. Add the beaten egg and mix well. Press into bottom and side of an 8-inch pie plate. Bake at 350 degrees for about 15 minutes or until crusty brown. Blend the soup, milk, mushrooms, and Worcestershire sauce in a saucepan and heat through. Reserve several hard-cooked egg slices for garnish. Fold in remaining eggs and pour into the corned beef shell. Garnish with reserved egg slices and parsley. Serve immediately. 6 servings.

## SUCCULENT BEEF HEART

1/2 lb. mushrooms, sliced
1/2 c. butter
1 beef heart
1 c. flour
1 tsp. garlic powder

1/2 tsp. basil
1/2 tsp. rosemary
1/2 tsp. thyme
2 c. Burgundy
1 env. onion soup mix

Saute the mushrooms in half the butter in a Dutch oven until lightly browned, then remove. Slice the heart and remove fat and ligaments. Combine the flour, garlic powder and herbs and dredge heart in flour mixture. Melt remaining butter in the Dutch oven. Add the heart and cook until brown. Add the Burgundy, mushrooms, soup mix and enough water to just cover and mix well. Cover the Dutch oven. Bake in 275-degree oven for 5 to 6 hours. 4-6 servings.

*Mrs. Willard H. Luff, Santa Monica, California*

## TEXAS KRAUT ROUND DOG TOSTADOS

| | |
|---|---|
| 1 med. green pepper, diced | 1 clove of garlic, crushed |
| 1 sm. onion, chopped | 1/4 tsp. oregano leaves |
| 1 tbsp. salad oil | 1/2 tsp. salt |
| 4 c. drained sauerkraut | 8 tortillas |
| 1/4 tsp. chili powder | Shortening |
| 1  8-oz. can tomato sauce | 8 frankfurters |
| 1  15-oz. can red kidney beans | 3/4 c. grated Cheddar cheese |

Saute the green pepper and onion in oil in a medium saucepan until light brown. Add the sauerkraut, chili powder and tomato sauce and cover. Cook over low heat for 30 minutes. Mash the undrained beans with garlic, oregano and salt in a saucepan and cook over low heat until thick, stirring occasionally. Fry the tortillas in 1 inch hot shortening in a skillet for about 1 minute, then drain on paper towels. Cut 10 slits in each frankfurter without cutting all the way through and place on broiler rack. Broil until brown on one side. Spread the bean paste over tortillas and place on heatproof platter or broiler rack. Top each with 1/2 cup sauerkraut mixture and a frankfurter, browned side down. Sprinkle the cheese in center. Broil for 1 minute or until cheese melts.

## BROILED LAMB KIDNEYS

| | |
|---|---|
| 1/2 c. red wine | 1/4 tsp. thyme |
| 1 tbsp. olive oil | 1/8 tsp. coriander |
| 1 clove of garlic, crushed | 4 lamb kidneys, cleaned |
| 1 tsp. salt | 2 strips bacon, halved |
| 1 tsp. dry mustard | |

Combine first 7 ingredients in a bowl. Cut the kidneys in half and place in the marinade. Marinate for 1 hour. Drain the kidneys. Wrap with bacon and secure with toothpicks. Place on broiler pan. Broil until bacon is crisp.

*Mrs. Rick Taylor, Tupelo, Mississippi*

## KIDNEYS FOR COMPANY

12 lamb or veal kidneys
Salt and white pepper to
  taste
Dry mustard and cayenne
  pepper to taste
1/2 c. flour
Olive oil
4 med. onions, chopped

4 c. beef stock
Worcestershire sauce to
  taste
Catsup to taste
1/2 lb. mushrooms, sliced
Butter
1 c. red wine (opt.)

Wash, skin and cut each kidney into eighths. Combine dry seasonings and flour and dredge kidneys with flour mixture. Brown in small amount of oil in heavy skillet until light brown. Add the onions and saute until tender. Add the stock, Worcestershire sauce and catsup and bring to a boil. Reduce heat and simmer until kidneys are tender. Saute the mushrooms in small amount of butter until light brown. Add to the kidney mixture. Add the wine just before serving. May be thickened, if desired.

*Mrs. Glen Davis, Raleigh, North Carolina*

## LIVER CRISPS AND ONIONS

1 lb. sliced liver
1/4 lb. sliced bacon
1/4 c. flour
1 tsp. salt

1/8 tsp. curry powder
1 lge. onion, sliced
4 tbsp. bacon drippings

Cut the liver into finger lengths about 1/2 inch thick. Place the bacon on a broiler pan. Broil until crisp, then drain on paper towels. Keep warm. Mix the flour with salt and curry powder. Dredge the liver with flour mixture. Saute the onion in bacon drippings in a skillet until lightly browned. Remove from skillet and keep warm. Fry liver in remaining bacon drippings in the skillet until done. Serve with onions and bacon. 4 servings.

*Naomi R. Stewart, Tonkawa, Oklahoma*

## LIVER LOAF

1 tbsp. butter
1 tbsp. flour
1 c. milk
2 c. ground beef liver
1 egg, beaten
1 tsp. salt
1/8 tsp. pepper

1/4 c. toasted bread
  crumbs
1/2 c. diced potatoes
1 green pepper, diced
1 onion, minced
3 slices bacon
3/4 c. tomato juice

Melt the butter in a saucepan and stir in the flour. Add milk gradually and cook over low heat, stirring constantly, until smooth and thickened. Cool. Mix the liver and egg in a bowl, then stir in the salt, pepper, bread crumbs, potatoes, green pepper and onion. Stir in the white sauce. Turn into a greased loaf pan and top with bacon slices. Bake in 400-degree oven for 1 hour, basting with tomato juice frequently.

*M. V. Tracy, Cayle, Oklahoma*

## QUICK LIVER STROGANOFF

1 lb. beef liver
1/3 c. flour
1 tsp. salt
1/8 tsp. pepper
1 tbsp. cooking oil
1 c. tomato juice

1 tbsp. instant minced
 onion
1/2 c. sour cream
Cooked rice
Chopped parsley (opt.)

Cut the liver into thin strips, removing veins and membranes. Mix the flour with salt and pepper and coat liver with flour mixture. Brown in hot oil in a skillet. Add the tomato juice and onion and cover. Simmer for 10 to 15 minutes. Stir in the sour cream and heat through. Place the liver mixture over rice on a heated platter. Sprinkle with parsley. About 4 servings.

## LIVER AND RICE PATTIES

1 lb. sliced beef liver
1 c. cooked rice
1/4 tsp. celery salt
1/2 tsp. chopped parsley
1/4 c. chopped celery

1 tbsp. grated onion
3/4 tsp. salt
Butter or cooking oil
Tomato sauce

Pour boiling water over liver in a pan and let stand for 3 minutes. Drain and grind through a food chopper. Place in a bowl. Add remaining ingredients except butter and tomato sauce and mix well. Shape into patties. Fry in a small amount of butter in a skillet until brown and done. Serve with tomato sauce.

*Mrs. George Pecsek, Virginia Beach, Virginia*

## FRIED SWEETBREADS

1/4 c. flour
1/2 tsp. salt
1/8 tsp. pepper

1 lb. sweetbreads
4 tbsp. butter

Combine the flour, salt and pepper in a paper bag. Clean the sweetbreads and separate into small pieces. Place in the bag and shake to coat. Melt the butter in a frying pan. Add the sweetbreads and cook until brown. Reduce heat and cover. Cook for 20 minutes.

*Mrs. Paul Bridges, Princeton, North Carolina*

## SWEETBREADS IN MUSHROOM SAUCE

| | |
|---|---|
| 1 lb. sweetbreads | 3 tbsp. butter |
| 1 tbsp. lemon juice | 3 tbsp. flour |
| 1 can mushrooms, drained | 1 c. milk |

Clean the sweetbreads. Place in boiling, salted water in a saucepan and add the lemon juice. Simmer for 20 minutes, then drain. Plunge into cold water and drain. Cut into 1/2-inch slices. Saute the mushrooms and sweetbreads in butter in a saucepan until lightly browned. Stir in the flour. Stir in the milk and cook over low heat, stirring constantly, until thickened.

*Mrs. Ben Richards, Columbia, South Carolina*

## SMOKED TONGUE DINNER

| | |
|---|---|
| 1 smoked beef tongue | 1/2 tsp. peppercorns |
| 1 onion, sliced | 6 onions |
| 1 stalk celery | 6 carrots, cut in quarters |
| 1 bay leaf | 1 1/2 lb. whole green beans |

Place the tongue in a kettle and cover with water. Add the sliced onion, celery, bay leaf and peppercorns. Bring to a boil and cover. Reduce heat and simmer until tender. Remove tongue from broth and cool. Remove skin and trim. Strain the broth and pour back into the kettle. Add the whole onions, carrots and beans. Slice the tongue and place on top. Cook for about 25 minutes or until vegetables are tender.

*Vergie V. Kahla, Port Bolivar, Texas*

## SWEET AND SOUR TONGUE

| | |
|---|---|
| 1 lemon, thinly sliced | 1 cinnamon stick |
| 1 c. cider vinegar | 8 whole cloves |
| 1 c. (packed) dark brown sugar | 1/3 c. blanched slivered almonds |
| 12 gingersnaps, crumbled | 1 sm. onion, sliced |
| 1 bay leaf | 1 can beef tongue |
| 1/2 c. raisins | |

Combine all ingredients except the tongue in a saucepan and cook over low heat for 10 minutes. Cut the tongue into thin slices and add to hot sauce. Heat through. Remove the lemon, cinnamon and cloves before serving.

*Mrs. J. W. Guy, Mt. Ulla, North Carolina*

# soups
# and stews

Soup's on!" This insistent call causes Southwesterners to perk up their ears and come a runnin'. They know that it summons them to hot, hearty fare and companionable dining. The cry also arouses curiosity, for Southwesterners may find almost any kind of soup on the table — from plain bean soup to elaborate shellfish gumbo.

Old-timers developed the simplest soups. They'd allow beef and meat bones to simmer for hours on the back of the stove. Then they would toss into the stock any food handy to increase rich flavor. Soon rules were added to soup-making procedure, and certain ingredients were used again and again. Beef, beans, and corn, you'll discover in these pages, are typical makin's for soups and stews.

More fanciful dishes give welcomed variety. Gumbo, a thick stew of Creole origin, was adapted into Southwestern cookery because of accessible Gulf water shellfish. Not to be outdone by their Creole neighbors, Southwesterners added to their gumbos a special native exuberance. One recipe that follows for Southwestern Gumbo specifies chicken, crab, shrimp, *and* oysters — not to mention the usual vegetables and seasonings! Southwesterners also adopted recipes for rich and hearty Brunswick Stew, made from game meat or poultry and vegetables.

Plain or fancy, Southwestern soups and stews are never run-of-the-mill. After all, just the call of "Soup's on!" makes natives high-tail it to chow — and that means fast!

## PENNY-SAVING PARTY STEW

| | |
|---|---|
| 1 c. green pepper, cut in 1/2-in. squares | 1   15-oz. can kidney beans |
| 2 tbsp. butter or margarine | 2 tsp. chili powder |
| 2   19-oz. cans beef stew | Corn bread or corn chips |

Cook the green pepper in the butter in a saucepan until tender. Add the stew, beans and chili powder and cook over low heat for 5 minutes, stirring occasionally. Serve with corn bread. 4 servings.

## BROWNED STEW WITH DUMPLINGS

| | |
|---|---|
| 3 tbsp. shortening | 4 c. boiling water |
| 2 lb. beef, cut in cubes | 1 tsp. lemon juice |
| 1 onion, diced | 1 1/2 tsp. baking powder |
| 1 1/8 c. flour | 1 egg |
| 2 tsp. salt | 2 to 3 tbsp. milk |
| 1/4 tsp. pepper | |

Melt the shortening in a Dutch oven. Add the beef and cook over medium heat until light brown. Add the onion and cook until tender. Sprinkle 2 tablespoons flour, 1 1/2 teaspoons salt and pepper over the beef mixture and stir well. Stir in the water and lemon juice and cover. Reduce heat and simmer for 3 hours to 3 hours and 30 minutes. Combine remaining flour, baking powder and remaining salt in a bowl. Add the egg and milk and mix well. Drop from a spoon on the stew and cover. Cook for 12 to 15 minutes or until dumplings are done.

*Mrs. Leroy J. Miller, Virginia Beach, Virginia*

## HAMBURGER-RICE SOUP

| | |
|---|---|
| 1 lb. ground beef | 1/2 c. diced onion |
| 2 tbsp. shortening | 2 tsp. salt |
| 2 c. canned tomatoes | 1/8 tsp. pepper |
| 2 c. diced potatoes | 1/4 c. rice |
| 1/2 c. diced carrots | 6 c. water |
| 1/2 c. diced celery | |

Brown the beef in shortening in a kettle over medium heat. Add remaining ingredients and cook over low heat for about 45 minutes, stirring occasionally and adding water, if needed.

*Mrs. Pat McEwen, Saperton, Georgia*

## INDIAN CORN STEW

| | |
|---|---|
| 1 med. onion, chopped fine | 1 can tomato soup |
| 1/2 green pepper, chopped fine | 2 tsp. sugar |
| 2 tbsp. butter | 1 tsp. salt |
| 1 lb. ground beef | 2 tbsp. flour |
| 1 No. 2 can whole kernel corn | 2 tbsp. cold water |

Cook the onion and green pepper in butter in a frying pan for 5 minutes. Add the beef and cook until brown, stirring frequently. Add the corn, soup, sugar and salt and simmer for about 15 minutes. Blend the flour with water and stir into the stew. Cook for 5 minutes longer.

*Mrs. Lucile O. Rowell, Elba, Alabama*

## OLD-TIME BEEF STEW

| | |
|---|---|
| 2 tbsp. shortening | 1/2 tsp. pepper |
| 2 lb. beef chuck | 1/2 tsp. paprika |
| 1 lge. onion, sliced | 2 bay leaves |
| 1 clove of garlic | Dash of allspice or cloves |
| 4 c. boiling water | 6 carrots, diced |
| 1 tbsp. salt | 1 lb. small white onions |
| 1 tbsp. lemon juice | 6 med. potatoes, diced |
| 1 tsp. sugar | 1/4 c. flour |
| 1 tsp. Worcestershire sauce | 1/2 c. cold water |

Heat the shortening in Dutch oven. Cut the beef in 1 1/2-inch cubes and add to the shortening. Cook until brown. Add the onion, garlic, boiling water, salt, lemon juice, sugar, Worcestershire sauce, pepper, paprika, bay leaves and allspice and bring to a boil. Reduce heat and cover. Simmer for 2 hours, stirring occasionally. Add the vegetables and simmer for about 30 minutes or until vegetables are tender. Discard bay leaf and garlic. Mix the flour and cold water until smooth and stir into the stew. Cook, stirring constantly, until thickened. 6-8 servings.

*Mrs. R. C. Thomas, Bruce, Mississippi*

## MEATBALLS WITH PEA SOUP

| | |
|---|---|
| 1 1/4 c. split peas | 8 c. water |
| 1/4 c. rice | 1/2 lb. hamburger |
| 3 med. onions, chopped | 2 beef bouillon cubes |
| 1 tsp. thyme | Salt and pepper to taste |

Cook the peas, rice, 1 cup onions and thyme in the water in a kettle for about 1 hour or until peas and rice are tender. Shape the hamburger into small balls and brown in a skillet. Remove from skillet. Cook remaining onions in hamburger drippings until tender. Add meatballs and onions to the rice mixture. Add the bouillon cubes and stir until dissolved. Add the salt and pepper and serve.

*Mildred Duke, Asheville, North Carolina*

## RANCH STEW

| | |
|---|---|
| 1  15-oz. can tomatoes | 1 med. onion, chopped |
| 1  15-oz. can cream-style corn | 2 tbsp. butter |
| 1  15-oz. can kidney beans | Salt and pepper to taste |
| 1 lb. ground beef | 1/2 tbsp. oregano |

Combine the tomatoes, corn and beans in a large saucepan and cook, until thickened. Brown the beef and onion in butter in a skillet, then stir in the salt, pepper and oregano. Stir into the corn mixture and simmer for 10 to 15 minutes.

*Mrs. Charles Johnson, Jesup, Georgia*

## MEXICAN STEW

| | |
|---|---|
| 1/2 c. suet | 4 potatoes, diced |
| 2 lb. beef, cut in cubes | 4 carrots, diced |
| 1/2 c. flour | Salt to taste |
| 8 c. water | 2 tbsp. chili powder |
| 6 onions, diced | 1 garlic clove, minced |

Cook the suet in a kettle over medium heat until fat is rendered. Roll the beef in flour and add to suet. Cook, stirring, until brown. Add the water and bring to a boil. Reduce heat and simmer until the beef is tender. Add remaining ingredients and cook until the vegetables are tender.

*Mrs. Helen Morris, Prescott, Arkansas*

## BRUNSWICK STEW

| | |
|---|---|
| 1 qt. chopped cooked pork | 2 tbsp. Worcestershire sauce |
| 1 qt. chopped cooked chicken | 1/2 c. catsup |
| 2 qt. chopped tomatoes | 1 tsp. mixed spices |
| 1 qt. cut corn | 1/4 tsp. red pepper |

**Salt and pepper to taste**          **1 tbsp. brown sugar**
**1 tbsp. white vinegar**             **Chicken stock**

Combine the pork, chicken, tomatoes, corn and remaining ingredients except stock in a large kettle and bring to a boil. Reduce heat and simmer until corn and tomatoes are done, stirring frequently and adding chicken stock, if needed. 16-20 servings.

*Mrs. Gary Burt, Moultrie, Georgia*

## BEEF STOCK LENTIL SOUP

**1 1/2 c. lentils**                  **1 onion, thinly sliced**
**6 c. beef stock**                   **2 tbsp. margarine**
**2 lge. tomatoes, chopped**          **1 tbsp. lemon juice**
**1 lge. onion, chopped**             **Salt to taste**
**1 clove of garlic, pressed**        **Allspice to taste**
**1 tsp. caraway seed**               **Lemon slices**

Rinse the lentils in cold water until the water is clear. Place in a saucepan and add the beef stock, tomatoes, chopped onion, garlic and caraway seed. Bring to a boil, then reduce heat and simmer for about 1 hour. Fry the sliced onion in the margarine until light brown, then drain on absorbent paper. Mash the soup through a strainer, then pour back into the saucepan and heat through. Season with lemon juice, salt and allspice. Serve with lemon slices and the fried onion.

## CHILI

| | |
|---|---|
| 1 c. dried pinto beans | 1 tbsp. salt |
| 2 lb. ground chuck | 1 tsp. pepper |
| 1 lge. onion, chopped | 1 tsp. Worcestershire sauce |
| 1 lb. green peppers, chopped | 1 tsp. comino seed |
| 2 cloves of garlic, minced | 1/3 c. parsley flakes |
| 1/3 c. chili powder | 1 tsp. monosodium glutamate |
| 2 No. 303 cans tomatoes | 1 sm. boiled potato |

Place the beans in a saucepan and cover with water. Bring to a boil and cook for 5 minutes. Drain. Cover with water and bring to a boil. Reduce heat and simmer until beans are almost done. Set aside. Saute the chuck, onion, green peppers and garlic in a kettle until vegetables are tender. Add the pinto beans and remaining ingredients except potato and simmer for 4 hours, stirring occasionally. Mash the potato and stir into the chili. Cook for 30 minutes longer. 8 servings.

*Mrs. R. E. DeLoach, Shreveport, Louisiana*

## FARMER'S CHOWDER

| | |
|---|---|
| 8 slices bacon | 1 1/4 c. packaged precooked |
| 1 c. diced ham |    rice |
| 1 1/2 c. mixed vegetables | 1 tsp. salt |
| 3 1/2 c. canned tomatoes | 1/8 tsp. pepper |
| 3 c. water | 1 tbsp. parsley flakes |

Fry the bacon in a large saucepan until crisp, then drain and crumble. Pour off all except 2 tablespoons bacon drippings from saucepan. Add the ham and saute until lightly browned. Add the bacon and remaining ingredients except parsley and bring to a boil. Reduce heat and simmer until rice is cooked, stirring occasionally. Add the parsley just before serving. 6-8 servings.

*Mrs. Betty DeVoe, Nashville, Tennessee*

## LAMB STEW WITH TOMATO DUMPLINGS

| | |
|---|---|
| 2 lb. lamb neck | 6 sm. white onions |
| 3 tbsp. shortening | 1 1/2 c. sifted all-purpose flour |
| 2 1/2 tsp. salt | 1 tbsp. baking powder |
| 1/8 tsp. pepper | 1 egg |
| 1/8 tsp. paprika | 1 tbsp. melted shortening |
| 4 c. water | 3/4 c. tomato juice |
| 6 sm. potatoes, halved | 2 tbsp. minced parsley |
| 6 sm. carrots, halved | |

Cut the lamb into 2-inch pieces. Place the shortening in a heavy skillet and brown the lamb in hot shortening. Add 1 1/2 teaspoons salt, the pepper, paprika and water. Cover the skillet and simmer for about 1 hour or until lamb is nearly tender. Add the vegetables and cook for about 45 minutes longer or until lamb is done. Sift flour, measure and sift again with 1 teaspoon salt and baking powder. Beat egg until light, adding the melted shortening and the tomato juice. Combine tomato juice liquid with flour, stirring only until flour is dampened. Drop the flour mixture, by spoonfuls, over the lamb and vegetables for dumplings. Cover and cook for 12 to 15 minutes without removing cover. Serve vegetables and dumplings around the lamb. Thicken the pan juices for gravy and pour over the lamb if desired. Garnish with parsley.

*Mrs. V. H. Stevens, Searcy, Arkansas*

## CHICKEN-PEPPER SOUP

1 broiler
1 tbsp. salt
5 white peppercorns
5 whole allspice
1 bay leaf
3 whole cloves
1 lge. carrot, diced
1 leek, chopped

4 lge. carrots, grated
2 lge. onions, chopped
2 c. shredded cabbage
1 sm. can tomato puree
1/2 tsp. minced chili pepper
1 c. ground peanuts
Cooked rice

Place the chicken in a saucepan and add enough water to cover. Bring to a boil and skim well. Add the salt, peppercorns, allspice, bay leaf, cloves, diced carrot and leek and cook for 35 to 40 minutes or until the chicken is tender. Remove chicken from broth and cool. Strain the broth and add enough water to make 4 cups liquid, if needed. Reserve 1/2 cup. Pour remaining broth back into the saucepan and bring to a boil. Add the grated carrots, onions, cabbage, tomato puree and chili pepper and cook until thickened, stirring frequently. Add the peanuts and cook for 15 minutes longer, stirring frequently. Remove the chicken from bones and cut in large pieces. Heat in the reserved broth. Place in a bowl. Place the rice in a bowl. Place rice, then chicken, then soup in soup bowls to serve.

## CHICKEN GUMBO

| | |
|---|---|
| 1 qt. sliced okra | 2 potatoes, diced |
| 2 med. onions, chopped | 1 pkg. frozen butter beans |
| 2  1-lb. cans tomatoes | 1 boned cooked chicken |
| 1  1-lb. can whole kernel | Salt and pepper to taste |
|    corn | Butter to taste |
| 1 bell pepper, finely chopped | |

Brown the okra and onions in small amount of bacon fat in a Dutch oven. Add the tomatoes, corn, bell pepper, potatoes, butter beans and chicken and bring to a boil. Add the salt, pepper, butter and enough boiling water to cover and reduce heat. Cover and simmer for 3 hours or longer, stirring frequently. Serve over rice. 8-10 servings.

*Mrs. Julian Brown, Jr., Clearwater, Florida*

## HOPKINS COUNTY CHICKEN STEW

| | |
|---|---|
| 1  4-lb. chicken, disjointed | 1/2 tsp. paprika |
| 1 tbsp. salt | 1/2 tsp. pepper |
| 6 med. onions, chopped | 1 tsp. chili powder |
| 10 med. potatoes, diced | 1  1-lb. can golden cream- |
| 3  1-lb. cans tomatoes |    style corn |
| 1/8 tsp. garlic powder | |

Place the chicken in a kettle and cover with water. Add the salt and bring to a boil. Reduce heat and cook for 1 hour or until tender. Remove chicken from broth and cool. Remove chicken from bones and dice. Add the onions, potatoes, tomatoes and seasonings to the broth and cook until vegetables are tender. Add the chicken and corn and simmer for 5 to 10 minutes to blend flavors, stirring occasionally. May be made a day ahead and reheated. 10 servings.

*Mrs. Pete Wright, Sulphur Springs, Texas*

## SOUTHWESTERN GUMBO

| | |
|---|---|
| 5 med. onions, chopped | 1 lb. okra, sliced |
| 4 garlic cloves, chopped | 12 bay leaves |
| 1 c. butter or margarine | 1 tsp. whole thyme |
| 1/2 c. flour | 1 sm. bunch parsley, chopped |
| 1  5-lb. chicken, disjointed | 1 pt. crab meat |
| 2 No. 2 cans tomatoes | 1 lb. cleaned shrimp |
| 4 qt. water | 1 pt. oysters |
| Salt and pepper to taste | |

Saute the onions and garlic in butter in a kettle until limp, then stir in the flour. Add the chicken, tomatoes, water, salt and pepper and bring to a boil. Reduce heat and cover. Simmer until chicken is tender. Remove chicken and cool. Remove chicken from bones and add to kettle. Add the okra, bay leaves, thyme and parsley and cook for 10 minutes. Stir in the crab meat, shrimp and oysters and cook for 30 minutes longer. Serve over rice. 3 gallons.

*Mrs. Travis Richard Coulter, Mabelvale, Arkansas*

## VEGETABLE-CHICKEN SOUP

2 lb. chicken legs
2 c. water
2 tsp. salt
5 white peppercorns
1 sm. onion, chopped
1 1/4 c. cocktail vegetable
 juice
3/4 c. broken spaghetti

1 pkg. frozen small green
 peas
Salt and pepper to taste
1/2 tsp. tarragon or chervil
Finely chopped parsley to
 taste
Grated Parmesan cheese

Place the chicken legs in a saucepan and add the water and salt. Bring to a boil and skim well. Add the peppercorns and onion and cover. Simmer for about 25 minutes or until chicken is tender. Remove chicken from broth and cool. Strain the broth and pour back into the saucepan. Add the vegetable juice and bring to a boil. Add the spaghetti and peas and cook for 12 to 15 minutes or until spaghetti is tender. Remove skin and bones from chicken and discard. Cut the chicken in small pieces and add to the soup. Add the seasonings and mix well. Sprinkle with parsley and serve with Parmesan cheese. 4 servings.

### TURKEY-MUSHROOM AND BARLEY CHOWDER

| | |
|---|---|
| 1 lb. fresh mushrooms | 1/8 tsp. pepper |
| 2 qt. chicken broth or water | 2 tbsp. butter or margarine |
| 1 c. diced onions | 4 tsp. flour |
| 1/2 c. diced celery | 1 c. pearl barley |
| 1/2 c. diced carrots | 1/2 c. milk |
| 1 1/2 tsp. salt | |

Rinse, pat dry and slice the mushrooms. Pour the broth into a large saucepan. Add 1/2 cup onions, celery, carrots, salt and pepper and bring to a boil. Reduce heat and cover. Simmer for 1 hour. Melt the butter in a large skillet. Add the mushrooms and remaining onions and saute for 5 minutes. Stir in the flour. Stir into the broth mixture, then stir in the barley. Cook for 1 hour to 1 hour and 30 minutes longer or until barley is tender. Add the milk slowly and heat through. Do not boil. Serve hot. Two 6 or 8-ounce cans sliced mushrooms may be substituted for fresh mushrooms. Add liquid to the chicken broth. 6-8 servings.

*Photograph for this recipe on page 60.*

### RABBIT STEW

| | |
|---|---|
| 1   3-lb. rabbit | Pepper to taste |
| 1 lge. onion, chopped | 1/2 tsp. rosemary |
| 2 tbsp. cooking oil | 1 No. 2 1/2 can tomatoes |
| 1 tsp. parsley | 2 lge. green peppers, chopped |
| 1/2 tsp. sweet basil | 1 can green beans |
| Garlic salt to taste | 1 can green peas |
| 1/4 tsp. oregano | |

Cut the rabbit into serving pieces. Cook the rabbit and onion in oil in a large saucepan until brown. Add seasonings and tomatoes and cook until the rabbit is tender. Add the vegetables and cook for 20 minutes longer. 4-6 servings.

*Mrs. Henry St. Amand, Las Vegas, Nevada*

### COWBOY SOUP

| | |
|---|---|
| 1 No. 2 can pork and beans | 1 c. water |
| 1 No. 2 can tomatoes | 3 slices bacon, diced |
| 2 cans Vienna sausage | |

Mix all ingredients in a saucepan and cook, stirring frequently, until thick. Serve with crackers. 4 servings.

*Mrs. Helen Gossmann, Arapaho, Oklahoma*

### CREAM OF POTATO SOUP SUPREME

| | |
|---|---|
| 4 med. potatoes, diced | 1/4 c. minced onion |
| 2 slices bacon, diced | 2 tbsp. butter |

| | |
|---|---|
| 1 tbsp. minced parsley | 1/4 tsp. dry mustard |
| 2 tsp. salt | 1/2 c. grated cheese |
| 1/2 tsp. nutmeg | 3 c. milk |
| Dash of red pepper | 1 tsp. Worcestershire sauce |

Cook the potatoes in boiling, salted water until tender, then drain. Mash. Saute the bacon and onion in butter in a large saucepan until light brown. Add the potatoes and remaining ingredients and cook over low heat until cheese is melted, stirring frequently. Serve immediately. 4-6 servings.

*Lois Demetro, Guymon, Oklahoma*

## FIRESIDE SEAFOOD CHOWDER

| | |
|---|---|
| 1 lb. fish fillets | Instant mashed potatoes |
| 2  6 1/2 or 7 1/2-oz. cans | for 4 servings |
| crab meat | 1 tbsp. basil |
| 1 c. thinly sliced celery | 1/2 tsp. paprika |
| 1 med. onion, finely chopped | 1/4 tsp. hot sauce |
| 1/2 c. butter | Salt and pepper to taste |
| 1 qt. milk | 1/2 c. chopped parsley |
| 3 c. water | |

Remove skin and bones from fish and cut fish into 1-inch pieces. Drain the crab meat and remove any remaining shell or cartilage. Saute the celery and onion in butter in a deep kettle until tender. Add the milk and water and bring to a boil. Blend in potatoes and cook, stirring constantly, until thickened. Add fish, crab meat and seasonings and simmer for 15 to 20 minutes or until fish flakes easily when tested with a fork. Sprinkle with parsley. 6 servings.

## AVOCADO SOUP WITH GARLIC

| | |
|---|---|
| 3 avocados | 1/2 tsp. salt |
| 1 1/2 c. chicken broth | 1 sm. clove of garlic, crushed |
| 2 tsp. lime juice | 1 1/2 c. heavy cream |

Puree the avocados with small amount of the broth, lime juice, salt and garlic. Combine with remaining broth and cream and chill thoroughly. Garnish with lemon slices or whipped cream seasoned with a dash of garlic powder. 6-8 servings.

*Photograph for this recipe on page 33.*

## HEARTY VEGETABLE SOUP

| | |
|---|---|
| 1 1/2 lb. stew beef | Sliced okra to taste |
| Salt to taste | 1 pkg. frozen cream-style corn |
| 1 med. onion, chopped | 2 c. canned tomatoes |
| 1 hot pepper | 2 tbsp. catsup |
| 6 potatoes, chopped | Pepper to taste |
| 1 pkg. frozen baby lima beans | Sugar to taste |

Place the stew beef in a kettle and cover with water. Season with salt. Add the onion and hot pepper and bring to a boil. Reduce heat and cover. Simmer until beef is tender. Add the potatoes, lima beans, okra and corn and simmer until vegetables are nearly done. Add the tomatoes, catsup, pepper and sugar and simmer for 20 to 30 minutes longer. 8 servings.

*Mrs. B. C. Fairley, Baton Rouge, Louisiana*

## TIP-TOP VEGETABLE SOUP

| | |
|---|---|
| 4 lb. beef shanks | 6 sprigs of parsley |
| 2 tbsp. shortening | 6 carrots, sliced |
| 2 qt. water | 2 c. cut green beans |
| 1 tsp. salt | 1 c. diced potatoes |
| 1 sm. onion, chopped | 1/2 c. chopped celery |
| 1  16-oz. can tomatoes | 1/4 c. rice or barley |

Brown the beef shanks in shortening in a kettle, then pour off excess fat. Add the water and bring to a boil. Add the salt and onion and reduce heat. Simmer for 2 hours. Add remaining ingredients and simmer for 1 hour longer. Remove beef shanks and cool. Remove beef from bones and return to soup. Reheat and serve. 8-10 servings.

*Claude W. Dodd, Durant, Mississippi*

## SPANISH CORN SOUP

| | |
|---|---|
| 1/4 c. butter | 1/4 c. chopped pimento |
| 1/2 c. chopped onion | 3 c. milk |
| 1/4 c. chopped green pepper | 1 tsp. salt |
| 1 No. 303 can yellow cream-style corn | 1/4 tsp. pepper |

Melt the butter in a saucepan. Add the onion and green pepper and cook until onion is transparent. Add the corn, pimento, milk, salt and pepper and bring to a boil. Remove from heat and serve. 6 servings.

*Mrs. Walter Griggs, Sapulpa, Oklahoma*

## SOPA DE MARISCOS

Olive or salad oil
2 med. onions, chopped
2 cloves of garlic, minced
3 tbsp. finely chopped
    parsley
2 tsp. crushed oregano
1 tsp. paprika
1 tbsp. chili powder
1/2 tsp. cumin
1/2 tsp. sage
1/2 can tomato paste
1   1-lb. 13-oz. can tomatoes
1/4 c. sherry
1/4 c. fresh lemon juice

1 tsp. grated lemon peel
1   8-oz. bottle clam juice
1 qt. water or fish stock
1 1/2 tsp. sugar
1 1/2 tsp. salt
1 lb. cod, cut in chunks
1/2 lb. cleaned shrimp
1 med. lobster in shell, cut
   in pieces
1 med. crab, cracked in
   pieces
1 doz. unshucked clams,
   scrubbed
Lemon slices

Heat 3 tablespoons oil in a large, heavy kettle or Dutch oven. Add the onions and garlic and saute until soft. Add the parsley and saute lightly. Combine next 5 ingredients in a cup. Add several drops of oil and blend well. Stir into sauteed mixture. Add the tomato paste and blend well. Cook for 3 minutes. Add remaining ingredients except the cod, shellfish and lemon slices and cover. Simmer for 35 to 40 minutes. Add the cod and cook for 5 minutes. Add the shrimp, lobster and crab and cook for 5 minutes. Add the clams and cook until clams open wide. Garnish with lemon slices. 6 servings.

# seafood

Outsiders who think the Southwest is a flat, dry expanse of plain and prairie are wrong, Southwestern natives claim. Theirs is a region sprinkled with clear creeks, rivers, and lakes and bordered by the glittering Mexican Gulf. Southwesterners can enjoy lazy inland fishing with pole and string or more challenging deep-sea sport. Whatever their preference, they're sure to bring home a successful day's catch, and you can bet they'll eat it for dinner that night.

They've created favorite recipes for the region's plentiful fish and shellfish. Perch, trout, bass, and other freshwater fish are popularly baked, fried, planked, and barbecued according to representative recipes in this section. You'll also find typical recipes for baked, broiled, and barbecued king mackerel, red snapper, flounder, and other Gulf fish.

Accessible shellfish include shrimp, oysters, lobsters, and crabs. Shrimp and oysters especially define coastal diet. Southwesterners favor oysters raw, though recipes for fried and scalloped oysters and oyster pie have become popular, too. There's regional agreement that shrimp should be fried.

Far more than an arid range, this is a region with inland and coastal waters, and enough fish and shellfish tomake an outsider envious.

## BAKED RED SNAPPER WITH TOMATO SAUCE

| | |
|---|---|
| 1  3-lb. dressed red snapper | 1 sm. onion, chopped |
| Salt and pepper | 1 tbsp. chopped green pepper |
| Margarine or butter | 1 tsp. sugar |
| 1 No. 2 can tomatoes | 1 tbsp. Worcestershire sauce |

Sprinkle the snapper inside and out with salt and pepper and place in a baking dish. Rub with margarine. Cook the tomatoes, onion, green pepper, sugar, 1/4 teaspoon salt and 1 tablespoon margarine in a saucepan for about 10 minutes. Add the Worcestershire sauce and cook for several minutes. Bake the snapper at 350 degrees for 1 hour, basting occasionally with tomato mixture. 4 servings.

*Mrs. Muriel Falkner, Bessemer, Alabama*

## SNAPPER-SHRIMP BAKE

| | |
|---|---|
| 4 red snapper fillets | 1 can frozen shrimp soup, |
| 2 cans shrimp, drained | thawed |
| Salt and pepper to taste | 1/2 c. buttered bread crumbs |
| 1/2 soup can water | |

Place the snapper fillets in a greased, shallow baking dish and sprinkle shrimp over fillets. Sprinkle with salt and pepper. Mix the water and soup and pour over fillets. Cover with bread crumbs. Bake at 350 degrees for 30 minutes.

*Mrs. Sharon Meadows, Arlington, Virginia*

## SNAPPER PUDDING

| | |
|---|---|
| 1  4-lb. red snapper | 1/2 c. flour |
| 1 bay leaf | 2 tsp. salt |
| 1 onion, sliced | 4 c. milk |
| 3 whole cloves | 1  8-oz. can sliced mushrooms |
| 5/8 c. butter | 1/2 c. grated Parmesan cheese |

Cook the snapper in boiling water with bay leaf, onion and cloves for 10 minutes, then cool in liquid. Drain. Remove bones from snapper and flake the snapper. Melt 1/2 cup butter in a saucepan and stir in flour. Add the salt and milk and cook until thickened, stirring constantly. Drain the mushrooms and add to the sauce. Add the snapper and mix well. Place in a greased casserole and cover with cheese. Dot with remaining butter. Bake at 350 degrees for 15 minutes.

*Mrs. Caroline Callaway, Chattanooga, Tennessee*

## BAKED HALIBUT

| | |
|---|---|
| 10 slices salt pork | 3 tbsp. flour |
| 1 lge. onion, sliced | 3 tbsp. butter |
| 3 bay leaves, crushed | 3/4 c. buttered cracker crumbs |
| 2 lb. halibut fillets | |

Place 6 slices salt pork in bottom of a baking pan and cover with onion and bay leaves. Place the halibut on the onion mixture. Mix the flour and butter and spread on the halibut. Cover with crumbs and remaining salt pork. Bake in 350-degree oven for 50 minutes.

*Mrs. Vernon Harrison, Albuquerque, New Mexico*

## BAKED STUFFED BASS

| | |
|---|---|
| 1/2 c. butter or salad oil | 1/2 tsp. dried sage |
| 1 1/2 c. minced onion | 1/2 tsp. dried thyme |
| 2 c. diced celery | 1 c. chopped stuffed olives |
| 3/4 c. chopped green pepper | 1   5 to 7-lb. bass |
| 2 2/3 c. cooked rice | Melted butter |
| Salt | 1 lemon, sliced |
| 1/2 tsp. pepper | 1/4 c. chopped parsley |

Melt the butter in a skillet. Add the onion, celery and green pepper and saute for 3 to 4 minutes or until tender. Add the rice, 1/2 teaspoon salt, pepper, sage, thyme and olives and mix well. Remove bone from bass. Rub bass inside and out with salt and melted butter. Place stuffing inside the bass and secure with skewers. Place the bass in a baking pan. Bake at 375 degrees for 1 hour and 30 minutes or until done. Arrange lemon slices on the fish, 1 slice overlapping another, and sprinkle with parsley. 7-10 servings.

*Celia J. Wilson, Florence, Alabama*

## HUKILAU FISH FEAST

| | |
|---|---|
| 2 med. California avocados | 1 whole baked fish, |
| Dash of hot sauce |    including head and tail |
| Dash of garlic salt (opt.) | 2 lge. lemons, thinly sliced |
| 1 tsp. lemon juice | |

Mash the avocados. Add the hot sauce, garlic salt and lemon juice and mix well. Spread on the body of fish with head and tail exposed. Arrange lemon slices on avocado spread and garnish with parsley.

## GOURMET HALIBUT WITH OYSTER SAUCE

| | |
|---|---|
| 6 tbsp. butter | 1/4 c. cream |
| 2 lb. halibut fillets | 1/4 tsp. salt |
| 1/2 pt. oysters | Cayenne pepper to taste |
| 1/2 c. white wine | 1/3 c. coarse cracker crumbs |
| 1 1/2 tbsp. flour | |

Melt 2 tablespoons butter in a frypan. Add the halibut and cook over low heat until halibut turns white. Place in a baking dish. Place the oysters in pan drippings. Add the wine and cook for 3 minutes. Drain and reserve liquid. Place the oysters on halibut. Melt 2 tablespoons butter in a saucepan and stir in the flour. Stir in the cream and reserved liquid and cook, stirring, until thickened. Stir in the salt and cayenne pepper and pour over oysters. Melt remaining butter and stir in cracker crumbs. Spread over sauce. Bake in 400-degree oven for 20 minutes.

*Mrs. Joseph L. Rawlinson, St. Petersburg Beach, Florida*

## HALIBUT STEAKS

| | |
|---|---|
| 2 lb. halibut steaks | 1 c. sliced onion |
| Salad oil | 1 c. cracker crumbs |
| 1 tsp. salt | 2 tsp. marjoram |
| 1/4 tsp. pepper | 1 1/2 c. light cream |

Brush the steaks with salad oil. Place in a baking dish and sprinkle with salt and pepper. Cook the onion in 1/4 cup oil in a saucepan until tender. Add the crumbs and marjoram and mix well. Spread on halibut and pour cream over top. Bake at 375 degrees for about 30 minutes. 4 servings.

*Mrs. John M. Kinney, Dallas, Texas*

## BAKED MACKEREL

| | |
|---|---|
| 1  2-lb. mackerel | Dash of thyme |
| 1/8 tsp. pepper | 1/4 c. lemon juice |
| 1/2 tsp. garlic salt | 1/2 c. water |
| 3 tbsp. cooking oil | 1/4 c. bread crumbs |
| 1 med. onion, finely chopped | 1 tsp. grated lemon peel |
| 1 green pepper, finely chopped | 1 tbsp. butter |
| 3 fresh tomatoes, finely chopped | |

Split the mackerel and place in a well-greased shallow baking dish. Sprinkle with pepper and garlic salt. Heat the oil in a saucepan. Add the onion, green pepper and tomatoes and saute for 5 minutes. Stir in the thyme, lemon juice and water and pour over mackerel. Combine bread crumbs, lemon peel and butter and sprinkle over mackerel. Bake at 350 degrees for 40 minutes.

*Mrs. R. E. Law, Maryville, Tennessee*

## BROILED MACKEREL

1/4 c. lemon juice
1/4 c. water
Salt to taste
4 lge. mackerel fillets

1/4 c. melted butter
Garlic salt to taste
Paprika to taste

Mix the lemon juice, water and salt in a bowl. Place the fillets in a baking dish. Broil 6 to 8 inches from heat for about 15 minutes or until brown, basting frequently with lemon mixture. Brush with butter and sprinkle with garlic salt and paprika. Garnish with lemon wedges and parsley.

*Mrs. Sarrah Glover, Quincy, Florida*

## JAUNTY HALIBUT STEAK PLATTER

2 lb. halibut steaks
1/2 c. melted butter
1/4 c. orange juice
1 tbsp. minced onion
1/2 tsp. paprika
1/4 tsp. hot sauce
1/4 tsp. salt

1   10-oz. package frozen carrot
    nuggets in butter sauce
1   10-oz. package frozen
    broccoli spears in butter
    sauce
Lemon cartwheel twists

Cut the steaks into 4 or 6 portions and place in a single layer on a well-greased broiler rack. Combine the butter, orange juice, onion, paprika, hot sauce and salt and mix well. Brush steaks generously with butter sauce. Broil, basting frequently with butter sauce, 3 to 4 inches from heat for 10 to 15 minutes or until fish flakes easily when tested with a fork. Prepare the carrots and broccoli according to package directions. Arrange the steaks on a warm platter with carrots and broccoli and add lemon twists.

## FRIED TROUT

| | |
|---|---|
| 1/4 c. evaporated milk | 1/4 c. cornmeal |
| 1 1/2 tsp. salt | 1 tsp. paprika |
| 1/8 tsp. pepper | 6 dressed trout |
| 1/2 c. flour | |

Combine the milk, salt and pepper in a shallow bowl. Combine the flour, cornmeal and paprika in another bowl. Dip the trout into milk mixture, then roll in flour mixture. Cook in small amount of fat in heavy iron skillet for 5 minutes or until brown. Turn carefully and cook for 5 minutes longer or until brown and fish flakes easily when tested with a fork. Drain on absorbent paper. Garnish with lemon slice twists, crab apples and parsley. Serve with creamed onions and glazed carrots.

## PLANKED TROUT

| | |
|---|---|
| 1   5-lb. trout, cleaned | 1/2 tsp. oregano |
| Salt and pepper | 1/3 c. milk |
| 1 c. diced onions | 4 slices bacon |
| 1/4 c. finely chopped celery | 1/2 c. chopped macadamia nuts |
| 3/4 c. butter | Juice of 1/2 lemon |
| 2 c. cracker crumbs | 1/2 c. dry sherry |

Place the trout on a rack in a 9 x 15-inch baking pan and season with salt and pepper inside and out. Cook the onions and celery in 1/4 cup butter in a saucepan until tender. Add the crumbs, 1/2 teaspoon salt, oregano, 1/4 teaspoon pepper and milk. Place in trout cavity and secure with skewers. Place the bacon over the trout. Bake at 350 degrees for 2 hours or until fish flakes easily when tested with a fork. Remove trout to a plank. Brown the macadamia nuts in remaining butter, then add lemon juice and sherry. Pour over the trout and garnish with mashed potatoes.

*Mrs. Pauline Olmstead, Waco, Texas*

## LAKE TROUT WITH FRENCH DRESSING

| | |
|---|---|
| 3 lb. lake trout fillets | 1 tsp. parsley flakes |
| Juice of 1 lemon | 1/2 c. French dressing |
| Salt and pepper to taste | 2 tbsp. melted butter |

Place the fillets, skin side down, in a shallow baking dish and sprinkle with lemon juice, salt, pepper and parsley. Pour remaining ingredients over the fillets. Bake at 350 degrees for 1 hour, basting several times with pan juices.

*Wendy Jennings, Alexandria, Louisiana*

## STUFFED TROUT

| | |
|---|---|
| 2 tbsp. olive oil | 1 c. bread crumbs |
| 1/4 c. chopped celery | Salt and pepper to taste |
| 1 clove of garlic, minced | 4 trout fillets |
| 1/4 c. chopped green onions | Flour |
| 1/2 c. chopped cooked shrimp | Melted butter |
| 1/2 c. lump crab meat | 1/4 c. lemon juice |

Heat the olive oil in a skillet. Add the celery, garlic and green onions and cook over low heat until soft but not brown. Add the shrimp and cook for several minutes, stirring constantly. Add the crab meat, bread crumbs, salt and pepper and mix. Dust trout with flour lightly and brush with butter. Season the trout fillets with salt and pepper. Place the stuffing on 2 fillets and cover with remaining fillets. Place in baking dish with a very small amount of water and brush with butter. Bake at 350 degrees until fish flakes easily when tested with a fork. Place on a platter. Mix 1/4 cup butter with the lemon juice and pour over the trout.

*Mrs. Alpha Hardcastle, Aransas Pass, Texas*

## BAKED PERCH FILLETS

| | |
|---|---|
| 1 pkg. frozen perch fillets | Grated rind of 1 lemon |
| 1/4 c. almonds | 1/2 tsp. paprika |
| 3 tbsp. soft butter or | 1/4 tsp. salt |
|    margarine | 1/4 tsp. pepper |

Thaw the perch fillets. Blanch the almonds in boiling water and drain. Remove skins and chop almonds. Mix with remaining ingredients. Place the fillets, skin side down, in a baking dish and spread with almond mixture. Bake at 350 degrees for 15 to 20 minutes or until fish flakes easily when tested with a fork.

*Fay Lightfoot, Austin, Texas*

## BARBECUED PERCH

| | |
|---|---|
| 2 tbsp. chopped onion | 1 tbsp. Worcestershire sauce |
| 1 tbsp. shortening | 2 tbsp. dark brown sugar |
| 3/4 c. catsup | 1/2 tsp. salt |
| 1/4 c. vinegar | 1 lb. perch fillets |

Cook the onion in shortening in a saucepan until light brown. Add remaining ingredients except the fillets and simmer for 5 minutes. Place the fillets in greased, shallow baking pan and pour sauce over fillets. Bake at 375 degrees for 30 minutes.

*Ercelle H. Cooper, Petersburg, Virginia*


## PUFFY PERCH FILLETS

| | |
|---|---|
| 1  12-oz. package frozen perch fillets, thawed | 2 tbsp. chopped pickle |
| Salt and pepper | 1 tbsp. chopped parsley |
| 2 egg whites | 2 tsp. lemon juice |
| 3 tbsp. mayonnaise | Dash of cayenne pepper |

Arrange the perch in a greased, shallow baking dish and sprinkle with salt and pepper to taste. Bake in 400-degree oven for 20 minutes. Combine remaining ingredients in a bowl and add 1/4 teaspoon salt and pepper to taste. Beat with an electric mixer until soft peaks form, then spread over perch. Bake for 5 minutes longer or until perch flakes easily with fork and topping is puffy and golden brown.

*Mrs. Karl Metts, Wheeling, West Virginia*


## POMPANO EN PAPILLOTES

| | |
|---|---|
| 1 lemon, sliced | 1 onion, minced |
| 1 bay leaf | Salt to taste |
| 1 sprig of thyme | 1 c. cooked shrimp, chopped |
| 6 pompano fillets | 1/2 c. crab |
| 2 tbsp. butter | 6 sliced mushrooms, sauteed |
| 3 tbsp. flour | 2 egg yolks, beaten |

Add the lemon, bay leaf and thyme to 3 cups boiling, salted water in a skillet. Add the pompano fillets and simmer for 15 minutes. Drain and reserve 1 1/2 cups stock. Place each fillet on a sheet of parchment paper. Melt the butter in a saucepan and stir in flour. Add the onion and salt and cook until flour is light brown. Add reserved stock and cook, stirring constantly, until smooth and thickened. Add the shrimp, crab and mushrooms and remove from heat. Cool slightly, then stir in egg yolks. Spoon onto pompano and fold pompano over. Fold parchment paper to encase pompano and place on a baking sheet. Bake at 400 degrees for 10 minutes.

*Mrs. Richard Smith, Dover, Delaware*

## BROILED FISH FILLETS WITH POTATO RING

| | |
|---|---|
| 1 pkg. frozen fish fillets | 3 tbsp. melted butter |
| 3 med. cooked potatoes, | Salt and pepper to taste |
|    sliced | Paprika to taste |

Let fillets thaw on refrigerator shelf. Separate the fillets and place, skin side down, in a greased broiling pan. Arrange the potato slices in the broiling pan and brush potatoes and fillets with part of the butter. Sprinkle with salt and pepper and sprinkle the potatoes with paprika. Broil 2 inches from heat for 6 to 10 minutes or until fish flakes easily when tested with a fork, brushing fillets and potatoes with remaining butter occasionally. Place the fillets on a platter and place the potatoes, overlapping, around the fillets. Garnish with parsley. 4 servings.

## SALMON PIE

| | |
|---|---|
| 3 c. mashed potatoes | 1 tbsp. lemon juice |
| 1/2 c. shredded Cheddar cheese | 1 c. milk |
| 1 egg yolk | 1/2 tsp. salt |
| 1/4 c. chopped onion | 1/4 tsp. pepper |
| 4 tbsp. butter | 2 tbsp. chopped pimento |
| 3 tbsp. flour | 1   1-lb. can salmon, drained |

Combine the potatoes, cheese and egg yolk. Place in a greased 1 1/2-quart baking dish, covering bottom and sides and making a ruffled edge around top. Cook the onion in butter in a saucepan for 5 minutes. Stir in flour. Add the lemon juice and milk and cook, stirring, until thickened. Stir in the salt, pepper and pimento. Break the salmon into large pieces and add to sauce. Pour into the casserole. Bake at 325 degrees for 25 minutes or until potato edge is brown. 4-5 servings.

*Mrs. Kay Armer, Jr., Cocoa, Florida*

## SALMON-STUFFED SOLE WHIRLS

| | |
|---|---|
| 4 med. fillets of sole | 1 tbsp. minced onion |
| 1  1-lb. can salmon | 2 tbsp. flour |
| 1 tbsp. lemon juice | 1 c. light cream |
| Butter | 1/2 tsp. dry dillweed |
| 1/2 tsp. salt | 1 tbsp. chopped parsley |
| Pepper to taste | Lemon slices |
| 1/4 lb. mushrooms, sliced | Parsley sprigs |

Preheat oven to 350 degrees. Cut the fillets in half lengthwise and remove the fine line of bones down the center of each. Pour the liquid from can of salmon into a shallow baking dish. Flake the salmon and spread about 2 tablespoons on each fillet. Roll up as for jelly roll and fasten each with a wooden pick. Reserve remaining flaked salmon. Arrange the fish rolls in the baking dish and sprinkle with lemon juice. Dot each roll with 1/2 teaspoon butter and sprinkle with salt and pepper. Cover with foil. Bake for 20 minutes. Saute the mushrooms and onion in 3 tablespoons butter in a saucepan for 5 minutes. Stir in the flour. Stir in the cream gradually and cook, stirring, until smooth and thick. Add the dillweed and chopped parsley and set aside. Place the salmon rolls on a warm serving platter. Drain juices from baking pan into the sauce and add reserved salmon. Cook over moderate heat, stirring, until heated through. Pour over the fish rolls and garnish with lemon slices and parsley sprigs. Sauce may be served separately, if desired. 4 servings.

## SALMON-BLUE CHEESE FIDEO

| | |
|---|---|
| 1 can cream of asparagus soup | 1 can drained salmon, flaked |
| 1 soup can water | 4 oz. noodles, cooked |
| 1 c. crumbled blue cheese | Crushed round cheese crackers |
| Dash of Worcestershire sauce | Butter |

Mix the soup, water and cheese in a saucepan and heat, stirring, until cheese is melted. Add the Worcestershire sauce, salmon and noodles and pour into a greased casserole. Cover with cracker crumbs and dot with butter. Bake at 350 degrees for 35 to 40 minutes. 6 servings.

*Mrs. Raymond M. Ball, Sanford, Florida*

## SALMON CROQUETTES WITH PIMENTO SAUCE

| | |
|---|---|
| 3 c. flaked salmon | 1 tbsp. finely chopped onion |
| 2 c. soft bread crumbs | 1 tbsp. chopped parsley |
| 2 eggs, well beaten | Salt and pepper to taste |
| 2 tbsp. melted butter | 2 tsp. baking powder |

Combine the salmon and bread crumbs in a bowl. Add the eggs, butter, onion, parsley, seasonings and baking powder and mix thoroughly. Shape into small croquettes. Fry in deep fat at 375 degrees until brown. Drain.

Sauce

| | |
|---|---|
| 4 tbsp. butter | 2 c. milk |
| 4 tbsp. flour | 1 pimento, finely chopped |

Melt the butter in a saucepan and stir in the flour. Stir in the milk and cook over low heat, stirring constantly, until thickened. Stir in the pimento and spoon over croquettes.

*Mrs. Burnette S. Spencer, Trinity, North Carolina*

## BAKED STUFFED FLOUNDER

| | |
|---|---|
| 1 1/2 lb. peeled deveined shrimp | 1/2 c. cooking oil |
| Salt and pepper to taste | 1/2 lb. crab meat |
| Cayenne pepper to taste | 4 eggs |
| 2 bay leaves | 1/2 c. cracker crumbs |
| 3 buns | 1/4 c. chopped green onion tops |
| 1/2 c. chopped celery | 1/4 c. chopped parsley |
| 1 c. chopped onion | 4 med. flounder |
| 2 cloves of garlic, minced | Melted butter |

Cook the shrimp in boiling water with salt, pepper, cayenne pepper and bay leaves for 10 minutes. Drain and chop. Soak the buns in 1 cup water. Cook the celery, onion and garlic in the oil in a kettle over medium heat until onions are wilted. Add the shrimp, crab meat, buns and eggs and mix well. Stir in the cracker crumbs, onion tops and parsley and season with salt, pepper and cayenne pepper. Split flounder lengthwise, removing backbone, and stuff with shrimp mixture. Place in a baking pan. Bake at 375 degrees for 45 minutes or until fish flakes easily when tested with a fork. Brush with butter and serve.

*Mrs. Frances H. Walter, Charleston, South Carolina*

## STUFFED FLOUNDER ROLLS

| | |
|---|---|
| 1  2-oz. can sliced<br>    mushrooms | 2 tbsp. finely chopped parsley<br>1/4 tsp. dried dillweed |
| 4 tbsp. margarine | 1 lb. flounder fillets |
| 1/4 c. finely chopped celery | Paprika |
| 2 tbsp. finely chopped onion | |

Drain the mushrooms. Melt 3 tablespoons margarine in a small skillet over low heat. Add the celery and onion and cook until tender but not brown. Add the mushrooms, parsley and dillweed and mix well. Spread over fillets. Roll fillets from narrow end and place, seam side down, in a shallow baking dish. Dot with remaining margarine and sprinkle with paprika. Bake in 400-degree oven for 20 minutes or until fish flakes easily when tested with a fork. 4 servings.

*Mrs. Doris Barkalow, Tampa, Florida*

## OLD-FASHIONED TUNA CUSTARD PIE

| | |
|---|---|
| 1/2 lb. sliced bacon | 3 eggs, slightly beaten |
| 1 sm. onion, sliced | 1 1/4 c. light cream |
| 1  6 1/2 or 7-oz. can tuna | 1/2 tsp. salt |
| 1/4 lb. Swiss cheese,<br>    shredded | Dash of hot sauce<br>Nutmeg to taste |
| 1 unbaked 9-in. pie shell | |

Fry the bacon in a skillet until crisp. Remove from skillet, then drain and crumble. Pour off most of the drippings from the skillet. Add the onion and cook until soft. Drain and flake the tuna. Place the cheese in bottom of the pie shell and top with bacon, onion and tuna. Mix the eggs with cream, salt and hot sauce and pour over tuna. Sprinkle with nutmeg. Bake in 425-degree oven for 15 minutes. Reduce temperature to 325 degrees and bake for 25 to 30 minutes longer or until a knife inserted in center comes out clean.

## CRUSTY TUNA SURPRISE

| | |
|---|---|
| **1 can cheese soup** | **2 cans grated tuna, drained** |
| **1/2 c. milk** | **3/4 c. corn flake crumbs** |
| **2 c. cooked rice** | **2 tbsp. melted butter** |

Combine the soup, milk and rice. Place alternate layers of tuna and rice mixture in a greased casserole. Combine the corn flake crumbs and butter and sprinkle over casserole. Bake at 425 degrees for 15 minutes. 4 servings.

*Mrs. R. C. Hansen, Pointblank, Texas*

## TUNA PIE WITH CHEESE ROLLS

| | |
|---|---|
| **1/2 c. chopped green pepper** | **1/2 tsp. salt** |
| **1/4 c. chopped onion** | **3 c. milk** |
| **6 tbsp. butter** | **1 lge. can tuna, drained** |
| **6 tbsp. flour** | |

Cook the green pepper and onion in butter in a saucepan until soft. Blend in the flour and salt. Add the milk slowly and cook, stirring, until thick. Place the tuna in a baking dish and pour the sauce over tuna.

### Cheese Rolls

| | |
|---|---|
| **1 1/2 c. flour** | **3 tbsp. shortening** |
| **3 tbsp. baking powder** | **1/2 c. milk** |
| **1/2 tsp. salt** | **3/4 c. grated cheese** |

Combine the flour, baking powder and salt in a bowl and cut in the shortening. Add the milk and mix well. Roll out on a floured surface into a rectangle about 1/2 inch thick. Cover with cheese and roll as for jelly roll, starting with long side. Cut into 1-inch slices and place over tuna mixture. Bake at 450 degrees for 30 minutes. 6 servings.

*Mrs. Grace Warwick, Cumberland, Maryland*

## TUNA PUFFS

| | |
|---|---|
| **1 can cream of mushroom soup** | **2 c. soft bread crumbs** |
| **1/2 c. cubed Velveeta cheese** | **2 sm. cans tuna, drained** |
| **2 eggs, separated** | **3 tbsp. chopped green pepper** |
| **1 c. chopped pitted ripe olives** | **Paprika** |

Place the soup and cheese in a saucepan and heat until cheese melts, stirring frequently. Cool slightly. Stir in the beaten egg yolks, olives, bread crumbs and tuna and cool. Add green pepper and fold in the stiffly beaten egg whites. Place in well-buttered ramekins and sprinkle with paprika. Bake at 350 degrees for 30 minutes. 6 servings.

*Leila Clark, Houston, Texas*

## WHITEFISH WITH ARTICHOKES

| | |
|---|---|
| 1  6-lb. whitefish, dressed | 1/2 tsp. savory |
| Salt | 1 1/2 c. fish or chicken |
| 1/2 tsp. pepper | stock |
| 1/4 c. lemon juice | 10 med. artichokes |
| 4 med. onions, sliced | 1 lge. onion, chopped |
| 2 lge. cloves of garlic, | 2 tbsp. butter |
| crushed | 2 vegetable bouillon cubes |
| 1 c. chopped parsley | 1/2 tsp. saffron stamens |
| 1 c. melted butter | 2 c. rice |
| 5 med. peeled tomatoes, | Lemon slices |
| diced | Parsley sprigs |
| 1/2 tsp. crushed rosemary | |

Sprinkle the whitefish with 2 teaspoons salt, pepper and lemon juice and place in a foil-lined shallow baking pan. Cook the sliced onions, garlic and 3/4 cup chopped parsley in the melted butter in saucepan over low heat for 5 minutes. Add the tomatoes, 1 cup water, rosemary, savory, fish stock and 2 teaspoons salt and simmer for 5 minutes, stirring occasionally. Pour over the whitefish. Bake at 350 degrees for 50 to 60 minutes, basting occasionally with sauce. Wash the artichokes. Cut off stems at base and remove small bottom leaves. Trim tips of leaves and cut off about 1 inch from top of artichokes. Stand artichokes upright in deep saucepan large enough to hold snugly. Add 2 to 3 inches boiling water and 2 1/2 teaspoons salt. Cover and simmer for 35 to 45 minutes or until base may be pierced easily with a fork, adding boiling water, if needed. Turn artichokes upside down to drain. Spread leaves gently and remove choke from center of artichokes with a metal spoon. Combine 4 cups cold water, chopped onion, butter, bouillon cubes, 2 teaspoons salt and saffron in a heavy saucepan and let stand for 5 minutes. Add the rice and bring to a boil, stirring frequently. Reduce heat and stir. Cover tightly and simmer for 12 to 14 minutes or until rice is tender. Fill artichokes with rice. Arrange the whitefish on a large platter with artichokes. Sprinkle the whitefish with remaining chopped parsley and garnish with lemon slices and parsley. Pour the sauce in baking pan into a bowl and serve with whitefish. Dry white wine may be substituted for fish stock.

*Photograph for this recipe on page 74.*

## CRAB MEAT DIVINE

| | |
|---|---|
| 2  10-oz. packages frozen | 1/8 tsp. pepper |
| broccoli | 2  6 1/2-oz. cans white crab |
| 2/3 c. sour cream | meat, drained |
| 1/3 c. French dressing | 2 hard-cooked eggs, chopped |
| 1/2 tsp. salt | 2 tbsp. grated Parmesan cheese |

Cook the broccoli according to package directions. Drain and arrange in a shallow baking dish. Mix remaining ingredients except cheese and place over broccoli. Sprinkle with cheese. Bake at 350 degrees for 15 to 20 minutes. Spinach may be substituted for broccoli. 4-6 servings.

*Mrs. Lorraine H. Mott, Tucson, Arizona*

## CRAB IMPERIAL

| | |
|---|---|
| 6 tbsp. butter | 2 1/2 c. thick white sauce |
| 3/4 c. finely chopped onions | 1 tsp. Worcestershire sauce |
| 2 tbsp. chopped pimento | 1 tsp. dry mustard |
| 1/4 tsp. salt | 3 egg yolks, beaten |
| Dash of cayenne pepper | Bread crumbs |
| 1 lb. crab meat | |

Melt the butter in a saucepan. Add the onions, pimento, salt and cayenne pepper and cook until onions are tender. Stir in the crab meat and cook for 2 minutes. Add the white sauce, Worcestershire sauce and mustard and stir well. Bring to a boil. Stir small amount of hot mixture into egg yolks, then stir back into the hot mixture. Place in a casserole and cover with bread crumbs. Dot with additional butter. Bake at 400 degrees until brown.

*Phoebe G. Fripp, Beaufort, South Carolina*

## DEVILED CRAB

| | |
|---|---|
| 1 c. milk | 1/3 tsp. dry mustard |
| 1 c. soft bread crumbs | 1/2 tsp. lemon juice |
| 2 c. cooked crab meat, flaked | 1/8 tsp. cayenne pepper |
| 2 hard-boiled eggs | 1/4 c. melted margarine |
| 1 1/2 tsp. salt | Buttered bread crumbs |

Combine the milk and bread crumbs in a bowl and stir in the crab meat and chopped egg whites. Blend in mashed egg yolks and remaining ingredients except buttered bread crumbs and place in a greased 10 x 6 x 2-inch baking dish. Sprinkle with buttered crumbs. Bake in 400-degree oven for 15 minutes. 6 servings.

*Joan M. Howlett, Greenville, South Carolina*

## CRAB TETRAZZINI

| | |
|---|---|
| 2 tbsp. butter or margarine | 2 tbsp. sherry |
| 2 tbsp. flour | 1/2 c. sour cream |
| 1/2 tsp. paprika | 1 egg yolk, beaten |
| 1/2 tsp. salt | 1/2 lb. crab meat |
| 1/8 tsp. pepper | 2 tsp. lemon juice |
| 1 c. thin cream | 1/3 c. finely chopped almonds |
| 1 tsp. instant minced onion | Hot cooked spaghetti |

Melt the butter in a saucepan over low heat and stir in the flour, paprika, salt and pepper. Stir in the cream and onion and cook over low heat, stirring constantly, until sauce comes to a boil. Remove from heat. Stir in sherry and sour cream, then the egg yolk. Stir in the crab meat and heat through. Add the lemon juice and half the almonds. Fill 6 individual casseroles about 1/2 full with spaghetti and spoon crab meat mixture over spaghetti. Sprinkle with remaining almonds. Bake at 400 degrees for 15 minutes.

*Ruth A. Sale, Charlotte, North Carolina*

## SPAGHETTI WITH CHINESE LOBSTER SAUCE

| | |
|---|---|
| 1   16-oz. package frozen lobster-tails, thawed | 1 lge. clove of garlic, minced |
| 1/4 c. oil | 3/4 c. cold water |
| 1 lb. ground pork | 2 tbsp. dry sherry (opt.) |
| 1 qt. chicken broth | 1/2 c. cornstarch |
| 1/4 c. soy sauce | Salt |
| 2 tbsp. sugar | 4 to 6 qt. boiling water |
| 2 tsp. monosodium glutamate | 1 lb. spaghetti |
| | 1 c. sliced scallions |

Remove lobster meat from shells and cut into bite-sized pieces. Heat the oil in large wok or skillet. Add the pork and cook, stirring frequently, until brown. Add the chicken broth, soy sauce, sugar, monosodium glutamate and garlic and simmer for 15 minutes. Add the lobster meat and bring to a boil. Blend the cold water with sherry and cornstarch and stir into the pork mixture. Simmer, stirring constantly, for about 5 minutes or until thickened. Season with salt to taste. Add 2 tablespoons salt to the boiling water and add the spaghetti gradually so that water continues to boil. Cook, stirring occasionally, until tender, then drain in a colander. Sprinkle with scallions and serve with lobster sauce. 8 servings.

## LOBSTER THERMIDOR

| | |
|---|---|
| 4   6-oz. frozen rock lobster-tails | 1/2 tsp. prepared mustard |
| Vinegar | 1 1/2 c. milk |
| 4 tbsp. butter or margarine | 1 c. heavy cream |
| 4 tbsp. flour | 1/2 tsp. grated onion |
| | 1 tsp. salt |

| | |
|---|---|
| 1/2 tsp. celery salt | 2 tsp. lemon juice |
| Dash of cayenne pepper | 1/4 to 1/3 c. sherry |
| 2 egg yolks, slightly beaten | Buttered crumbs |

Drop the lobster-tails into boiling water and add 1 tablespoon vinegar for each quart of water. Bring to a boil and cook for 9 minutes. Drain and plunge into cold water. Drain. Cut away thin under membranes with kitchen scissors. Pull out lobster meat and cut into small pieces. Reserve outer shells. Melt the butter in a saucepan over low heat, then blend in flour. Add the mustard. Remove from heat. Stir in milk gradually and cook, stirring constantly, until thickened. Add the heavy cream, onion, salt, celery salt and cayenne pepper and mix. Blend small amount of hot sauce into egg yolks, then stir back into remaining sauce. Stir in the lemon juice, sherry and lobster meat. Fill reserved shells with lobster mixture and cover with buttered crumbs. Place on a baking sheet. Broil until light brown.

*Celia Stansbury, Asheville, North Carolina*


## SCALLOPED OYSTERS

| | |
|---|---|
| 1 pt. oysters | 2 c. cracker crumbs |
| Milk | Salt and pepper to taste |
| 1 tsp. Worcestershire sauce | 1/2 c. melted butter |
| 2 tbsp. cooking sherry (opt.) | |

Drain the oysters and reserve liquid. Add enough milk to reserved liquid to make 1 cup liquid and stir in the Worcestershire sauce and sherry. Combine the cracker crumbs, salt, pepper and butter and sprinkle 1/3 of the mixture in a greased casserole. Cover with half the oysters. Sprinkle with half the remaining crumb mixture, then add remaining oysters. Sprinkle with remaining crumb mixture and pour the milk mixture over top. Bake in 400-degree oven for 30 minutes or until brown. 6 servings.

*Mary M. Brightwell, Brooksville, Florida*


## OYSTER PIE

| | |
|---|---|
| 2 c. sifted flour | 2 tbsp. butter |
| 1 1/2 tsp. salt | 1 pt. oysters, drained |
| 2/3 c. shortening | 1 c. cracker crumbs |
| 5 tbsp. water | 1 tsp. Worcestershire sauce |
| 2 green onions, finely chopped | 1/2 tsp. hot sauce |
| 1 clove of garlic, minced | 2 tbsp. lemon juice |

Place the flour and 1 teaspoon salt in a mixing bowl and cut in the shortening. Stir in the water, small amount at a time, and mix well. Roll out half the dough on a floured surface and place in a pie pan. Cook the green onions and garlic in butter in a saucepan until golden brown. Remove from heat. Place the oysters in the pastry-lined pan and sprinkle the cracker crumbs over oysters. Add the Worcestershire sauce, hot sauce, remaining salt and lemon juice to the onion mixture and mix well. Place over cracker crumbs. Roll out remaining pastry on the floured surface and place over pie. Seal edge and cut slits in center. Bake at 400 degrees for 10 minutes. Reduce temperature to 350 degrees and bake for 40 minutes longer. Serve hot.

*Lorraine Steele, Houston, Texas*

## FRIED OYSTERS

1 pkg. crackers
1 pt. select oysters, drained

2 eggs, beaten

Crush the crackers fine. Dip the oysters in eggs and roll in cracker crumbs. Fry in hot, deep fat until golden brown.

*Fay Parnell, New London, North Carolina*

## SHRIMP WIGGLE

4 tbsp. butter
4 tbsp. flour
1/2 tsp. salt
1/8 tsp. pepper
1/2 tsp. celery salt
1 tbsp. paprika

2 c. milk
1/2 tsp. onion juice
3 drops of hot sauce
2 c. cleaned cooked shrimp
2 c. tiny green peas
Holland rusk

Melt the butter in a saucepan and blend in the flour, salt, pepper, celery salt and paprika. Add the milk and onion juice and cook until thickened, stirring constantly. Add the hot sauce, shrimp and peas and heat through. Serve on Holland rusk. 6 servings.

*May Archibald, Chattanooga, Tennessee*

## SHRIMP NEWBURG

1 lb. cleaned cooked shrimp
3 tbsp. sherry
1/4 c. butter or margarine
1 1/2 tbsp. flour
1 1/2 c. light cream
2 egg yolks, well beaten

Dash of cayenne pepper
1/2 tsp. salt
1 tbsp. lemon juice
1 tsp. Worcestershire sauce
1/2 c. canned mushrooms

Place the shrimp in a bowl and sprinkle with sherry. Melt the butter in top of a double boiler. Add the flour and blend well. Add the cream slowly, and cook over low heat, stirring constantly, until thickened. Stir small amount of sauce into the egg yolks, then stir back into remaining sauce. Place over boiling water. Add the seasonings and stir well. Add the mushrooms and shrimp and stir gently until heated through. Serve immediately over toast triangles. 6 servings.

*Mrs. W. E. Emish, Dallas, Texas*

## SWEET-SOUR SHRIMP

1 c. sliced celery
1 c. green pepper strips
1/2 c. sliced onion
1/4 c. salad oil
2 tbsp. flour
1 1/2 c. tomato juice

1/4 c. (packed) brown sugar
1/2 tsp. salt
1 tbsp. grated lemon rind
1/4 c. lemon juice
1 1/2 lb. cleaned cooked shrimp

Saute the celery, green pepper and onion in hot oil in a saucepan for about 10 minutes or until lightly browned. Stir in the flour. Add the tomato juice slowly and cook, stirring, until thickened. Add the brown sugar, salt, lemon rind and lemon juice and stir until blended. Cook for about 5 minutes, stirring occasionally. Add the shrimp and heat through. Serve with rice and garnish with lemon quarters. Yield: 4-6 servings.

*Mary Bagley, Grand Junction, Colorado*

## SHRIMP OLE

| | |
|---|---|
| 1 lb. shrimp | 1 No. 2 can tomatoes |
| 1  4-oz. can chopped mushrooms | 1 bay leaf |
| 2 tbsp. vegetable oil | 1/2 tsp. oregano |
| 3 med. onions, sliced | 1 1/2 tsp. chili powder |
| 1 clove of garlic, minced | 2 pimentos, sliced |
| 1 c. sliced celery | 1 tsp. salt |
| 1/2 green pepper, sliced | 1/8 tsp. pepper |
| 1 tbsp. flour | Corn chips or hot cooked rice |

Shell and devein the shrimp. Drain the mushrooms. Heat the oil in a large frying pan. Add the onions, garlic, celery and green pepper and cook until onions and celery are tender. Sprinkle with flour and cook, stirring constantly, until mixture is lightly browned. Add the tomatoes, bay leaf, oregano, chili powder, mushrooms, pimentos, salt and pepper and cook for at least 10 minutes. Add the shrimp and bring to a boil. Reduce heat and simmer for about 3 minutes. Serve on corn chips. 4 servings.

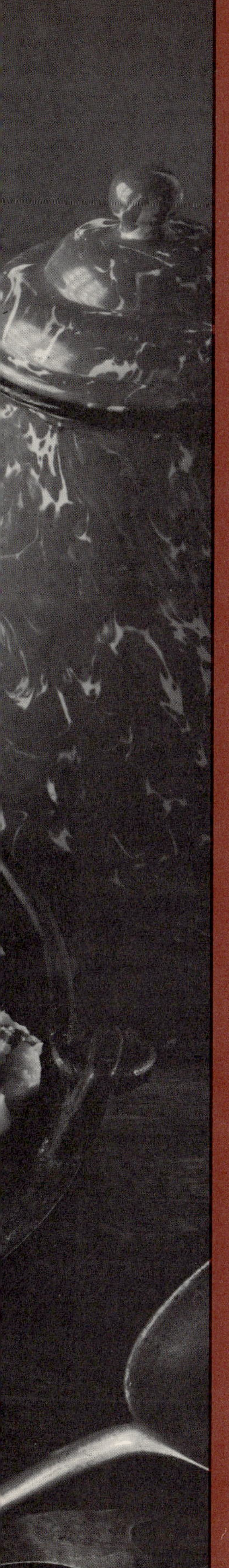

# poultry and game birds

Southwesterners have some strong ideas about poultry and game birds, and it'd take a lot of convincing to change them. According to Southwestern natives, poultry tastes most delicious when cooked outdoors over coals or used in certain dishes of Mexican origin. And game birds should be bagged skillfully, dressed properly, and cooked right, which means cooked simply and plainly and not "fancied up."

In this section you'll find recipes that illustrate the Southwestern attitude toward poultry and game birds. There are recipes for grilling poultry outdoors. The Mexican influence is conspicuous in recipes such as arroz con pollo, chicken with rice; chicken enchiladas; chicken tacos; chicken tamale pie; and chicken hot tamales. A recipe for Chili Chicken alternates layers of zesty onion, pepper, chili powder, and tomato sauce with chicken.

Game bird recipes are less elaborate. Characteristic regional favorites tell how to bake, roast, braise, and fry game birds like dove, duck, goose, pheasant, and quail. Game pies are popular, and Southwestern hunters aren't adverse to stuffed and baked game. Southwesterners, in fact, have many delicious recipes for the game birds so plentiful in this region.

The following recipes for poultry and game birds will have you thinking like native Southwesterners and enjoying poultry and game birds the way that they do!

## TOSTADOS CON POLLO

1 med. head western iceberg
  lettuce
1  8-oz. can tortillas
1/2 c. salad oil
2  1-lb. cans kidney beans,
  drained
1/4 tsp. garlic powder
Salt and pepper to taste
Hot sauce to taste

1  12-oz. can boned chicken,
  sliced
2 peeled avocados, sliced
1 c. grated Parmesan cheese
1 med. tomato, thinly sliced
2 seeded canned green chilies
1 med. tomato, quartered
1 sm. onion, quartered

Core the lettuce. Wash in cold water and drain well. Shred the lettuce with a sharp knife. Fry the tortillas in hot oil in a skillet for about 3 seconds, then drain on paper towels. Drain off all except 2 tablespoons oil from the skillet. Add the beans and garlic powder and cook, mashing the beans, until thick. Stir in the salt and pepper. Spread the bean mixture on half the tortillas and sprinkle with hot sauce. Top with chicken, avocado slices, Parmesan cheese, remaining tortillas, sliced tomato and lettuce. Combine the green chilies, quartered tomato and onion in an electric blender container and blend until smooth. Place on lettuce. 6 servings.

## ARROZ CON POLLO

1  2 1/2 to 3-lb. chicken
Seasoned flour
1/3 c. fat or salad oil
1 med. onion, chopped
1 clove of garlic, minced

1 c. rice
3 1/2 to 4 c. canned tomatoes
1 tsp. salt
1 green pepper, sliced
  in rings

Cut the chicken in serving pieces and dip in seasoned flour. Cook in hot fat in a skillet until brown and arrange in a greased 3-quart casserole. Cook the onion and garlic in remaining fat in the skillet until soft and add to chicken. Sprinkle the rice around chicken and add tomatoes and salt. Cover tightly. Bake in 350-degree oven for 1 hour and 10 minutes. Add the green pepper and bake for 20 minutes longer. 4-6 servings.

*Ruby Danzy Harris, Guntersville, Alabama*

## BAKED CHICKEN AND OREGANO RICE

| | |
|---|---|
| 1 broiler, disjointed | 1/4 c. chopped green pepper |
| 1 c. melted butter or margarine | 1   3-oz. can mushrooms, drained |
| 1 box round cheese crackers, rolled fine | 3/4 tsp. oregano |
| Pepper and paprika to taste | 1 can beef consomme |
| 6 green onions, chopped | 1 consomme can water |
| | 1 c. rice |

Dip the chicken in half the butter and roll in cracker crumbs. Place in a shallow casserole in a single layer. Sprinkle with pepper and paprika. Bake at 350 degrees for 55 minutes. Do not turn. Saute the onions, green pepper and mushrooms in remaining butter in a saucepan until onions are tender. Add remaining ingredients and cover. Simmer for 40 minutes. Place in mounds on a platter and place chicken on rice mixture. 6-8 servings.

*Mrs. Clarence Geist, Hope, Arkansas*

## BAKED CHICKEN WITH POTATO STUFFING

| | |
|---|---|
| 1   5-lb. roasting chicken | 2 tsp. instant minced onion |
| 1 c. mashed potato flakes | 1 tsp. parsley flakes |
| 1 c. chopped celery | 1/2 tsp. salt |
| 3 tbsp. melted butter or margarine | 1/4 tsp. poultry seasoning |

Have the chicken at room temperature. Combine the potato flakes, celery, butter and seasonings in a bowl and mix thoroughly. Spoon into cavity of chicken and secure opening. Tie the drumsticks to tail. Place in large brown paper bag. Fold over opening of bag and secure with gem clips. Place in a baking pan. Bake in 325-degree oven for 2 hours and 30 minutes. 6 servings.

*Mrs. Charles J. Maddox, Sumter, South Carolina*

## BROILED CHICKEN

| | |
|---|---|
| 2   2-lb. chickens, halved | 1/2 tsp. pepper |
| Melted butter | 1/2 tsp. monosodium glutamate |
| 2 tsp. salt | |

Place the chickens, skin side down, on a broiler pan and brush with butter. Season with salt, pepper and monosodium glutamate. Broil 5 to 7 inches from heat for 15 to 25 minutes or until lightly browned, brushing with butter occasionally. Turn and broil for 15 to 25 minutes longer or until brown, brushing with butter occasionally. 4 servings.

*Mrs. N. R. Veazey, Nashville, Tennessee*

## CAMPFIRE CHICKEN WITH RAISIN DUMPLINGS

| | |
|---|---|
| 1/2 c. flour | 2 carrots |
| 2 tsp. salt | 2 c. water |
| 1/8 tsp. pepper | 1 c. California seedless |
| 2  2 1/2-lb. frying chickens | raisins |
| 1/4 c. cooking oil | 2 c. biscuit mix |
| 1 onion | 3/4 c. milk |
| 1 stalk celery | |

Combine the flour, salt and pepper in a paper bag. Cut the chickens into serving pieces. Add the chicken, a piece at a time, to flour mixture and shake until well coated. Shake off excess flour gently and place chicken pieces on a flat surface without overlapping until ready to cook. Heat the oil in a Dutch oven. Add the chicken, several pieces at a time, and cook over high heat until brown on all sides, adding more oil, if needed. Slice the onion, celery and carrots. Return all pieces of browned chicken to the Dutch oven. Add the vegetables and water and cover. Simmer for 30 to 45 minutes or until largest pieces of chicken are tender. Mix the raisins and biscuit mix in a bowl. Add the milk and stir until well mixed. Drop by spoonfuls onto chicken mixture and cook over low heat for 10 minutes. Cover and cook for 10 minutes longer. 8 servings.

*Photograph for this recipe on page 94.*

## CHICKEN AND DUMPLINGS

| | |
|---|---|
| 1  6-lb. stewing hen, | Monosodium glutamate |
| disjointed | 2 c. flour |
| 2 lge. stalks celery | 1/2 tsp. baking powder |
| Parsley to taste | 1 c. cream |
| Salt and pepper | |

Brown the chicken in a kettle in small amount of fat. Add the celery, parsley, salt and pepper to taste and desired amount of monosodium glutamate and cover with water. Bring to a boil and reduce heat. Cover and simmer for 2 to 3 hours or until chicken is tender. Drain the chicken and reserve the broth. Chill the reserved broth and skim off 1/2 cup fat. Mix the flour, baking powder and 1/8 teaspoon salt in a bowl and cut in the chicken fat. Stir in enough broth to make a stiff dough. Roll out thin on a floured surface and cut in small squares. Bring remaining broth to a boil in the kettle and drop in dumplings. Reduce heat and cook for 15 minutes. Stir in the cream and cook for 10 minutes longer. Arrange the chicken and dumplings on a serving platter and cover with dumpling liquid. 8 servings.

*Beth Mohn, Richmond, Virginia*

## CHICKEN DIVAN

| | |
|---|---|
| 1 pkg. onion soup mix | 2 c. cooked sliced white |
| 1 pt. sour cream | chicken |
| 2 pkg. frozen broccoli, | 1 c. whipped cream |
| cooked | Grated Parmesan cheese |

Blend the soup mix with sour cream. Arrange the broccoli in a casserole and spoon half the sour cream mixture over broccoli. Cover with chicken slices. Fold the whipped cream into remaining sour cream mixture and spread over chicken. Bake at 350 degrees for 20 minutes or until bubbly. Sprinkle with cheese and broil until brown. 6-8 servings.

*Mrs. Mildred Fry, Corinth, Mississippi*

## COLOMBIAN CHICKEN

1 broiler-fryer chicken, disjointed
3 tsp. salt
1/4 c. butter or margarine
2 med. onions, sliced
2  20-oz. cans tomatoes
1 c. water
1 c. chopped celery with leaves
1/4 tsp. dried leaf marjoram
1/4 tsp. thyme
1/4 tsp. basil
1/4 tsp. hot sauce
1  1-lb. can whole kernel corn
1  10-oz. package frozen lima beans
1 tbsp. cornstarch
1/2 c. shredded Monterey Jack cheese
Hot corn bread sticks

Sprinkle the chicken with 1 teaspoon salt. Melt the butter in a deep kettle. Brown the chicken in the butter and remove from kettle. Add the onions and brown lightly. Return chicken to kettle. Add the tomatoes, water, celery, remaining salt, herbs and hot sauce and cover. Simmer for 45 minutes. Add the corn and lima beans and cook for 20 minutes longer or until chicken is tender. Blend the cornstarch with small amount of cold water and stir into the stew. Cook for 2 minutes or until thickened. Turn into a serving dish and sprinkle with cheese. Serve in soup plates with corn bread sticks. Mild Cheddar cheese may be substituted for Monterey Jack cheese. 4 servings.

## CHICKEN BREASTS SUPREME

| | |
|---|---|
| 2 c. sour cream | 1/2 tsp. pepper |
| 1/4 c. lemon juice | 2 tsp. paprika |
| 1 tbsp. Worcestershire | 2 garlic cloves, minced |
|   sauce | 6 chicken breasts, halved |
| 1 tbsp. celery salt | 1 1/2 c. dry bread crumbs |
| 1 tbsp. salt | 1/2 c. melted margarine |

Mix the sour cream, lemon juice, seasonings and garlic in a large bowl. Place chicken breasts in sour cream mixture and cover. Refrigerate overnight. Remove chicken breasts from sour cream mixture and coat with crumbs. Place in a shallow 9 x 12-inch baking pan. Pour half the margarine over chicken. Bake at 350 degrees for 45 minutes. Turn and pour remaining margarine over the chicken. Bake for 15 minutes longer or until brown.

*Mrs. Edna Derrick, Charlotte, North Carolina*

## CHICKEN ENCHILADAS

| | |
|---|---|
| 1  2 1/2-lb. chicken, | 1 sm. can chili peppers, chopped |
|   disjointed | 1 sm. can chili |
| 1 lge. onion, chopped | 1/4 tsp. pepper |
| 1/4 c. margarine | 18 tortillas |
| 1 can cream of chicken soup | 1/2 lb. grated cheese |

Cook the chicken in boiling, salted water until tender. Drain and reserve 1/4 cup broth. Remove chicken from bones and cut in bite-sized pieces. Saute onion in margarine in a saucepan until tender. Add the chicken, reserved broth and remaining ingredients except tortillas and cheese and mix well. Place layers of tortillas and chicken mixture in 10-inch casserole and sprinkle cheese on top. Bake at 350 degrees for 20 minutes. 6 servings.

*Juanita Ham, Shallowater, Texas*

## CHICKEN FRICASSEE

| | |
|---|---|
| 1/4 c. finely chopped salt pork | 1 tsp. capers |
| 1/2 c. finely chopped cured ham | 1/4 c. tomato sauce |
| 2 tbsp. lard | 1 tsp. oregano |
| 1 lge. onion, chopped | 1 tbsp. salt |
| 1/2 green pepper, chopped | 1  3-lb. chicken |
| 1 tomato, chopped | 1 lb. peeled potatoes, diced |
| 1 sweet chili pepper, chopped | 1 lge. can green peas |
| 8 green olives, pitted | 1 tbsp. butter or margarine |

Cook the salt pork and ham in the lard in a kettle over high heat for 5 minutes, stirring occasionally. Add the onion, green pepper, tomato, chili pepper, olives, capers, tomato sauce, oregano and salt and mix well. Cut the chicken in serving pieces and add to ham mixture. Add the potatoes. Drain the peas and reserve liquid. Add enough water to reserved liquid to make 3 cups liquid and stir into chicken mixture. Bring to a boil and cover. Cook over moderate heat for 30 minutes. Uncover. Add peas and butter and stir. Cook over low heat for 15 minutes longer. Serve with rice. 6 servings.

*Mrs. Wylodine F. Reed, Aberdeen, Mississippi*

## CHICKEN LOAF

| | |
|---|---|
| 4 c. chopped cooked chicken | 1 c. cracker crumbs |
| 1 c. cooked rice | 2 c. chicken broth |
| 1/4 c. diced pimento | 4 eggs, beaten |
| 1 tsp. grated onion | 1 tsp. salt |
| 1 c. milk | 1 tsp. pepper |
| 1 c. bread crumbs | 1/2 tsp. poultry seasoning |

Combine all ingredients and place in a shallow 2-quart baking dish. Bake at 325 degrees for about 1 hour or until knife inserted in center comes out clean. Serve with mushroom sauce, if desired. 12 servings.

*Dr. Carmen Burns, Toccoa, Georgia*

## CHICKEN HASH

| | |
|---|---|
| 2 tbsp. butter | 1/4 c. light cream |
| 1 1/2 tbsp. flour | 2 c. chopped cooked chicken |
| 3/4 c. chicken broth | Salt and pepper to taste |

Melt the butter in a saucepan and stir in the flour. Add the chicken broth and cream and cook over low heat, stirring constantly, until thickened. Stir in the chicken and season with salt and pepper. Turn into buttered shallow casserole. Bake at 375 degrees until lightly browned. Serve over toast points. 4 servings.

*Mrs. Owen Swafford, Cleveland, Tennessee*

## CREAMED CHICKEN TACOS

| | |
|---|---|
| 1 can enchilada sauce | 1 c. grated cheese |
| 1 c. evaporated milk | 1 pkg. corn chips |
| 1 can cream of mushroom soup | 1 diced cooked chicken |
| 1 c. tomato juice | 2 c. grated mild cheese |

Combine the enchilada sauce, milk, soup, tomato juice and cheese in a double boiler and cook until heated through, stirring frequently. Place half the corn chips in a casserole. Add the chicken, then the cheese. Pour sauce mixture over the cheese and top with remaining corn chips. Bake at 350 degrees for 40 minutes. 8 servings.

*Mrs. Frances Wheelwright, Ogden, Utah*

## CHICKEN NARANJA

| | |
|---|---|
| 1  3-lb. frying chicken, disjointed | 2 1/2 c. orange juice |
| Salt and pepper to taste | 1/4 tsp. cinnamon |
| 4 tbsp. butter | 1/8 tsp. cloves |
| 1/2 c. blanched slivered almonds | 1/8 tsp. nutmeg |
| | 1 orange |
| 1/2 c. raisins | 1 tbsp. flour |
| | 2 tbsp. water |

Sprinkle the chicken with salt and pepper and cook in the butter in a skillet until golden brown. Add the almonds, raisins, orange juice, cinnamon, cloves and nutmeg and cover. Simmer for about 25 minutes. Cut the orange in 1/4-inch slices and cut each slice in half. Add to the chicken mixture and cook for 15 minutes longer or until chicken is tender. Mix the flour and water and stir into the pan juices. Cook, stirring frequently, for 10 minutes longer or until sauce is thick. 4 servings.

## CHICKEN TAMALE PIE

| | |
|---|---|
| 1 lge. stewing chicken | 1 can tomato sauce |
| 2 cloves of garlic | 1 tbsp. cumin powder |
| 4 chili pequins | 1 tbsp. chili powder |
| 1 c. butter | 2 c. pitted ripe olives |
| 1 1/2 c. flour | 1 1/2 c. yellow cornmeal |
| 1 lge. can tomatoes | 1 c. cold water |

Cook the chicken in a large amount of boiling, salted water with garlic and chili pequins until tender. Drain the chicken and reserve broth. Strain the reserved broth, then chill. Remove fat from top. Cool the chicken, then remove chicken from bones in large pieces. Melt the butter in a saucepan and add flour gradually. Add the tomatoes, tomato sauce and enough chicken broth to make a thick mixture. Season with cumin powder and chili powder and cook, stirring, until thick. Stir in the chicken and olives. Mix the cornmeal and 1 cup cold water in a saucepan. Heat 4 cups chicken broth and stir into the cornmeal mixture. Cook, stirring, until thick. Place in a large baking pan. Place the chicken mixture over cornmeal mixture. Bake at 400 degrees for 45 minutes to 1 hour.

*Mary Frazzini, Reno, Nevada*

## CHILI CHICKEN

| | |
|---|---|
| 2   3-lb. fryers, disjointed | 3 tsp. chili powder |
| 2 tbsp. butter or margarine | 1/4 c. flour |
| 2 tbsp. olive or vegetable oil | 1   2-lb. can Italian tomatoes |
| 1 lge. onion, chopped | 3 tsp. salt |
| 1 lge. green pepper, chopped | 1 tsp. sugar |
| 1 lge. red pepper, chopped | 1/4 tsp. pepper |

Brown the chicken in butter and olive oil in a large frying pan. Remove from frying pan and set aside. Stir the onion, green pepper and red pepper into drippings in the frying pan and cook until soft. Stir in the chili powder and cook for 1 minute. Sprinkle flour over top and stir well. Stir in tomatoes, salt, sugar and pepper and cook, stirring constantly, for 1 minute or until thickened. Layer the chicken and tomato sauce in a 3-quart baking dish until all ingredients are used, then cover. Bake in 350-degree oven for 1 hour. Uncover and bake for 30 minutes longer or until chicken is tender. Garnish with red and green pepper rings, if desired. 8 servings.

*Mrs. Peggy Evans Escue, Lubbock, Texas*

## COUNTRY CAPTAIN

| | |
|---|---|
| 6 chicken breasts | 2 tsp. curry powder |
| 1/3 c. flour | 1/2 tsp. thyme |
| 1/2 tsp. salt | 1 tsp. chopped parsley |
| Pepper | 4 c. canned tomatoes |
| 1/2 c. shortening | 2 c. cooked rice |
| 1 c. chopped onions | 1/4 c. currants |
| 1 c. chopped green pepper | 1/2 c. chopped almonds |
| 1 1/2 tsp. garlic salt | |

Remove skin from chicken. Mix the flour with salt and pepper to taste and roll chicken in seasoned flour. Brown on all sides in hot shortening in a skillet, then remove from skillet. Place the onions and green pepper in same skillet and cook until tender. Add the garlic salt, 1 teaspoon pepper, curry powder, thyme, parsley and tomatoes and mix thoroughly. Place in a casserole and add chicken. Add enough water to cover chicken and cover the casserole. Bake in 350-degree oven for 45 minutes or until chicken is tender. Place chicken in center of a large heated platter and place rice around chicken. Add currants to hot liquid in casserole and pour over chicken and rice. Sprinkle with almonds.

*Mrs. D. K. Martin, Jemison, Alabama*

## ELEGANT CHICKEN PIE

2 c. flour
2 tsp. baking powder
1 tsp. salt
2/3 c. shortening
1/2 c. hot water
1 tbsp. lemon juice
1 egg yolk, beaten

Sliced cooked chicken
Sauteed mushrooms
2 c. thickened chicken broth
1 to 2 tsp. chicken-seasoned
   stock base
1 egg, slightly beaten

Sift first 3 ingredients together. Mix the shortening, water, lemon juice and egg yolk and stir into flour mixture. Roll half the dough out on lightly floured cloth and place in 9-inch pie pan. Fill with chicken slices and mushrooms. Combine broth with stock base and pour over chicken mixture. Roll out remaining pastry and place over chicken mixture. Cut slits in pastry and seal edge. Brush pastry with egg. Bake at 425 degrees for 25 to 30 minutes and serve hot. 4-6 servings.

*Mrs. John Faulk, Albany, Georgia*

## HERBED CHICKEN

1  5-oz. can water
   chestnuts
3 lge. chicken breasts,
   halved
Salt and pepper to taste
1/4 c. butter or margarine
1 can cream of chicken soup

3/4 c. cooking sauterne
1 can cream of mushroom
   soup
2 tbsp. chopped green
   pepper
1/4 tsp. crushed thyme

Drain and slice the water chestnuts. Season the chicken with salt and pepper. Brown in butter in a skillet over low heat, then place, skin side up, in 11 1/2 x 7 1/2 x 1 1/2-inch baking dish. Add the chicken soup to drippings in skillet and stir in the sauterne slowly. Stir in the water chestnuts and remaining ingredients and heat to boiling point. Pour over the chicken and cover with foil. Bake at 350 degrees for 25 minutes. Uncover and bake for 25 to 35 minutes longer or until chicken is tender. Serve with rice. One 3-ounce can broiled-in-butter mushrooms, drained, may be substituted for the mushroom soup. 6 servings.

*Mrs. Judy Murphy, East Point, Georgia*

## HOT TAMALES

1  3-lb. stewing chicken
3 onions, chopped fine
3 med. tomatoes, chopped
Salt to taste
Red pepper to taste

Yellow cornmeal
30 ripe olives, pitted
Corn husks, soaked in warm
   water

Place the chicken in a saucepan and cover with boiling water. Simmer until chicken is tender. Drain and reserve broth. Remove chicken from bones and chop fine. Place in a saucepan and add the onions, tomatoes, salt and red pepper.

Add enough reserved broth to moisten and simmer for 10 minutes. Bring remaining broth to boiling point and stir in enough cornmeal until mixture is the consistency of mush. Spread 1/2 inch cornmeal mixture over each corn husk and top with 2 tablespoons chicken mixture. Add 2 olives and roll so that chicken mixture is covered by cornmeal mush and mush is wrapped in husk. Tie ends of corn husks and steam for 30 minutes. Serve in husks. 15 servings.

*Mrs. Frances Caddell, Daytona Beach, Florida*

## MIRACLE CHICKEN-IN-A-BAG

| | |
|---|---|
| 1   6 1/2-oz. can crab meat | 1/4 tsp. tarragon |
| 1 1/2 c. chive-onion sour cream | 2   2-lb. chickens |
| 1 c. cooked rice | 1/2 c. flour |
| 1 1/2 tsp. salt | 1/2 tsp. paprika |
| 3/4 tsp. celery salt | 1/2 c. salad dressing |
| | 2/3 c. sesame seed |

Combine the crab meat, sour cream, rice, 1/2 teaspoon salt, 1/4 teaspoon celery salt and tarragon and place in cavities of the chickens. Secure openings with toothpicks. Combine the flour, paprika and remaining salt and celery salt in a paper bag. Shake chickens, one at a time, in seasoned flour. Brush the chickens with salad dressing and shake in another paper bag containing sesame seed. Place in a large paper bag and fasten bag securely. Place on a rack in a baking pan. Bake in 325-degree oven for 1 hour and 20 minutes without opening oven door. Remove from oven and let stand for 10 to 15 minutes. Remove from bag and remove toothpicks. Cut chickens in half. 4 servings.

*Mrs. J. Wilmer Marshall, Upperco, Maryland*

## OVEN-FRIED CHICKEN AND DRESSING

| | |
|---|---|
| 1   4-lb. chicken | 2 tbsp. chopped onion |
| Seasoned flour | 1/2 c. melted butter or margarine |
| 6 c. dry bread cubes | 1 can cream of chicken soup |
| 1 tsp. salt | |
| Dash of pepper | 2 tbsp. flour |
| 1 1/4 tsp. sage | |

Cut the chicken into serving pieces and dredge with seasoned flour. Brown in small amount of fat in a skillet, then place around edge of a Dutch oven. Combine the bread cubes, salt, pepper, sage, onion, butter and 1/2 cup soup and place in center of the Dutch oven. Pour off all the drippings from the skillet except 2 tablespoons, then heat. Stir in the flour. Add enough water to remaining soup to make 2 cups liquid. Stir into the flour in the skillet and cook, stirring, until thickened. Pour over chicken. Cover. Bake at 350 degrees for 1 hour. 6 servings.

*Mrs. Mabel H. Simons, Hot Springs, Arkansas*

## OVEN PECAN CHICKEN

1   3-lb. frying chicken
1 c. prepared biscuit mix
1 tsp. salt
1 tsp. paprika
1/2 tsp. poultry seasoning

1/2 c. finely chopped
   pecans
1 c. evaporated milk
1/2 c. butter or margarine

Preheat oven to 400 degrees. Cut the chicken into serving pieces. Combine the biscuit mix, seasonings and pecans. Dip each chicken piece into evaporated milk, then roll in pecan mixture. Melt the butter in a shallow baking pan and place the chicken in a single layer in the pan. Bake for 40 minutes. Turn and bake for about 20 minutes longer or until chicken is tender. 4 servings.

*Mrs. Vance Hickman, Winston-Salem, North Carolina*

## SPICY CHICKEN

1 egg, beaten
3 tbsp. milk
2/3 c. flour
1/2 tsp. salt
1/8 tsp. pepper
1/8 tsp. paprika

1/4 tsp. ginger
1/4 tsp. cloves
1/8 tsp. nutmeg
1   2 1/2-lb. fryer,
   disjointed
6 tbsp. margarine

Mix the egg and milk. Mix the dry ingredients in a plastic bag. Dip chicken in egg mixture, then shake in the bag until coated. Melt the margarine in an electric skillet at 340 degrees. Place the chicken in the skillet and cover. Cook for 20 minutes. Turn and cook for 20 minutes longer.

*Mrs. L. M. Geib, Takoma Park, Maryland*

## SOPA CON POLLO

1 pkg. tortillas
1 cooked chicken
1 sm. onion, grated
Grated cheese
1 can cream of chicken soup

1 can cream of mushroom soup
1/2 can tomatoes and green
   chilies
Salt and pepper to taste

Cut the tortillas in strips. Remove chicken from bones and dice. Place alternate layers of tortillas, chicken, onion and cheese in a greased casserole. Mix the soups with tomatoes and pour over casserole. Sprinkle with salt and pepper. Bake at 375 degrees for 45 minutes. 6-8 servings.

*Augusta Jannett, Yoakum, Texas*

## BARBECUED TURKEY

4 tbsp. shortening
2 sm. onions, chopped

2 cloves of garlic, minced
1/4 c. parsley flakes

| | |
|---|---|
| 4 tsp. lemon juice | 1/2 c. white vinegar |
| 1/4 tsp. pepper | 1 1/2 c. water |
| 2 tbsp. brown sugar | 1 tsp. hot sauce |
| 2 tsp. dry mustard | 3 tbsp. Worcestershire sauce |
| 2 tsp. paprika | 1   5-lb. turkey, halved |
| 1 c. chili sauce | Salt to taste |

Melt the shortening in a saucepan. Add the onions and garlic and cook until golden. Add remaining ingredients except turkey and salt and blend well. Cover and simmer for 15 minutes. Sprinkle the turkey with salt and place in a shallow roasting pan, skin side up. Pour 1 cup barbecue sauce over turkey. Bake at 300 degrees for 2 hours and 30 minutes to 3 hours or until tender. Pour remaining sauce over the turkey and broil until brown. 8 servings.

*Mrs. Clarence Tisdale, San Saba, Texas*

## TURKEY CUTLETS PACIFICA

| | |
|---|---|
| 1 egg, slightly beaten | 1   1-lb. can tomatoes, drained |
| 1/2 c. milk | 1 sm. can tomato puree |
| 6 thick slices cooked turkey | 1/2 tsp. oregano |
| Flour | 1/2 tsp. sugar |
| Dry bread crumbs | 6 slices mozzarella or |
| 1/4 c. butter |    Swiss cheese |
| Salt and pepper to taste | 2 California avocados |

Mix the egg and milk. Coat the turkey slices with flour, then dip in egg mixture. Roll in bread crumbs. Melt the butter in a large, heavy skillet. Add the turkey cutlets and cook until brown on both sides. Sprinkle with salt and pepper and place in a shallow baking dish. Mix the tomatoes, tomato puree, oregano and sugar and spoon over cutlets. Top with cheese. Broil for several minutes or until cheese is bubbly. Peel and slice the avocados and arrange on cutlets. 6 servings.

## ROAST TURKEY WITH CORN BREAD DRESSING

| | |
|---|---|
| 6 cold biscuits, crumbled | 1 tsp. rosemary |
| 2 c. hot turkey broth | 1 tsp. pepper |
| 1 c. cooked diced turkey giblets | 1 tsp. salt |
| 3 eggs, beaten (opt.) | 1 sm. can pimento strips, drained |
| 1 med. onion, chopped | 1 recipe baked corn bread |
| 1 c. chopped celery | 1   10 to 13-lb. broad-breasted turkey hen |
| 1 tsp. sage | |

Mix all ingredients except the turkey and place in turkey cavity loosely. Place in a roaster and cover. Bake at 500 degrees for 15 minutes. Reduce temperature to 350 degrees and bake for 15 to 25 minutes per pound depending on size of the turkey, basting with the pan juices occasionally. Remove cover and bake until brown. Place any remaining dressing in a casserole. Place in the oven to bake 1 hour before the turkey is done. 15 servings.

*Mrs. Paul W. Weiss, San Antonio, Texas*

## ROAST WILD TURKEY AND STUFFING

| | |
|---|---|
| 1   10-lb. wild turkey and giblets | 1/4 tsp. ground mace |
| 10 to 12 slices bread, crumbled | 2 c. chopped pecans |
| 2 tsp. celery salt | 4 hard-cooked eggs, chopped |
| 1 tsp. nutmeg | 1 1/2 c. chopped mushrooms |
| 4 tbsp. chopped parsley | 1 lge. onion, chopped fine |
| Salt and pepper to taste | 1/2 c. butter |
| | 2/3 to 1 c. sherry |

Parboil the giblets until tender, then drain and chop fine. Add the bread crumbs and blend in seasonings. Add the pecans and eggs and mix well. Saute the mushrooms and onion in the butter until onion is tender, then stir into the bread mixture. Moisten with enough sherry to hold ingredients together. Stuff turkey with the bread mixture and place in a roaster. Roast at 325 degrees for 2 hours and 30 minutes to 3 hours, basting several times with pan juices. 8-10 servings.

*Mrs. Philip Lee, Vicksburg, Mississippi*

## TURKEY A LA KING

| | |
|---|---|
| 1   8 1/2-oz. can peas | 1/4 tsp. salt |
| 1   2 1/2-oz. can mushrooms | Dash of pepper |
| 1   4-oz. can pimento strips | 1 chicken bouillon cube |
| 2 tbsp. butter or margarine | 2 tbsp. sherry |
| 2 tbsp. flour | 2 c. chopped turkey |
| 1 c. milk | |

Drain the peas, mushrooms and pimento strips. Melt the butter in top of a double broiler over low heat, then stir in the flour. Add the milk and cook, stirring constantly, until thick and smooth. Add the salt and pepper and cover. Place over boiling water and cook for 5 to 8 minutes. Add the peas, mushrooms, pimento strips and remaining ingredients and mix well. Cook until heated through. Serve over toast or in patty shells. 6 servings.

*Mary Jo Trevey, Lexington, Kentucky*

## TURKEY AND CORN PUDDING

| | |
|---|---|
| 2 c. diced cooked turkey | 1/4 tsp. dry mustard |
| 2 tbsp. flour | 1/4 c. minced green pepper |
| 3 c. milk | 1 2/3 c. canned whole |
| 3 eggs, well beaten |    kernel corn |
| 1 1/2 tsp. salt | 1/4 c. minced onion |
| 1/8 tsp. pepper | 1/4 c. chopped parsley |

Place the turkey in a greased 2-quart casserole. Mix the flour with small amount of milk, then stir in remaining milk and eggs. Stir in remaining ingredients and pour over turkey. Bake at 325 degrees for 1 hour and 15 minutes or until knife inserted in center comes out clean. 6-8 servings.

*Mrs. Victor Erickson, McArthur, California*

## TURKEY PILAF

| | |
|---|---|
| 2 tbsp. butter or margarine | 2 c. water |
| 3/4 c. rice | 1/2 c. chopped cooked |
| 1 env. onion soup mix |    turkey |

Melt the butter in a skillet. Add the rice and cook, stirring, until golden. Add soup mix and stir in the water. Cover and simmer for 20 to 25 minutes or until water is absorbed and rice is tender. Add the turkey and heat through. Serve with coconut, chopped peanuts, raisins or chutney. 4 servings.

*Mrs. Lillian Funderburk, Pasadena, Texas*

## DOVE IN SOUR CREAM

| | |
|---|---|
| 12 dove | 3 or 4 slices bacon |
| Salt and pepper to taste | 1 c. chicken broth or |
| Flour |    water |
| Oil or butter | 1 c. sour cream |

Wash and dry the dove thoroughly. Season with salt and pepper and roll in flour. Cook in small amount of oil in a skillet until lightly browned. Place the bacon in a casserole and top with dove. Add the chicken broth and cover. Bake at 350 degrees for 50 minutes. Uncover. Spoon the sour cream over the dove and bake for 10 minutes longer.

*Mrs. W. C. Lindley, Chandler, Arizona*

## ARIZONA-STYLE WHITE WING DOVES

| | |
|---|---|
| 1 doz. doves | Salt and pepper to taste |
| Flour | 1 c. warm water |
| Cooking oil | 1  8-oz. can mushrooms |
| 1/2 c. sherry | 1 clove of garlic, minced |

Dredge the dove with flour and brown in small amount of oil in a pressure cooker. Add the sherry, salt, pepper, water, mushrooms and garlic and cook for 20 minutes at 15 pounds pressure.

*Mrs. Nellie Hammond, Yuma, Arizona*

## BRAISED DUCK

| | |
|---|---|
| 1  4 to 5-lb. duck | Salt and cayenne pepper |
| 1/4 lb. salt pork | to taste |
| 1 sprig of parsley | 3 c. boiling water or |
| 1 bay leaf | stock |
| 2 stalks celery, chopped | 2 tbsp. butter |
| 1 carrot, diced | 2 tbsp. flour |
| 1 onion, sliced | |

Cut the duck into serving pieces. Dice the salt pork and cook in a skillet over low heat until fat is rendered. Remove the salt pork. Cook the duck in fat in the skillet until brown, then place in a baking pan. Add the parsley, bay leaf, vegetables, seasonings and water and cover tightly. Bake at 350 degrees for 1 hour and 30 minutes to 2 hours or until tender, adding water, if needed. Place the duck on a platter. Strain the broth, then skim off fat. Bring the broth to a boil. Mix the butter and flour and stir into the broth. Cook until thickened and serve with duck. 4 servings.

*Lavycie M. Coward, Danville, Virginia*

## DUCK PIE

| | |
|---|---|
| 12 sm. ducks | 1 c. cooked chopped celery |
| 1 tsp. salt | 2 c. cooked diced potatoes |
| 1/2 tsp. pepper | 1 c. cooked green peas |
| 1 lge. onion, finely | 1/2 lb. sliced bacon, fried |
| chopped | and crumbled |
| 3 whole cloves | 4 tbsp. butter |
| 2 tbsp. flour | 1 recipe pie crust |
| 1 c. sour cream | |

Cut the ducks in half and place in a saucepan. Add 2 cups water, salt, pepper, onion and cloves and simmer until ducks are tender. Remove ducks from broth. Mix the flour with 2 tablespoons water and stir into the duck broth. Cook until thickened, then stir in the sour cream. Place the ducks in a single layer in a large baking dish and add the vegetables. Sprinkle with bacon and pour sour cream mixture over top. Dot with butter and cover with pie crust. Bake at 375 degrees until crust is well browned. 8-10 servings.

*Frances J. Martin, Dodson, Texas*

## DUCK A LA ORANGE

3 oranges
1 6-lb. duck
Salt and pepper to taste
4 tbsp. butter

1/2 c. stock
1/2 c. orange juice
1 tsp. cornstarch

Peel 2 oranges and cut in quarters. Scrape white inner pulp from the peel and cut enough peel in thin strips to make 1 tablespoon. Rub the duck with salt and pepper and cook in the butter in a Dutch oven until well browned. Add the stock, orange quarters and orange peel and cover. Simmer for about 1 hour and 30 minutes or until tender. Remove the duck and place on a hot platter. Keep warm. Mix 1/2 cup pan juices with orange juice and bring to boiling point. Mix the cornstarch with 2 tablespoons cold water and stir into the orange juice mixture. Cook until slightly thickened. Season with salt and pepper and pour over duck. Slice remaining orange thin and garnish the duck with orange slices. 6 servings.

*Mrs. W. F. McGurk, Minden, Louisiana*

## RICE WITH DUCK

1 4 to 5-lb. duck
2 tbsp. butter or margarine
1 tbsp. salt
1/4 c. instant minced onion
2 tsp. ground cumin seed

1/2 tsp. ground marjoram
1/4 tsp. instant garlic
 powder
1/16 tsp. ground red pepper
1 c. long grain rice

Remove excess fat from the duck and cut duck into 4 pieces. Brown in butter in a Dutch oven or heavy, deep skillet over medium heat. Add 1 cup boiling water and salt. Cover and cook for 45 minutes or until duck is tender. Skim off excess fat. Add the spices, seasonings and 2 cups boiling water and mix well. Add the rice and cover. Cook for 20 minutes longer or until rice is tender. Serve hot. 4 servings.

## GOOSE STUFFED WITH SAUERKRAUT

| | |
|---|---|
| 1 goose | 1 potato, grated |
| 1 lge. can sauerkraut | Salt and pepper to taste |

Place the goose in a baking pan. Bake in 400-degree oven for 20 minutes. Place the sauerkraut and potato in a saucepan and cook for 20 minutes. Salt and pepper inside of the goose and stuff with sauerkraut mixture. Decrease temperature to 300 degrees and bake until done.

*Clara Brady, Johnson City, Tennessee*

## BAKED PHEASANT IN CREAM

| | |
|---|---|
| 1 pheasant | 2 tbsp. butter or margarine |
| Salt to taste | 1 pt. half and half |

Cut the pheasant in half and rub with salt. Brown in the butter in a skillet. Place in a Dutch oven and pour the half and half over pheasant. Cover. Bake at 350 degrees for 1 hour. Uncover and baste. Bake for 30 minutes longer.

*Mrs. Wallace Browder, Houston, Texas*

## SCALLOPED PHEASANT

| | |
|---|---|
| 2 pheasant | 1 onion, chopped |
| 1 loaf day-old bread | 3 tbsp. flour |
| 1 c. chopped celery | 4 eggs |
| 1 tsp. sage | 1 qt. milk |
| 1 tsp. salt | Buttered bread crumbs |
| 1 tsp. pepper | |

Place the pheasant in a kettle and cover with water. Bring to a boil and reduce heat. Simmer until pheasant are tender. Drain and reserve broth. Chill the reserved broth. Remove fat from broth and reserve 1/4 cup fat. Remove pheasant from bones and cut pheasant in large pieces. Crumble the bread and add the celery, sage, salt, pepper and onion. Add enough broth to moisten and place in a casserole. Cover with pheasant. Melt reserved fat in a saucepan and stir in flour. Beat eggs well and add milk. Add to the flour mixture and cook until the consistency of custard. Pour over pheasant and cover with buttered bread crumbs. Bake at 350 degrees for 40 minutes or until set. 20 servings.

*Mrs. C. M. McAlister, Humboldt, Tennessee*

## BAKED QUAIL WITH DRESSING

| | |
|---|---|
| 1 onion, diced | 2 eggs, beaten |
| 4 tbsp. butter | Salt and pepper to taste |
| 4 c. toasted bread cubes | 8 quail |
| 1 can cream of mushroom soup | 8 strips bacon |

Saute the onion in butter until tender. Add bread cubes, soup, eggs, salt and pepper and mix well. Stuff quail with dressing and wrap each quail with a strip of bacon. Place in a baking pan and add a small amount of water. Bake at 350 degrees for 1 hour and 30 minutes.

*Mrs. Wayne Hasenfrat, Perry, Oklahoma*

## COUNTRY-FRIED QUAIL

| | |
|---|---|
| 12 quail | 2 eggs, well beaten |
| Salt and pepper to taste | Flour |
| 1/4 c. milk | 1 qt. peanut oil |

Cut the quail in half and season with salt and pepper. Combine the milk and eggs. Dip quail in the milk mixture, then in flour. Fry in hot oil until golden brown. Serve hot.

*Mrs. John W. Matthews, Milledgeville, Georgia*

## QUAIL COOKED IN WINE

| | |
|---|---|
| 2 shallots, chopped | 2 c. white wine |
| 2 cloves of garlic, minced | 4 tbsp. flour |
| 1/2 bay leaf | 1/2 tsp. salt |
| 1 tsp. peppercorns | 1/8 tsp. pepper |
| 2 whole cloves | Dash of cayenne pepper |
| 3/4 c. butter | 1 tsp. minced chives |
| 6 quail | |

Cook the shallots, garlic, bay leaf, peppercorns and cloves in 1/2 cup butter in a saucepan over low heat for 8 minutes, stirring constantly. Add the quail and cook until well browned. Add the wine and simmer for 30 minutes. Remove the quail. Strain the wine mixture. Melt remaining butter in a saucepan and blend in the flour. Stir in reserved sauce slowly and cook until thick. Add remaining ingredients and quail and cover. Bring to boiling point.

*Mrs. Douglas Buchanan, Post, Texas*

## QUAIL WITH RICE

| | |
|---|---|
| 12 frozen quail breasts | 3 tbsp. melted butter |
| 3/4 c. flour | 1 clove of garlic, minced |
| Salt and pepper to taste | 1 med. onion, chopped |
| Paprika to taste | 2 1/2 c. chicken broth |
| 1 1/2 c. instant rice | |

Thaw the quail breasts in salted water for 2 to 3 hours, then drain. Mix the flour, salt, pepper and paprika and place in a bag. Add the quail breasts and shake until coated. Brown the quail breasts in 1 inch of hot fat in a heavy skillet, turning to brown on all sides. Remove from skillet and set aside. Cook the rice in butter over medium heat until lightly browned, stirring constantly. Place in a buttered baking dish and sprinkle with salt and pepper. Add the garlic and onion. Place the quail on top and pour chicken broth over all. Cover. Bake at 325 degrees for 1 hour.

*Mrs. Virgil Mathews, Spearman, Texas*

# vegetables

The rich soil, hot sunshine, and ample rainfall of many parts of the Southwest produce big and tasty vegetables. Southwesterners have been quick to take advantage of their land's rich yield and have made vegetables an important part of their cookery. Southwestern vegetable recipes emerged from the many influences that shaped the whole regional cuisine, including that of the American Indian, Mexican, Spaniard, Southerner, and Wild West cowboy.

In this section you'll find recipes representative of each of these influences. From the heritage of the American Indian comes favorite ways to prepare corn, yams, squash, pumpkins, beans, tomatoes, potatoes, and onions. Like their Indian predecessors, modern Southwesterners love to husk bright plump ears of corn and roast them over hot coals until juicy and tender. From the neighboring Mexicans, Southwesterners learned to make chile rellenos, or stuffed green peppers, and the Spanish introduced them to zesty vegetables dishes.

The influence of the South is seen in barbecued vegetables, which Southwesterners have been fast to adopt. And the Wild West cowboy left his brand on still popular recipes for pinto beans.

All of these recipes and more are collected in the pages that follow. They illustrate a varied medley of regional vegetables — and also a medley of lasting influences.

## CREAMED ASPARAGUS ON CHOW MEIN NOODLES

| | |
|---|---|
| 1/4 c. butter or margarine | 1/2 tsp. marjoram (ground) |
| 1/4 c. flour | 1/8 tsp. pepper |
| 1 c. milk | 2 lb. cooked asparagus |
| 1 c. chicken bouillon | 1  3-oz. can chow mein |
| 6 hard-cooked eggs, quartered | noodles |
| 1 tsp. grated onion | 12 strips crisply fried bacon, |
| Salt to taste | crumbled |

Melt the butter in a saucepan and blend in flour. Add the milk and chicken bouillon gradually and cook until thickened, stirring constantly. Add the eggs, onion, salt, marjoram and pepper and mix thoroughly. Heat through. Arrange asparagus on noodles and spoon egg mixture over asparagus. Sprinkle with bacon. 6-8 servings.

*Mrs. C. G. Bartsch, Aurora, Colorado*

## DELICIOUS ASPARAGUS CASSEROLE

| | |
|---|---|
| 1 lge. can cut asparagus, | 1 sm. jar pimento strips, drained |
| drained | 1 tsp. salt |
| 2 eggs, beaten | 1/4 tsp. pepper |
| 1 c. grated cheese | 1 1/4 c. round buttery cracker |
| 1 can sliced mushrooms, | crumbs |
| drained | 1/4 c. melted butter |

Combine all ingredients except butter and mix lightly. Place in a greased baking dish and pour butter over top. Bake at 325 degrees for 30 minutes. 6 servings.

*Mrs. Albert Rosasco, Valle Crucis, North Carolina*

## GREEN BEAN AND ALMOND CASSEROLE

| | |
|---|---|
| 2 No. 303 cans French-cut | 1 can cream of mushroom soup |
| green beans, drained | 1  8-oz. package frozen onion |
| 1  3 1/2-oz. package blanched | rings |
| slivered almonds | |

Pour 1 can beans into 2-quart baking dish and sprinkle with 1/2 of the almonds. Spread 1/2 can soup over almonds and add 1/2 of the onion rings. Repeat layers. Bake at 350 degrees for 35 minutes. 8-10 servings.

*Mrs. Myrtle D. Mitchell, Columbia, North Carolina*

## WESTERN BAKED BEANS

| | |
|---|---|
| 1 lb. pinto beans | 3 tbsp. brown sugar or |
| 6 c. water | molasses |
| 1/2 c. chopped onions | Pinch of oregano |
| 1 tbsp. cooking oil | 1 tsp. salt |
| 1 can tomatoes and chilies | 1/8 tsp. pepper |

Cook the beans in boiling water until tender, adding water as needed. Pour into a casserole. Saute the onions in the oil until tender. Stir in remaining ingredients, then stir into beans. Cover. Bake at 325 degrees for 30 minutes. Uncover and bake for 30 minutes longer. 8-10 servings.

*Mrs. D. J. Hume, Avondale, Arizona*

## RANCH-STYLE FRIJOLES

| | |
|---|---|
| 2 lb. pinto beans | 1 can taco sauce |
| 2 tsp. salt | 1 can roasted green chilies, |
| 2 lge. onions, diced | chopped |
| 2 cloves of garlic, diced | 1 can tomatoes |
| 1/2 tsp. pepper | 1/2 tsp. chili powder (opt.) |
| 1/2 tsp. comino seed | |

Soak the pinto beans in cold water overnight. Drain, then add enough water to cover by 2 inches. Add the salt and cook over medium heat for about 1 hour. Add remaining ingredients and cook over low heat for 1 hour to 1 hour and 30 minutes or until beans are tender.

*Mrs. Barry Goldwater, Scottsdale, Arizona*

## MARIACHI

| | |
|---|---|
| 1/4 c. green pepper strips | 1  16-oz. can pork and beans |
| 1/4 tsp. chili powder | with tomato sauce |
| 1 tbsp. butter or margarine | 1 c. cubed cooked chicken |

Cook the green pepper with chili powder in butter in a saucepan until green pepper is tender. Add remaining ingredients and heat through, stirring occasionally. 2-3 servings.

## BARBECUED LIMA BEANS

1 c. dried lima beans
1/4 c. chopped onion
1/4 tsp. finely chopped garlic
1/4 c. diced salt pork
2 1/4 tsp. mustard
1/8 tsp. salt

1/2 tsp. Worcestershire sauce
1/2 tsp. chili powder
1/2 c. tomato soup
1 tbsp. vinegar
1 tsp. brown sugar

Place the beans in a saucepan and cover with water. Bring to a boil and cook for 2 minutes. Remove from heat and let soak for 1 hour or overnight. Cover beans with water and bring to a boil. Reduce heat and simmer until beans are tender. Drain and reserve 1/2 cup liquid. Brown the onion and garlic in half the salt pork. Stir in remaining salt pork, beans, reserved liquid and remaining ingredients and place in a baking pan. Bake at 400 degrees for 30 minutes. 4-6 servings.

*Mrs. L. R. Rodgers, Baltimore, Maryland*

## REFRIED BEANS

2 c. dried red beans
1 onion, chopped
1 clove of garlic, minced
6 c. cold water
1 tsp. salt

6 tbsp. bacon drippings
Shredded lettuce
Onion rings
Grated cheese

Simmer the beans, onion and garlic in the water in a saucepan until beans are tender. Add salt and cook until liquid has evaporated. Heat the bacon drippings in a skillet. Add the beans and mash with a potato masher. Cook, stirring, until dry, then press beans with back of a spoon into shape of a pancake. Brown, then flip over and brown. Turn out onto a large platter. Sprinkle generously with lettuce. Top with onion rings and cheese.

*Mrs. Ann Banning, Fort Smith, Arkansas*

## HARVARD BEETS

1/2 c. sugar
1 tbsp. cornstarch
1/2 tsp. salt
1/2 c. white vinegar

2 tbsp. margarine
1 No. 2 can sliced beets,
   drained

Mix the sugar, cornstarch and salt in a saucepan. Stir in the vinegar and cook over medium heat for 5 minutes, stirring constantly. Add margarine and pour over beets.

*Mrs. Sam Speir, Manchaca, Texas*

## RED CABBAGE SUPREME

1 head cabbage
1 tbsp. shortening
1/4 c. vinegar

1/4 c. sweet pickle juice
1 tsp. salt
1/4 c. sugar

| | |
|---|---|
| 1/4 c. currant jelly | Salt and pepper to taste |
| 1 apple, chopped (opt.) | |

Shred the cabbage and combine with remaining ingredients in a saucepan. Simmer for about 1 hour, stirring occasionally. Flavor improves when reheated. 6-8 servings.

*Mrs. William Graves, Montgomery, Alabama*


## CREAMED CABBAGE

| | |
|---|---|
| 1 lge. cabbage, chopped | 1/8 tsp. pepper |
| 2 tbsp. butter | 1 c. milk |
| 2 tbsp. flour | 1/4 tsp. dry mustard |
| 1/4 tsp. salt | 1/2 c. diced cheese |

Parboil cabbage for 5 minutes and drain. Melt the butter in a saucepan over low heat. Blend in flour and seasonings and cook, stirring, until smooth and bubbly. Stir in the milk and mustard and bring to a boil, stirring constantly. Cook for 1 minute. Add the cheese and stir until melted. Place the cabbage in a casserole and pour sauce over cabbage. Bake in 350-degree oven for 35 minutes.

*Mrs. Dolan P. Klunpitu, New Iberia, Louisiana*


## SCALLOPED CABBAGE

| | |
|---|---|
| 1 head cabbage, chopped | 2 c. milk |
| 1 1/2 tsp. salt | 1 tbsp. butter |
| 1/2 tsp. sugar | 1/2 lb. cheese, grated |
| 4 tbsp. flour | Paprika |

Place the cabbage in a saucepan and add small amount of water, 1 teaspoon salt and sugar. Cook until tender, stirring occasionally. Place the flour in a saucepan and stir in the milk, small amount at a time. Add remaining salt and remaining ingredients except paprika and cook until blended and thickened, stirring constantly. Place the cabbage in a baking dish and pour sauce over cabbage. Sprinkle with paprika. Bake at 400 degrees until brown. 6 servings.

*Mrs. Jane Littleton, Dade City, Florida*


## SPICED CARROTS

| | |
|---|---|
| 1 pkg. carrots | 1/4 c. melted butter |
| 2 tbsp. vinegar | 4 or 5 whole cloves |
| 2 tbsp. sugar | Salt and pepper to taste |

Cook the carrots in boiling water until done, then drain. Combine the vinegar, sugar, butter and cloves. Pour over the carrots and season with salt and pepper. 4-6 servings.

*Mrs. Raymond Lierly, Fayetteville, Arkansas*

## CARROT SOUFFLE

| | |
|---|---|
| 5 med. carrots | 1/8 tsp. pepper |
| 3 tbsp. butter or margarine | 1/4 tsp. nutmeg |
| 2 tbsp. minced onion | 1 c. milk |
| 3 tbsp. flour | 3 eggs, separated |
| 1/2 tsp. salt | |

Preheat oven to 350 degrees. Wash and scrub the carrots with a vegetable brush. Cut into 1 1/2-inch pieces. Cook, covered, in boiling, salted water for about 20 minutes or until tender, then drain. Puree enough carrots to make 3/4 cup. Melt the butter in a saucepan. Add the onion and cook over low heat until tender but not brown. Stir in the flour, salt, pepper and nutmeg. Stir in the milk gradually and cook, stirring, until thick. Cool slightly. Beat the egg yolks until thick and lemon-colored and stir into carrot mixture. Beat the egg whites until stiff peaks form and fold into the carrot mixture. Turn into a 1-quart baking dish. Bake for 35 to 40 minutes or until golden brown and firm. 4-6 servings.

*Mrs. Lena Stroud, San Antonio, Texas*

## HOT PICKLED CAULIFLOWER

| | |
|---|---|
| 1 med. head cauliflower | 2 tbsp. chopped green pepper |
| 3 tbsp. wine vinegar | 1 tsp. sugar (opt.) |
| 2 tbsp. butter or margarine | 1/4 tsp. salt |
| 2 tbsp. diced pimento | |

Separate the cauliflower into flowerets. Cook in a small amount of boiling, salted water for about 10 minutes, then drain. Combine remaining ingredients in a small saucepan and cook over low heat for 5 minutes. Pour over the cauliflower. 4-6 servings.

*Mrs. Eloise Dykes, Laurel, Mississippi*

## CORN AND KIDNEY BEANS

| | |
|---|---|
| 1 sm. green pepper, chopped | 1  12-oz. can whole kernel corn, drained |
| 1 med. onion, chopped | |
| 3 tbsp. oil | 1  3-oz. can sliced mushrooms |
| 1 tsp. chili powder | 1  8-oz. can tomato sauce |
| 1  1-lb. can chili without beans | 1 c. grated Cheddar cheese |
| 1  1-lb. can kidney beans, drained | |

Saute the green pepper and onion in oil until tender and add chili powder. Place in a 2-quart casserole. Add remaining ingredients in order listed. Bake at 325 degrees for 1 hour. 6 servings.

*Mrs. Irene Knudsen, Crescent City, California*

## CORN FRITTERS

| | |
|---|---|
| 1 c. flour | 1 tsp. salt |
| 1 tsp. baking powder | 2 eggs |

**1 tbsp. melted shortening**  
**1/4 c. milk**

**2 c. cooked corn**

Sift the flour with baking powder and salt into a bowl and stir in the eggs, shortening and milk. Stir in the corn. Drop by spoonfuls into deep, hot fat and cook for 3 to 5 minutes or until brown. 6 servings.

*Mrs. Dwight Hightower, Winnsboro, Texas*

## AVERY CORN PUFF

**1 c. milk**  
**1 bay leaf**  
**2 whole cloves**  
**1 garlic clove**  
**3 sprigs of parsley**  
**4 tbsp. butter or margarine**  
**1 tbsp. chopped onion**

**1 tbsp. flour**  
**1/2 tsp. salt**  
**1/2 tsp. hot sauce**  
**2 c. cooked whole kernel corn, drained**  
**3 eggs, separated**  
**Paprika**

Scald the milk in a saucepan with bay leaf, cloves, garlic and parsley, then strain. Melt the butter in a saucepan. Add the onion and saute until golden. Blend in the flour, salt and hot sauce. Add the milk and cook, stirring constantly, until thickened. Remove from heat and stir in the corn. Stir in the beaten egg yolks and fold in the stiffly beaten egg whites. Pour into a shallow 1 1/2-quart baking dish and sprinkle with paprika. Bake in 350-degree oven for about 25 minutes. Serve immediately. 4-6 servings.

## CHILI CORN COBS

| | |
|---|---|
| 6 to 8 ears of fresh corn | 1/4 tsp. hot sauce |
| 1/4 lb. butter or margarine | 1/4 tsp. salt |
| 1/2 tsp. chili powder | |

Husk the corn and remove silks. Plunge corn into a large kettle of rapidly boiling water and cover. Cook over high heat for 8 to 10 minutes. Remove from water and drain well. Melt the butter in a small saucepan and stir in remaining ingredients. Serve corn at once with butter mixture.

*Photograph for this recipe on page 121.*

## COMANCHE CORN

| | |
|---|---|
| 1/4 c. minced onion | 1/2 c. shredded dried beef |
| 1/4 c. chopped green pepper | 2 c. whole kernel corn |
| 1  2 1/2-oz. can mushroom | 1 tbsp. chopped pimento |
|    stems and pieces, drained | Salt and pepper to taste |
| 1/4 c. margarine | |

Saute the onion, green pepper and mushrooms in margarine in a saucepan until the onion is tender. Add the dried beef and cook for 3 to 5 minutes. Add the corn, pimento, salt and pepper and cover. Cook over low heat until the corn is tender, stirring frequently. 4 servings.

*Mrs. Lola H. Lehman, Liggott, Arkansas*

## MEXICAN CORN

| | |
|---|---|
| 2 c. whole kernel corn | 1/4 c. chopped celery |
| 2 tsp. chili powder | 1 3/4 c. tomatoes |
| 1/4 c. grated cheese | 1/2 c. cracker crumbs |
| 2 tbsp. cooking oil | Salt and pepper to taste |
| 1 onion, chopped | |

Combine all ingredients and pour into a baking dish. Bake at 350 degrees for 30 minutes.

*Mrs. Charles Lookabaugh, Watonga, Oklahoma*

## TEXAS CORN

| | |
|---|---|
| 1/4 c. melted margarine | 6 ears of corn |
| 1 tbsp. chili powder | Salt and pepper to taste |
| 1 tsp. paprika | |

Combine the margarine, chili powder and paprika. Brush each ear of corn with the margarine mixture and sprinkle with salt and pepper. Place each ear of corn on a sheet of foil. Fold foil and seal. Place on a cookie sheet. Bake at 350 degrees for 1 hour. May be cooked on a grill.

*Mrs. Bill Garrison, Lancaster, Texas*

## OLD-FASHIONED CORN PUDDING

| | |
|---|---|
| 2 eggs, beaten | 1 pt. cut corn |
| 2 tsp. flour | 1 c. milk |
| 1 tsp. salt | 2 tbsp. melted butter or |
| 1 tsp. white pepper (opt.) | margarine |
| 1 tbsp. sugar | |

Preheat oven to 375 degrees. Mix the eggs, flour, salt, pepper, sugar and corn in a bowl. Add the milk and butter and mix. Pour into a greased casserole. Bake for 45 minutes. 6 servings.

*Mrs. Marguerite W. Boone, Nashville, North Carolina*

## TAMALE CORN

| | |
|---|---|
| 2 sm. cans green chilies | 1 tsp. garlic salt |
| 2 eggs, beaten | 1/2 tsp. baking powder |
| 2 No. 2 1/2 cans cream-style | 1/4 c. salad oil |
| corn | 1/2 lb. sharp cheese, grated |
| 1/3 c. cornmeal | |

Drain and chop the green chilies. Combine the eggs, corn, cornmeal, garlic salt, baking powder and oil. Place in a greased baking dish alternately with cheese and green chilies, beginning and ending with corn mixture. Bake at 350 degrees for 45 minutes. 6-8 servings.

*Ermina Campbell, Sacaton, Arizona*

## SPINACH LOAF

| | |
|---|---|
| 1 No. 2 can spinach | 2 c. bread crumbs |
| 1 c. chopped celery | 1/2 tsp. salt |
| 1 onion, chopped | 1/2 tsp. pepper |
| 1 egg, beaten | 1/2 tsp. sage |
| 1/2 lb. bulk sausage | |

Drain the spinach and reserve liquid. Cook the celery and onion in small amount of water until tender, then drain. Add remaining ingredients and mix well. Stir in enough reserved liquid to moisten and place in a baking dish. Bake at 350 degrees for 45 minutes or until done. 6 servings.

*Mrs. Tryon C. Lewis, Fayetteville, Arkansas*

## HOMINY CASSEROLE

| | |
|---|---|
| 2 cans hominy | 1 onion, chopped |
| 2 c. grated cheese | 1 can cream of celery soup |
| 2 green peppers, chopped | |

Place 1 can hominy in a baking dish and sprinkle 1/2 of the cheese, 1/2 of the green peppers and 1/2 of the onion over hominy. Repeat layers and cover with the soup. Bake at 300 degrees for 1 hour.

*Mrs. Robert Souser, Otis, Colorado*

## BAKED STUFFED CUCUMBERS

3 med. cucumbers  
1 c. flaked canned salmon  
1/2 c. white sauce  
1/3 c. chopped celery  

1 tbsp. chopped parsley  
1 tbsp. chopped green pepper  
1 tbsp. chopped onion  

Peel the cucumbers and cut into halves lengthwise. Remove seeds and part of the pulp. Cook in boiling, salted water for 5 minutes, then drain. Combine remaining ingredients and place in cucumber shells. Place in a baking pan. Bake at 400 degrees for 30 minutes.

*Mrs. Roberta McWilliams, Memphis, Tennessee*

## DIRTY RICE

1 lb. rice  
1/2 lb. chicken livers, chopped  
1 lge. onion, finely chopped  
3 sprigs of parsley, minced  

Salt and pepper to taste  
1 lb. lean ground beef  
1/3 lb. bulk pork sausage  
3 stalks celery, finely chopped  

Cook the rice according to package directions. Combine remaining ingredients in a large saucepan and cook until done, stirring frequently. Add the rice and heat thoroughly. 16 servings.

*Mrs. H. D. Allday, Dallas, Texas*

## VEGETABLE RICE

1 1/3 c. packaged precooked  
   rice  

1 1/2 c. cooked mixed  
   vegetables  

1/2 tsp. salt
1 1/2 c. boiling water
2 tbsp. finely chopped onion

3 tbsp. butter
Dash of pepper

Add the rice, vegetables and salt to the boiling water in a saucepan and bring to a boil. Simmer for 5 minutes, then remove from heat. Saute the onion in butter in a saucepan. Add to the rice mixture. Add the pepper and mix well. 4-6 servings.

## GOURMET MUSHROOMS

3 slices bread
1 lb. large fresh mushrooms
3 tbsp. butter or margarine
3/4 c. finely chopped onions
Salad oil
Seasoned salt to taste
1 tbsp. parsley flakes
1/2 tsp. salt

1/8 tsp. pepper
1/4 tsp. marjoram
1/4 tsp. thyme
1 tsp. Worcestershire sauce
3 tbsp. sherry or bouillon
1 egg, slightly beaten
1/4 c. toasted slivered
  almonds

Remove the crusts from bread and cut the bread into small cubes. Wash and stem the mushrooms and dry on paper towels. Chop the stems fine. Melt the butter in a saucepan. Add stems and onions and saute until onions are transparent. Brush outside of mushroom caps with oil and arrange, hollow side up, in a shallow baking dish. Sprinkle insides of caps with seasoned salt. Add the bread cubes and remaining ingredients to the onion mixture and mix well. Fill mushroom caps with bread mixture. Bake at 425 degrees for about 15 minutes or until mushrooms are tender but not limp.

*Georgia Alford, Tampa, Florida*

## OKRA AND TOMATOES

1 med. onion, chopped
1 sm. green pepper, chopped
1 clove of garlic, chopped
1 tbsp. cooking oil

3 lge. peeled tomatoes,
  chopped
Salt and pepper to taste
2 lb. okra, ends trimmed

Cook the onion, green pepper and garlic in the oil over low heat for 10 minutes. Add the tomatoes, salt and pepper and blend well. Add the okra and simmer for 30 minutes. Pour into a serving dish and garnish with chopped parsley. 6 servings.

*Mrs. Dexter C. Gulledge, Collins, Mississippi*

## ONIONS IN TOMATO SAUCE

6 lge. onions
1/2 c. chopped celery
2 tbsp. chopped green pepper

1 1/2 c. tomato juice
Salt and pepper to taste
2 tbsp. melted butter

Place the onions in a casserole. Mix remaining ingredients and pour over onions. Cover. Bake at 350 degrees for about 1 hour.

*Mrs. Nola Y. Coates, Brandenton, Florida*

## BUTTERED STUFFED ONIONS

| | |
|---|---|
| 6 med. onions | 1/2 tsp. marjoram |
| Salt | 1 c. bread crumbs |
| 3 tbsp. melted butter | 1 tbsp. chopped pimento |
| 3 tbsp. chopped parsley | 2 tbsp. grated Parmesan cheese |

Preheat oven to 400 degrees. Cut tops off onions and peel. Remove centers, leaving a shell about 3/4 inch thick and sprinkle inside of shells with small amount of salt. Chop half the onion removed from centers and saute in 2 tablespoons butter in a saucepan until tender. Add the parsley, marjoram, bread crumbs, pimento, 1/2 teaspoon salt and cheese and mix well. Spoon into onion shells and brush with remaining butter. Place in a casserole and cover. Bake for 40 minutes or until tender.

*Mrs. A. W. Hemphill, Summit, Mississippi*

## CREAMED ONIONS WITH DRIED BEEF

| | |
|---|---|
| 2 lb. small onions | 2 c. milk |
| 4 tbsp. butter | 1/4 lb. sliced dried beef, |
| 2 tbsp. flour | shredded |
| 1/2 tsp. salt | 1 c. bread crumbs |

Cook the onions in boiling, salted water for 10 minutes, then drain. Place in a 1 1/2-quart baking dish. Melt 2 tablespoons butter in a saucepan and stir in the flour and salt. Add the milk gradually and cook, stirring, until thickened. Cover the beef with boiling water and drain immediately. Add to the sauce and pour over onions. Melt remaining butter and toss with the bread crumbs. Sprinkle over beef mixture. Bake at 425 degrees for 12 to 15 minutes or until brown. 6 servings.

*Clara Deiter, Clay, Louisiana*

## SPANISH POTATO OMELET

| | |
|---|---|
| 1 1/2 lb. cooked potatoes | 8 eggs |
| 3 tbsp. olive oil | 1/2 c. sliced pimento-stuffed |
| 4 tbsp. butter or margarine | olives |
| 1 med. onion, chopped | 1/8 tsp. pepper |

Peel and dice the potatoes. Heat 2 tablespoons oil and 2 tablespoons butter in a 10-inch seasoned skillet or omelet pan over medium heat. Add the potatoes and onion and saute until potatoes are brown. Remove from skillet. Wipe the skillet clean, add remaining oil and 1 tablespoon butter and heat. Beat the eggs until light and mix in the olives, potato mixture and pepper. Pour into the skillet. Cook over low heat, running a spatula around edges occasionally to allow uncooked egg to go to bottom, until omelet is almost firm. Loosen around edges and invert plate over top of skillet. Turn omelet out onto the plate. Clean out any bits that stick to the skillet and add remaining butter. Slide omelet back into the skillet. Cook over low heat until lightly browned. Invert onto a serving plate or serve from skillet. 6 servings.

*Photograph for this recipe on page 114.*

## POTATO SOUFFLE

| | |
|---|---|
| 1 c. milk | 1 tsp. salt |
| 1/4 c. margarine | 1 tsp. dry mustard |
| 3 c. instant mashed potatoes | Pepper to taste |
| 1/2 c. grated American cheese | 2 eggs, separated |

Place the milk and margarine in a saucepan and bring to a boil over low heat. Remove from heat. Stir in the potatoes and beat until light and fluffy. Stir in the cheese, salt, mustard and pepper. Beat the egg yolks until lemon-colored and fold into the potato mixture. Beat the egg whites until stiff peaks form and fold into potato mixture. Turn into a greased 1 1/2-quart casserole. Bake at 350 degrees for 45 to 50 minutes. Serve immediately. 6-8 servings.

*Phyllis J. Dixon, Las Cruces, New Mexico*

## POTATOES ANNA

| | |
|---|---|
| 3 lb. potatoes | 2 tsp. salt |
| 1/2 c. melted butter or margarine | 1/8 tsp. pepper |

Peel the potatoes and slice thin. Pour about 1 tablespon butter into a 9 x 9 x 2-inch baking pan and arrange overlapping rows of potatoes in the pan. Combine the salt and pepper and sprinkle 1/4 of the mixture over potatoes. Drizzle 1/4 of the butter over potatoes. Repeat to make 4 layers of potatoes, ending with butter. Press down with a pancake turner and cover tightly with heavy-duty aluminum foil. Bake in 375-degree oven for 1 hour. Let stand for 5 minutes. Run a knife around edges and turn out on a serving platter. About 8 servings.

## POTATO DUMPLINGS

| | |
|---|---|
| 1 c. bread crumbs | 1 tsp. baking powder |
| 1 c. mashed potatoes | Salt to taste |
| 1 egg, beaten | Chicken broth |
| 1 c. flour | |

Combine the bread crumbs, potatoes, egg, flour, baking powder and salt in a bowl and stir in enough chicken broth for a thick consistency. Drop by spoonfuls into boiling chicken broth and cook over low heat for about 15 minutes or until dumplings are done. 6 servings.

*Mrs. Ruth M. Hader, Roswell, New Mexico*

## POTATO PANCAKES

| | |
|---|---|
| 4 potatoes | 1 tsp. salt |
| 1 onion | 1/2 tsp. pepper |
| 4 tbsp. flour | 2 beaten eggs |

Wash and peel the potatoes, then grate and drain. Grate the onion and mix with the potatoes. Add the flour, seasonings and eggs and mix well. Drop by spoonfuls into deep, hot fat and cook until brown on both sides.

*Mrs. Edward J. Riester, Triadelphia, West Virginia*

## WILTED LETTUCE

| | |
|---|---|
| 2 lge. bunches leaf lettuce | 1/4 c. vinegar |
| Dash of salt and pepper | 2 tbsp. water |
| 2 tsp. sugar | 1 egg, beaten |
| 8 slices bacon, chopped | |

Shred the lettuce into a bowl and add the seasonings. Fry the bacon in a skillet until crisp, then remove from skillet. Mix the vinegar, water and egg and stir into the bacon fat. Cook until thickened, stirring constantly. Add to the lettuce and toss until mixed. Sprinkle with the bacon. 6 servings.

*Marlene Downey, Atlanta, Georgia*

## DEVILED ENGLISH PEAS

| | |
|---|---|
| 1   1-lb. can English peas, drained | 1 c. grated cheese |
| 4 hard-cooked eggs, sliced | 1 can cream of mushroom soup |
| 1/2 c. chopped pimento | 1 can French-fried onion rings |

Arrange layers of half the peas, eggs, pimento and cheese in a casserole and spread half the soup over the cheese. Repeat layers. Bake at 350 degrees for 25 minutes. Cover with onion rings and bake until onion rings are crisp. 6-8 servings.

*Mrs. Opal Ramage, McAdams, Mississippi*

## GOOD-LUCK BLACK-EYED PEAS

4 strips bacon, chopped
1/2 c. chopped onions

1/2 c. chopped bell pepper
2 cans black-eyed peas

Fry the bacon until light brown. Add the onions and bell pepper and saute for about 15 minutes. Add the peas and liquid and simmer for about 20 minutes or until liquid has evaporated. 6 servings.

*Mrs. Eugene Taylor, Midland, Texas*

## FRENCH-STYLE GREEN PEAS

2 to 3 lb. fresh peas
6 lettuce leaves
12 sm. white onions
1/4 c. butter
1 tsp. sugar

Salt to taste
3 tbsp. water
2 sprigs of parsley
2 sprigs of fresh chervil

Shell the peas. Shred the lettuce fine and peel the onions. Place half the lettuce in a large saucepan and add the onions, peas and remaining ingredients. Top with remaining lettuce and cover. Cook over low heat for 20 to 25 minutes or until peas and onions are tender, shaking pan occasionally while cooking. Remove parsley and chervil sprigs and toss ingredients in pan until well mixed. One or 2 10-ounce packages frozen peas may be used instead of fresh peas. 4-6 servings.

## SPINACH MADELEINE

| | |
|---|---|
| 2 pkg. frozen spinach | 1 tsp. Worcestershire sauce |
| 4 tbsp. butter | Crushed red pepper to taste |
| 2 tbsp. flour | 1/2 tsp. pepper |
| 2 tbsp. chopped onion | 1 c. Cheddar cheese, cut in |
| 1/2 c. evaporated milk | cubes |
| 3/4 tsp. garlic salt | Bread crumbs |
| 1/2 tsp. salt | |

Cook the spinach according to package directions. Drain and reserve 1/2 cup liquid. Melt 2 tablespoons butter in a saucepan over low heat. Add the flour and stir until smooth. Add the onion and cook, stirring, until soft. Stir in the reserved liquid slowly. Stir in the milk and cook, stirring constantly, until smooth and thick. Add the seasonings and cheese and stir until cheese is melted. Stir in the spinach and place in a casserole. Cover with bread crumbs and dot with remaining butter. Bake at 325 degrees for 15 to 20 minutes or until bubbly and brown. 6 servings.

*Mrs. Harold R. Haase, New Orleans, Louisiana*

## SUCCOTASH

| | |
|---|---|
| 1/2 lb. sliced bacon, chopped | 1 can tomato soup |
| 1 sm. onion, chopped | 1 c. cream |
| 1 green pepper, chopped | 1 tsp. salt |
| 1 qt. lima beans | 1 c. buttered bread crumbs |
| 1 can whole kernel corn | |

Cook the bacon in a skillet over low heat until crisp. Drain off most of the drippings. Add the onion and green pepper to the skillet and cook until onion is tender. Stir in the beans, corn, soup, cream and salt. Pour into a large casserole and cover with bread crumbs. Bake at 350 degrees for 40 minutes. 12 servings.

*Mrs. A. E. Duke, Arlington, Virginia*

## CHILES RELLENOS

| | |
|---|---|
| 1/4 lb. Cheddar cheese | 1 egg, separated |
| 1  4-oz. can roasted peeled | 1 tsp. flour |
| green chilies | 1/4 tsp. salt |

Slice the cheese and cut into oblong strips. Cut the green chilies into strips. Wrap strip of green chili around each piece of cheese and secure with toothpicks. Beat the egg yolk well, then stir in the flour and salt. Beat the egg white until stiff peaks form, then fold in the egg yolk mixture. Dip each strip into egg mixture carefully and remove from egg mixture with a slotted spoon. Place in a skillet in a small amount of fat and cook over low heat until golden brown. Drain on absorbent paper.

*Margaret Wells, Marietta, Georgia*

## STUFFED GREEN PEPPERS

| | |
|---|---|
| **4 med. green peppers** | **1/4 c. chili sauce** |
| **2 tbsp. margarine** | **1/2 c. grated cheese** |
| **1/4 c. chopped celery** | **1/4 tsp. salt** |
| **1 c. cooked rice** | **Buttered crumbs** |

Cut stem ends from green peppers and remove seeds. Cook the green peppers in boiling, salted water for 5 minutes, then drain. Melt the margarine in a saucepan. Add the celery and cook until tender. Add the rice, chili sauce, cheese and salt. Fill green peppers with rice mixture and cover with crumbs. Place in a baking dish in 1/2 inch water. Bake at 350 degrees for about 30 minutes or until green peppers are tender and crumbs are brown.

*Mrs. Bill Crews, Lawrenceburg, Tennessee*

## RED AND GREEN PEPPER POT

| | |
|---|---|
| **3 red peppers** | **12 tomatoes** |
| **3 green peppers** | **1/4 c. margarine** |
| **6 yellow onions** | **Salt and pepper to taste** |

Cut the tops off the red and green peppers and remove seeds. Cut the peppers in rings and large pieces. Cut the onions and tomatoes in wedges. Saute the peppers and onion in the margarine over low heat for 10 minutes, stirring frequently. Add the tomato wedges, salt and pepper and simmer for 10 minutes longer. May be frozen.

### STUFFED ZUCCHINI

| | |
|---|---|
| 1 lb. ground beef | 1/4 tsp. dried mint |
| 1/2 c. chopped onion | 1/4 tsp. dried dill |
| 1/3 c. packaged precooked rice | 8 med. zucchini |
| 3/4 c. milk | 2  8-oz. cans seasoned |
| 2 tsp. salt | tomato sauce |
| 1/2 tsp. pepper | |

Mix first 8 ingredients well. Trim both ends from zucchini. Cut zucchini in half lengthwise and scoop out centers, leaving shells. Chop centers. Fill zucchini loosely with beef mixture. Shape any remaining beef mixture into balls. Heat the tomato sauce in a skillet. Add stuffed zucchini, chopped centers and meatballs and cover. Simmer for 30 minutes or until zucchini are tender.

*Jean Starling, Baton Rouge, Louisiana*

### MUSHROOM-STUFFED BAKED TOMATOES

| | |
|---|---|
| 6 med. tomatoes | 1/2 tsp. salt |
| 1 1/2 c. sliced fresh | 1/8 tsp. pepper |
|    mushrooms | 1 egg yolk, beaten |
| 4 tbsp. butter | 1/4 c. grated Parmesan |
| 2 tbsp. tomato paste | cheese |
| 2 tbsp. water | |

Cut tops from tomatoes and scoop out pulp. Place tomato shells in a shallow baking dish. Saute the mushrooms in 3 tablespoons butter in a heavy skillet for 3 minutes. Combine tomato paste, water, salt and pepper in a small saucepan and cook over moderate heat until heated through. Cool for 4 minutes, then stir in the egg yolk. Stir in the mushrooms. Stuff the tomatoes with the mushroom mixture. Sprinkle with cheese and dot with remaining butter. Bake at 425 degrees for 10 minutes.

*Mrs. Loy Miller, Hickory, North Carolina*

### PRONTO SPANISH RICE

| | |
|---|---|
| 2 tbsp. bacon drippings | 1 c. hot water |
| 1/4 c. diced onion | 1  8-oz. can tomato sauce |
| 2 1/2 tbsp. diced green pepper | 1/2 tsp. salt |
| 1 c. packaged precooked rice | 1/8 tsp. pepper |

Melt the bacon drippings in a large skillet. Add the onion, green pepper and rice and cook over medium heat until lightly browned, stirring constantly. Add remaining ingredients and bring to a boil. Reduce heat and simmer for 5 minutes. One 16-ounce can tomatoes may be substituted for hot water and tomato sauce. 3 servings.

*Mrs. Laura Cushing, Richmond, Virginia*

## FRIED RICE WITH SHRIMP

| | |
|---|---|
| 1 c. rice | 1/2 lb. cleaned cooked shrimp |
| Salad oil | 2 eggs, beaten |
| 1 pkg. chicken-noodle soup mix | Salt and pepper to taste |
| 2 1/2 c. boiling water | 1 1/2 tbsp. soy sauce |

Brown the rice in 1/4 cup oil. Stir in the soup mix and water and simmer until most of the liquid is absorbed. Saute the shrimp in 1 tablespoon oil for several minutes. Add the eggs, salt, pepper and soy sauce and cook, stirring, until eggs are set. Stir in the rice and place in a serving dish. Garnish with chopped green onions. 4 servings.

*Mrs. David Marlowe, Jackson, Tennessee*

## MEXIA SPANISH RICE

| | |
|---|---|
| 1/4 lb. sliced bacon, diced | 1 tsp. salt |
| 1 med. green pepper | Dash of pepper |
| 1 med. onion, minced | 1/2 tsp. prepared mustard |
| 2 c. packaged precooked rice | 1 can consomme |
| 2   8-oz. cans tomato sauce | Tomato wedges |

Cook the bacon in a glass-ceramic saucepan until brown, then remove from saucepan. Cut the green pepper in half. Mince half the green pepper and add to the saucepan. Add the onion and rice and cook, stirring, until lightly browned. Add the tomato sauce, salt, pepper and mustard and mix well. Stir in the consomme and bring to a boil. Reduce heat and cover. Simmer until rice is tender and liquid is absorbed. Cut remaining green pepper into strips. Garnish the rice mixture with tomato wedges and green pepper strips. May be prepared day before serving and chilled. Bake at 325 degrees for 25 minutes, then garnish. 6 servings.

## FRIED SWEET POTATOES

| | |
|---|---|
| 3 med. sweet potatoes, sliced | 1/2 to 3/4 c. sugar |
| 3/4 c. cooking oil | |

Fry the sweet potatoes in the oil in a skillet over low heat until brown, turning frequently. Drain on paper towels, then sprinkle with sugar. 4 servings.

*Mrs. Wendell Franke, Paint Rock, Texas*

## NUT-COVERED SWEET POTATO BALLS

| | |
|---|---|
| 2 c. mashed cooked sweet potatoes | 8 slices pineapple, drained |
| Salt and pepper to taste | 1/2 c. sugar |
| 1/2 c. finely crushed corn flakes | 2 tbsp. butter |
| Chopped nuts | 2 tbsp. honey |
| | 1 tbsp. water |

Season the sweet potatoes with salt and pepper, then combine with corn flake crumbs. Shape into 8 balls and roll in nuts. Chill for at least 40 minutes or overnight. Arrange the pineapple slices in a greased 8 x 10 x 2-inch baking dish and top each slice with a sweet potato ball. Bake in 375-degree oven for 15 minutes. Combine the sugar, butter, honey and water in a small saucepan and bring to a boil over low heat, stirring frequently. Cook for 1 minute. Spoon over the potato balls and bake for 5 minutes longer.

*Thelma Davis, Murray, Oklahoma*

## TURNIP GREENS

| | |
|---|---|
| 2 lb. young turnip greens | Salt and pepper to taste |
| 1/2 lb. salt pork | |

Wash the turnip greens thoroughly. Wash and score the salt pork. Place in a large saucepan and cover with water. Bring to a boil and cook for 15 minutes. Add the turnip greens, salt and pepper and bring to a boil. Reduce heat and simmer until the turnip greens are tender.

*Mrs. Fletcher Wharton, Columbus, Mississippi*

## STUFFED EGGPLANT

| | |
|---|---|
| 1 lge. eggplant | 1 tsp. chopped parsley |
| 1 sm. onion, chopped | 1 tsp. Worcestershire sauce |
| 3 tbsp. butter or margarine | 1 1/4 c. round buttery cracker crumbs |
| 1 can cream of mushroom soup | |

Cut a 1-inch thick slice lengthwise from the eggplant. Remove pulp from the eggplant, leaving 1/2-inch thick shell. Peel and chop the 1-inch slice. Chop the pulp. Cook the chopped eggplant, covered, in small amount of boiling water for 5 minutes or just until tender, then drain. Saute the onion in 2 tablespoons butter until soft and stir into the eggplant. Add the soup, parsley and Worcestershire sauce and fold in 1 cup cracker crumbs. Place in the eggplant shell and place the shell in a shallow baking pan. Sprinkle with remaining crumbs and dot with remaining butter. Pour hot water into the pan to a depth of 1/4 inch. Bake at 375 degrees for 45 minutes. 6 servings.

*Mrs. C. R. Cox, Shelbyville, Kentucky*

## EGGPLANT SUPREME

| | |
|---|---|
| 2 eggplant | 1 tsp. oregano |
| 1/4 c. salad oil | 1 tsp. basil |
| 1 sm. onion, sliced | 1 tsp. salt |
| 1/4 c. green pepper strips | Pepper to taste |
| 1 clove of garlic, minced | 1/4 c. parsley sprigs |
| 2 tomatoes, cut in wedges | |

Cut the eggplant in half lengthwise and scoop out pulp, leaving 1/2-inch shells. Dice the pulp and set aside. Cook the eggplant shells in boiling, salted water until just tender, then drain. Place in a baking dish, cut side up. Heat the oil in a saucepan. Add the onion, green pepper, garlic, diced eggplant, tomatoes, oregano, basil, salt and pepper and cook for about 3 minutes or until heated through, stirring frequently. Spoon into eggplant shells and sprinkle with parsley. Bake at 350 degrees for 25 minutes.

# casseroles

**S**outhwestern casseroles emerge from a diversified hodgepodge of ingredients. Sometimes ingredients are characteristic regional favorites; sometimes not-so-typical foods are used. Southwestern casseroles combine certain ingredients for either conventional flavor or for more unusual dishes. The result is potluck, and that's just what this section offers you.

You'll find recipes that use ground beef, short ribs, chicken, oysters, shrimp, tomatoes, and rice — foods that appear again and again in Southwestern cookery. But there are also recipes that show Southwestern willingness to try less common foods. Some casseroles call for wild rice, cheese, and noodles — certainly not typical regional ingredients but nevertheless accepted in a flavorful casserole.

Some of the casseroles use familiar food combinations that have been adopted all over the country, and by Southwestern natives, too. Examples are rice and beef, ham and macaroni, pork and apple, chicken and almond casseroles. However, more unusual casseroles accompany these, and you'll find intriguing recipes that combine chicken and green chilies, turkey and chili, oysters and corn — all of which carry a definite Southwestern brand.

In this section Southwesterners introduce you to a whole new world of casseroles, where you can choose from varied ingredients.

### LOCAS DE CREMA

| | |
|---|---|
| 1 lb. ground chuck | 1 tomato sauce can water |
| 1 med. onion, chopped | 1 pkg. tortillas |
| Dash of garlic salt | American cheese slices |
| Dash of pepper | 1 can green chili peppers |
| Dash of oregano | 1 carton sour cream |
| 1 can tomato sauce | |

Brown the ground chuck and onion in a skillet. Add the garlic salt, pepper, oregano, tomato sauce and water and simmer for 15 minutes. Soften the tortillas in small amount of fat in a skillet, then place a slice of cheese on each tortilla. Drain the peppers and cut in strips. Place a strip on each slice of cheese. Roll up tortillas and place close together in a casserole. Add sour cream to the beef mixture and heat through. Pour over tortillas and cover. Bake in 350-degree oven for 45 minutes.

*Mrs. Joseph W. Lunn, Valparaiso, Florida*

### OKLAHOMA CASSEROLE

| | |
|---|---|
| 1 1/2 lb. lean ground beef | 1 No. 303 can whole kernel corn |
| 2 tbsp. salad oil | 1  1/2-lb. package noodles, |
| 2 tsp. salt |    cooked |
| 1  3 or 4-oz. can mushrooms, | 2 c. tomato juice |
|    chopped | 1 c. cheese, grated |

Brown the beef in hot oil, then sprinkle with salt. Arrange all the ingredients in a large casserole in the order listed. Bake in 325-degree oven for about 1 hour. 6-8 servings.

*Mrs. Allen Moffat, Piedmont, Oklahoma*

### SPANISH RICE AND BEEF

| | |
|---|---|
| 4 slices bacon, chopped | 1 No. 2 1/2 can tomatoes |
| 1 med. onion, chopped | 3/4 c. rice |
| 1 1/4 lb. ground beef | 1/2 tsp. paprika |
| 1 1/2 tsp. salt | |

Saute the bacon in a skillet until browned and crisp. Remove from skillet and pour off half the fat. Brown the onion in the remaining bacon fat, then add ground beef and salt. Cook until beef is lightly browned. Add the tomatoes, bacon, rice and paprika, then turn into a greased casserole. Cover. Bake at 350 degrees for 1 hour and 30 minutes or until rice is tender, adding hot water if needed.

*Mrs. A. H. Foote, Barber, Arkansas*

### WILD RICE CASSEROLE

| | |
|---|---|
| 2 c. boiling water | 1 can sliced mushrooms |
| 1 c. wild rice | 1/2 c. water |
| 1 can chicken gumbo | 1 tsp. salt |

1 bay leaf
1/4 tsp. celery salt
1/4 tsp. garlic salt
Pepper to taste
Onion salt to taste

Paprika to taste
3 tbsp. chopped onion
3 tbsp. salad oil
1 lb. lean ground beef

Pour the boiling water over rice in a bowl and cover. Let stand for 15 minutes, then drain. Place in a 2-quart casserole. Add the gumbo, mushrooms and liquid, water and seasonings and mix. Let stand for several minutes. Saute the onion in the oil in a skillet until tender and add to rice mixture. Add the beef to oil remaining in the skillet and cook until brown. Add to rice mixture and cover. Bake at 350 degrees for 1 hour and 15 minutes.

*Mrs. James Woods, Bedford, Kentucky*

## HOT MONTERREY SALAD

1 lb. ground beef
1 clove of garlic, minced
1 tbsp. butter or margarine
2 tsp. salt
1/4 tsp. hot sauce
1 tbsp. lemon juice
1 c. mayonnaise

3 c. cooked rice
2 c. sliced celery
1 c. chopped green pepper
1 c. chopped onions
3 med. tomatoes, cut into
  eighths
1 c. corn chips

Cook the beef and garlic in butter in a skillet for 10 minutes or until brown. Mix the salt, hot sauce, lemon juice and mayonnaise and add to the beef mixture. Add remaining ingredients except corn chips and mix lightly. Turn into a greased 2-quart casserole and place the corn chips around edge of casserole. Bake at 375 degrees for 25 to 30 minutes. 8 servings.

## BEEF SHORT RIB CASSEROLE

3 tbsp. fat
3 med. onions, chopped
3 lb. beef short ribs
1 carrot, sliced
2 c. canned tomatoes

1/2 c. rice
1/4 tsp. pepper
1 1/2 tsp. salt
1 tsp. sugar

Melt the fat in a frying pan, then add the onions and ribs and cook until brown. Transfer the onions and ribs to a casserole and add the carrot, tomatoes and rice. Sprinkle with the pepper, salt and sugar. Add enough hot water to cover. Cover. Bake at 275 degrees for about 3 hours, adding more water if necessary.

*Mrs. J. A. Frazier, Booneville, North Carolina*

## CHUCK WAGON CASSEROLE

2 c. cooked beef, cut in cubes
1   1-lb. can whole kernel
   corn, drained
1 can tomato soup
1 c. shredded Cheddar cheese

1 tbsp. instant minced onion
1 tsp. chili powder
1 pkg. refrigerator biscuits
2 tbsp. melted butter
1/4 c. cornmeal

Combine the beef, corn, soup, cheese, onion and chili powder in a shallow 2 1/2-quart casserole. Bake at 400 degrees for 10 minutes. Dip the biscuits into the melted butter, then into the cornmeal and arrange on the casserole. Bake for 20 to 25 minutes longer or until biscuits are golden brown. 4-6 servings.

*Mrs. Harold Lee Howdyshell, Staunton, Virginia*

## SPANISH-STYLE STEAK CASSEROLE

1 lb. round steak
1 c. chopped onions
1 c. diced carrots
1 c. diced green peppers
1 c. chopped celery

2 c. quartered potatoes
1 No. 303 can tomatoes
Dash of Worcestershire sauce
Salt and pepper to taste

Brown the steak on both sides in small amount of fat in a frying pan, then add the onions, carrots, green peppers, celery and potatoes. Pour the tomatoes over the top and add Worcestershire sauce, salt and pepper. Bake, covered, at 300 degrees for 2 hours. 4-6 servings.

*Mrs. Conrad H. Hicks, Charlottesville, Virginia*

## ROUND STEAK OVEN DINNER

1   2-lb. round steak, 1 in.
   thick
2 tsp. salt
Dash of pepper

Flour
3 med. onions, sliced
1/4 c. fat
3 lge. potatoes, halved

| | |
|---|---|
| **1 bay leaf** | **1 No. 303 can French-style** |
| **1 can tomato soup** | **green beans** |

Cut the steak in serving pieces. Season with salt and pepper and dredge with flour. Cook the onions in hot fat in a skillet until tender but not brown and remove from skillet. Brown steak on both sides in same skillet, then place in a 3-quart casserole. Add onions, potatoes, bay leaf and soup and cover. Bake at 350 degrees for 1 hour and 45 minutes or until steak is tender. Drain the beans and add to casserole. Bake for 10 to 15 minutes longer. 6-8 servings.

*Mrs. Ronald F. Snyder, Fairmont, West Virginia*

## MEXICAN MEATBALL SKILLET

| | |
|---|---|
| **2 tbsp. butter** | **1 can beans in tomato sauce** |
| **1 tbsp. oil** | **1 can meatballs in sauce** |
| **2 green peppers, sliced** | **1/4 tsp. garlic salt** |
| **1 can tomatoes** | **1/2 tsp. Mexican spices** |

Heat the butter and oil in a skillet. Add the green peppers and cook until brown. Add the tomatoes and liquid and cook until thickened. Add the beans and meatballs and stir well. Season with the garlic salt and Mexican spices and heat through.

## QUICK BEEF CASSEROLE

| | |
|---|---|
| 1 pkg. frozen peas and carrots | 1 tsp. salt |
| 1 can cooked potatoes | 1/4 tsp. pepper |
| 1 can white onions | 3 c. roast beef and gravy |
| 1/4 tsp. thyme | 2 c. canned tomatoes |

Cook the peas and carrots in boiling water in a covered saucepan for 5 minutes, then drain. Place the peas and carrots, potatoes, onions and seasonings in a buttered casserole. Mix the beef, gravy and tomatoes and pour over the onion mixture. Bake at 375 degrees for 20 to 30 minutes. 6 servings.

*Mrs. W. O. Tune, Vernon Hill, Virginia*

## HAM AND MACARONI CASSEROLE

| | |
|---|---|
| 4 oz. elbow macaroni | 1 clove of garlic, crushed |
| 2 c. smoked ham, cut in cubes | 2 c. canned tomatoes |
| 2 tbsp. chopped onion | Salt and pepper to taste |
| 2 tbsp. chopped green pepper | 1 c. grated sharp cheese |
| 2 tbsp. chopped celery | 4 tbsp. buttered bread crumbs |

Cook the macaroni according to package directions, then drain and return to the same pan. Add remaining ingredients except cheese and bread crumbs. Mix well and pour into a 2-quart casserole. Cover with the cheese, then the bread crumbs. Bake for 35 minutes in 350-degree oven. 4 servings.

*Mrs. Katherine M. Thompson, Falls Church, Virginia*

## HAM-RICE CASSEROLE

| | |
|---|---|
| 2 cans cream of celery soup | 4 c. cooked rice |
| 1 c. light cream | 4 c. cooked ham, cut in cubes |
| 1 c. grated Cheddar cheese | 1   10-oz. package frozen green peas |
| 1/2 c. grated Parmesan cheese | |
| 1 1/2 tbsp. minced onion | 1   3 1/2-oz. can French-fried onion rings |
| 1 tbsp. prepared mustard | |
| 1/8 tsp. pepper | |

Combine the celery soup and cream in a saucepan and stir until smooth. Cook over low heat until heated through. Stir in cheeses. Blend in the onion, mustard and pepper and remove from heat. Combine the sauce with the rice and ham. Place alternate layers of the ham mixture and the green peas in a 3-quart casserole and sprinkle with onion rings. Bake at 350 degrees for 15 to 20 minutes. 10 servings.

*Mrs. Martha Jo Bredemyer, Lancaster, Texas*

## CHOPS AND POTATOES CASSEROLE

| | |
|---|---|
| 4 pork chops | 1/2 c. sour cream |
| 1 can cream of mushroom soup | 1/4 c. water |

**2 tbsp. chopped parsley**      **Salt and pepper to taste**
**4 c. thinly sliced potatoes**

Brown the pork chops in a skillet. Blend the soup with sour cream, water and parsley. Place half the potatoes in a 2-quart casserole and sprinkle with salt and pepper. Add half the soup mixture. Add remaining potatoes and sprinkle with salt and pepper. Add remaining soup mixture and top with pork chops. Cover. Bake in a 375-degree oven for 1 hour and 15 minutes. 4 servings.

*Mrs. Thomas L. Williams, Mobile, Alabama*

## FILLET OF PORK ON VEGETABLES

**1   3 1/2-lb. pork tenderloin**      **3 red peppers**
**Salt and pepper to taste**          **3 green peppers**
**3/4 c. bouillon**                    **Olive oil**
**1/2 tsp. sage**                      **1/2 tsp. basil**
**1 1/2 lb. onions**                   **1/2 c. grated Parmesan cheese**
**1 1/2 lb. tomatoes**                 **Margarine**

Preheat oven to 350 degrees. Season the pork with salt and pepper and place in a baking pan. Pour the bouillon into a saucepan and add the sage. Bring to a boil and pour over the pork. Bake for 45 minutes, basting occasionally. Turn and bake for 45 minutes longer, basting occasionally. Peel the onions and tomatoes and cut in wedges. Remove seeds from the red and green peppers and cut in strips. Fry the onions in small amount of oil until tender. Add remaining vegetables except the tomatoes and season with the basil, salt and pepper. Cover and simmer for about 10 minutes. Add the tomato wedges and simmer for 5 minutes. Pour into a casserole. Slice the pork and arrange around edge of casserole. Sprinkle with the cheese and dot with margarine. Cover with foil. Bake at 400 degrees for about 20 minutes. Garnish with sliced black olives and chopped parsley. 10 servings.

## PORK AND APPLE CASSEROLE

| | |
|---|---|
| 4 pork loin chops | 2 tbsp. brown sugar |
| 1 1/2 tsp. Kitchen Bouquet | 1/2 tsp. basil |
| 1 tbsp. cooking oil | 1/8 tsp. ground cloves |
| 1 tsp. salt | 3 tbsp. lemon juice |
| 1 qt. diced tart red apples | 3 tbsp. water |
| 1/2 c. seedless raisins | |

Brush the pork chops with Kitchen Bouquet. Brown in oil in a heavy skillet over moderate heat, then sprinkle with salt. Place the apples and raisins in a mixing bowl and sprinkle with the sugar and spices. Toss lightly. Sprinkle with the lemon juice and toss again. Place in a well-greased 6 x 10 x 2-inch baking dish. Remove the pork chops from the skillet and add water to pork chop drippings, then pour over the apples. Top with the pork chops and cover with foil. Bake at 350 degrees for 30 minutes. Uncover and bake for 1 hour longer. 4 servings.

*Mrs. June Williams, Clinton, Arkansas*

## TAMALE CASSEROLE

| | |
|---|---|
| 3 c. diced cooked veal | 1 tbsp. chili powder |
| 1/4 c. minced onion | 12 ripe olives, pitted |
| 2 tbsp. salad oil | 2 1/2 c. water |
| 1 1/2 tsp. salt | 1/2 c. yellow cornmeal |
| Dash of pepper | 2 eggs, well beaten |
| 1/2 c. tomato juice | 2 tbsp. butter or margarine |
| 1 c. catsup | |

Brown the veal and onion in oil in a skillet and stir in 1/2 teaspoon salt, pepper, tomato juice, catsup and chili powder. Chop the olives and add to the veal mixture. Cook for 3 to 4 minutes, then pour into a 2-quart casserole. Mix the water and remaining salt in a saucepan and bring to a boil. Stir in cornmeal slowly and cook until thickened, stirring constantly. Beat in eggs and spread over veal mixture. Dot with butter. Bake at 375 degrees for 45 minutes or until brown. 6-8 servings.

*Mrs. Tom Shofner, Jr., Crawford, Texas*

## TEXAS CASSEROLE

| | |
|---|---|
| 2 lb. veal round steak | 2 cans cream of chicken soup |
| 1/3 c. flour | 1 soup can water |
| 1 tsp. paprika | Butter-Crumb Dumplings |
| 1/2 c. salad oil | 1 c. sour cream |
| 1 3/4 c. small canned onions | |

Coat the steak with the flour and sprinkle with the paprika, then pound the steak. Cut the steak into 2-inch cubes, then brown in hot oil in a skillet. Place the browned veal cubes in a deep casserole and cover with the onions. Combine 1 can soup and water and add to skillet in which steak was browned. Bring to a boil and pour over the veal. Bake at 300 degrees for 45 minutes or until tender. Top with Butter-Crumb Dumplings. Bake at 425 degrees for 25 minutes or until dumplings are brown. Combine remaining soup with the sour cream in a saucepan and heat through. Serve with casserole.

## Butter-Crumb Dumplings

| | |
|---|---|
| 2 c. flour | 1 tsp. dried onion flakes |
| 4 tsp. baking powder | 1 c. milk |
| 1/2 tsp. salt | 1/4 c. melted butter |
| 1 tsp. poultry seasoning | 1 c. bread crumbs |
| 1 tsp. celery seed | |

Sift flour, baking powder, salt and poultry seasoning together in a large bowl, then add celery seed, onion flakes and milk. Stir just until moistened. Combine the melted butter and crumbs in a skillet. Drop the dough by rounded tablespoonfuls into the crumb mixture and roll until well coated.

*Mrs. A. W. Bertram, Needville, Texas*

## VEAL-RICE CASSEROLE

| | |
|---|---|
| 1 lb. veal round, diced | 1 can cream of mushroom soup |
| 1 lge. onion, chopped | 1 can cream of chicken soup |
| 1 c. diced celery | 1  8-oz. can button mushrooms |
| 1/4 lb. butter | 1 c. salted cashew nuts |
| 3/4 c. rice | |

Cook the veal, onion and celery in butter in a skillet over low heat until the onion is clear but not brown. Cover the rice with water in a bowl and let set for 20 minutes. Combine the soups, 1 cup water and mushrooms and mix well. Drain the rice and add to the soup mixture. Add veal, celery and onion. Place in a large buttered casserole and cover. Bake for 1 hour and 15 minutes in a 325-degree oven. Remove the cover and add the cashew nuts. Mix and bake for 15 minutes longer. 8 servings.

*Mrs. A. H. Magie, Pine Bluff, Arkansas*

## BAKED CHICKEN-RICE CASSEROLE

| | |
|---|---|
| 1 1/2 c. rice | 1 can sliced mushrooms |
| 1 can cream of mushroom soup | 1/2 c. slivered almonds |
| 1 can cream of chicken soup | 12 chicken breasts |
| 1 can cream of celery soup | Salt and pepper to taste |
| 1 1/2 soup cans water | 1/2 c. melted margarine |

Place the rice in a buttered pan and add the soups, water, mushrooms and almonds. Sprinkle the chicken with salt and pepper, then dip in margarine and place on the rice mixture. Cover. Bake at 350 degrees for 1 hour and 30 minutes.

*Mrs. Carl Goodwin, Jr., DeWitt, Arkansas*

## CHICKEN-ALMOND CASSEROLE

2 1/2 c. diced cooked chicken
2 c. diced celery
3/4 c. slivered almonds
1 c. mayonnaise
4 tbsp. diced onion
2 tbsp. lemon juice
2 cans cream of chicken soup
1 sm. can pimento strips, drained
5 hard-cooked eggs, diced
Salt and pepper to taste
1 c. crushed potato chips

Combine all ingredients except potato chips in a deep 2 1/2-quart casserole and mix well, then sprinkle with potato chips. Bake at 350 degrees for 1 hour. 10 servings.

*Mrs. Fred F. Denny, New Castle, Kentucky*

## GREEN CHILI AND CHICKEN CASSEROLE

2 doz. tortillas
1 c. hot shortening
1 cooked chicken
4 lge. canned green chili peppers, chopped
1 lge. tomato, diced
1 clove of garlic, chopped
2 tbsp. chopped onion
1 1/2 c. chicken broth
1 lge. can evaporated milk
Salt and pepper to taste
1 lb. Jack cheese, grated

Dip the tortillas in shortening and arrange 6 tortillas in a 13 x 9 x 2-inch baking pan. Remove chicken from bones and cut in large pieces. Add remaining ingredients except cheese and mix well. Place 1/4 of the chicken mixture over tortillas in the pan and sprinkle with 1/4 of the cheese. Repeat layers 3 times. Bake in a 350-degree oven for about 30 minutes. Cut in squares and garnish with lettuce and olives. Serve with frijoles. 6-8 servings.

*Mrs. Nina Weisling, Morenci, Arizona*

## CHICKEN SPAGHETTI SUPREME

1   4-lb. hen
8 oz. spaghetti
2 med. onions, chopped
1 c. chopped celery
3 tbsp. margarine
1 can cream of mushroom soup
1 sm. bottle olive pieces, drained
1 tbsp. Worcestershire sauce
Salt and pepper to taste
1 c. chopped nuts
2 c. grated hoop cheese

Cook the hen in boiling water to cover until tender, then remove from broth and cool. Cook the spaghetti according to package directions. Cook the onions and celery in the margarine in a 3-quart saucepan until clear. Add 1 quart broth and simmer for 15 minutes. Add the soup and spaghetti to the broth mixture and let stand for 1 hour. Shred the hen and combine with olives, Worcestershire sauce, salt, pepper and nuts. Mix with the spaghetti mixture. Place in a casserole and sprinkle with cheese. Bake at 350 degrees for 30 minutes. 8 servings.

*Mrs. Sam Rollins, Milan, Tennessee*

## CHICKEN-NOODLE CASSEROLE

| | |
|---|---|
| 1  2-lb. chicken | 1 can mushroom soup |
| 2  5-oz. packages noodles | 1 soup can water |
| 1  6-oz. jar stuffed | 1 tsp. salt |
|    olives, drained | 2 c. grated American cheese |
| 8 hard-cooked eggs, sliced | |

Cook the chicken in boiling water to cover until tender. Remove chicken from bones and discard the bones. Dice enough chicken to measure 3 cups. Cook the noodles according to package directions. Cut the olives in quarters. Place half the noodles in a greased 2-quart casserole. Add a layer of chicken, olives and eggs, then remaining noodles. Combine the soup, water and salt and pour over the noodles. Bake at 350 degrees for 25 minutes. Top with grated cheese and bake for 5 minutes longer. 10 servings.

*Mrs. Jerome Johnson, Heber Springs, Arkansas*

## TURKEY WONDER

| | |
|---|---|
| 1 can Chinese noodles | 1 c. coarsely chopped celery |
| 2 c. chopped cooked turkey | 1/2 c. chopped onion |
| 1 can cream of mushroom soup | 1 c. chopped cashew nuts |
| 1 c. water | 1/2 c. crumbled potato chips |
| 1 can mushrooms | 1/2 c. grated cheese |

Place the Chinese noodles in a buttered casserole. Combine the remaining ingredients except potato chips and cheese in a bowl and pour over the noodles. Top with the potato chips and cheese. Bake at 350 degrees for 10 to 12 minutes. 10 servings.

*Mrs. Louis King, Jefferson, Texas*

## TURKEY-CHILI CASSEROLE

| | |
|---|---|
| 1  4-oz. can green chilies | 1 can cream of chicken soup |
| 1 med. onion | 9 corn tortillas |
| 1 lb. sharp Cheddar cheese | 4 tbsp. (about) soft butter |
| 4 c. diced  cooked turkey | 1 c. chicken broth |

Drain the green chilies. Chop the green chilies and the onion fine and shred the cheese. Combine the turkey, green chilies, onion and soup. Spread the tortillas with butter and cut each in half. Arrange 6 halves in a 9 x 13-inch baking pan. Spread 1/3 of the turkey mixture over the tortillas and top with 1/3 of the cheese. Repeat layers 2 times and pour chicken broth over all, then cover. Bake at 400 degrees for 25 to 30 minutes. Cut into squares and remove with spatula. 6-8 servings.

*Mrs. Gordon C. Holmes, Bishop, California*

## TURKEY IN THE STRAW

1 sm. jar pimentos
1 can cream of mushroom soup
1 sm. can evaporated milk
1 c. cubed cooked turkey

1 sm. can broiled-in-butter
  mushrooms
1  4-oz. can shoestring
  potatoes

Drain the pimentos and cut in strips. Combine the soup and milk in a casserole and stir until smooth. Add the pimentos, turkey, mushrooms and 2/3 of the potatoes and mix gently. Place the remaining potatoes on top. Bake at 325 degrees for 40 minutes. 3-4 servings.

*Mrs. G. C. Crawford, Oklawaha, Florida*

## LAMB AND EGGPLANT CASSEROLE

1 med. eggplant
2 c. ground lamb
1/2 c. chopped onion
3 tbsp. chopped parsley

1 tsp. salt
1/4 tsp. paprika
1/2 tsp. curry powder
1 c. chopped canned tomatoes

Pare the eggplant and chop fine. Add the remaining ingredients and mix well. Place in a buttered casserole and cover casserole. Bake at 350 degrees for about 45 minutes. Remove the cover and bake until browned.

*Jacqueline Huffman, New Castle, Virginia*

## LAMB AND VEGETABLE BOUQUET

1 c. dried lge. lima beans
2 1/2 lb. lamb stew meat
4 c. water
Salt and pepper to taste
1/4 tsp. thyme

2 onions, chopped
2 or 3 potatoes, cubed
3 carrots, cubed
3 tbsp. instant flour

Cover the lima beans with water and soak overnight. Drain the beans. Brown the lamb in a small amount of fat in a skillet, then add the beans, water, salt, pepper and thyme. Cover the skillet. Simmer for 1 hour and 30 minutes or till the beans and lamb are tender. Add the onions, potatoes and carrots and place in a baking dish. Add water, if necessary, to cover the lamb mixture and sift flour over the top. Bake at 350 degrees for 1 hour or till the vegetables are tender.

*Edith Cinelli, Galveston, Texas*

## LAMB CHOP CASSEROLE

6 shoulder lamb chops
1/3 c. melted butter or margarine
2 c. finely chopped onions

1 clove of garlic, crushed
2 tsp. salt
1/2 tsp. pepper

| | |
|---|---|
| **1 c. canned chicken broth** | **4 whole cloves** |
| **2 parsley sprigs** | **1 lb. potatoes** |

Preheat oven to 350 degrees. Brown the lamb chops on both sides in butter in a large skillet, then place in a 13 x 9 x 2-inch baking dish. Saute the onions and garlic in remaining drippings in the skillet for about 5 minutes or until tender. Sprinkle onion mixture over the chops, then sprinkle with 1 teaspoon salt and 1/4 teaspoon pepper. Pour on chicken broth and add parsley sprigs and cloves. Bake, covered, for 30 minutes. Pare the potatoes, slice thin and arrange over the chops. Sprinkle with remaining salt and pepper and bake, covered, for 30 minutes or until the potatoes are tender. Uncover and bake for 30 minutes longer or until the potatoes are golden brown. 6 servings.

*Teresa McMackin, Bruceton, Tennessee*

## SKILLET LAMB CHOP CASSEROLE

| | |
|---|---|
| **4 shoulder lamb chops, 3/4 to 1 in. thick** | **1/8 tsp. pepper** |
| **2 tbsp. salad oil** | **1/2 tsp. soy sauce** |
| **1 med. onion, chopped** | **1 c. water** |
| **1 or 2 cloves of garlic, crushed** | **1 can tomato soup** |
| **1 tsp. salt** | **1 med. green pepper, cut in strips** |
| **1/4 tsp. oregano** | **1  1-lb. 4-oz. can white kidney beans** |
| **1/4 tsp. thyme leaves** | |

Brown the lamb chops in oil in a large skillet, then drain off oil. Add the onion, garlic, seasonings and water and cover. Simmer for 30 minutes or until lamb is tender, then remove lamb chops. Stir the soup into pan liquid. Add the green pepper and place chops on top. Rinse and drain the beans and add to the lamb mixture. Bake at 350 degrees for about 20 minutes.

## BAKED FISH FILLETS

| | |
|---|---|
| 1 lb. frozen fish fillets | 1 can cream of mushroom soup |
| 1   1-lb. can sliced potatoes, drained | 1 1/2 c. shredded Cheddar cheese |
| 1   1-lb. can whole green beans, drained | 2 tbsp. chopped parsley |
| 1/4 tsp. salt | 2 tsp. grated lemon rind |
| | Tomato slices |

Thaw the fish fillets and drain on absorbent toweling. Arrange the potatoes in a 1 1/2-quart buttered shallow baking dish and place the beans over potatoes. Place the fish over beans and sprinkle with salt. Combine the soup, cheese, parsley and lemon rind in a mixing bowl and spoon over fish. Bake in a 350-degree oven for 30 minutes. Top with tomato slices and bake for 10 minutes longer. Let stand for 10 minutes before serving. 6-8 servings.

## SUNSHINE CHEDDAR CASSEROLE

| | |
|---|---|
| 1   7-oz. can tuna | 1 1/2 c. milk, scalded |
| 2 c. grated carrots | 3 eggs, slightly beaten |
| 1 1/2 c. cooked rice | 1 tsp. salt |
| 1 1/2 c. shredded Cheddar cheese | 1/2 tsp. pepper |
| 1 tbsp. minced onion | 6 Cheddar cheese strips |
| | Parsley |

Place the tuna and liquid in a bowl, then add the carrots, rice, cheese and onion and toss until well mixed. Turn into a 2-quart casserole. Pour a small amount of the hot milk into the beaten eggs in a bowl, stirring constantly. Add the remaining milk, salt and pepper and pour over the rice mixture. Bake for 50 to 60 minutes at 350 degrees or until a knife inserted near the center comes out clean. Garnish with strips of Cheddar cheese and chopped parsley. 6 servings.

*Mrs. Orpha Johnson, Russell Springs, Kentucky*

## WESTERN TUNA CASSEROLE

2 tbsp. chopped celery
1 tsp. curry powder
3 tbsp. margarine
1/4 c. sifted flour
2 c. milk
1 tsp. seasoned salt

2 tsp. instant minced onion
1 tsp. lemon juice
1  7-oz. can tuna
1 canned green chili
Thin tomato slices

Cook the celery and curry powder in margarine in a saucepan until celery is soft, then stir in the flour. Add the milk gradually and cook, stirring, until thick and smooth. Add the seasoned salt, onion, lemon juice and tuna and cook over low heat until heated through. Chop the green chili and add to the tuna mixture, then turn into a baking dish. Top with tomato slices.

### Almond Crumbs

1/2 c. soft bread crumbs
2 tbsp. melted margarine

1/4 c. chopped almonds

Combine all ingredients and sprinkle over casserole. Bake at 375 degrees for 20 minutes. 5 servings.

*Mrs. Arlie Weaver, Chinle, Arizona*

## FRIDAY RICE SPECIAL

1  7 3/4-oz. can salmon
1 1/3 c. packaged precooked
   rice
1/2 c. milk
2 c. grated Cheddar cheese

3/4 tsp. salt
Dash of pepper
1/4 c. chopped stuffed
   olives

Drain and flake the salmon. Cook the rice according to package directions in a double boiler. Combine the milk, cheese, salt and pepper and cook, stirring occasionally, until well blended and smooth. Arrange layers of rice, salmon, olives and cheese sauce in a buttered 1 1/2-quart casserole, ending with sauce. Bake, uncovered, for 30 minutes in a 350-degree oven. 6 servings.

*Mrs. Leo D. Long, Wilburn, Arkansas*

## SALMON-CORN CASSEROLE

1 tall can red salmon,
   drained
1 No. 2 can cream-style corn
1 sm. green pepper, chopped

1 1/2 tsp. salt
1/4 tsp. pepper
1/3 c. bread crumbs
1 1/2 tsp. butter

Remove the bones from the salmon, then arrange the salmon in a greased casserole. Combine the corn, green pepper, salt and pepper and arrange over the salmon. Top with the bread crumbs and dot with butter. Bake in 350-degree oven for about 45 minutes or until bubbly and brown.

*Mrs. John F. Baker, Umbarger, Texas*

## SOUTHERN SEAFOOD BAKE

| | |
|---|---|
| 1 lb. frozen scallops | 1/4 c. butter or margarine |
| 1   10-oz. package frozen | 1/4 c. minced onion |
|    shelled deveined shrimp | 1/2 c. catsup |
| 4 eggs, lightly beaten | 1 tsp. celery salt |
| 4 c. cooked rice | 1 tsp. (about) curry powder |

Thaw the scallops and shrimp in container on refrigerator shelf for 6 hours or at room temperature for 2 hours. Drain the scallops and reserve 1/4 cup liquid. Cut the scallops into smaller pieces, if large. Cook the shrimp in boiling, salted water for 3 to 5 minutes, then drain. Combine the reserved scallop liquid, or shrimp stock, if preferred, with the eggs in a bowl. Add the rice, scallops and shrimp. Melt the butter in a saucepan. Add the onion and brown lightly. Add the catsup, celery salt and curry powder, then stir into the rice mixture. Place in a buttered, shallow 2-quart baking dish. Bake in 350-degree oven for 30 minutes or until firm. Garnish with whole olives, if desired. 8 servings.

## OYSTER-CORN CASSEROLE

| | |
|---|---|
| 2 pt. oysters | 2/3 c. melted butter |
| 2 cans cream-style corn | 1 tsp. salt |
| 5 c. crushed round buttery | Red pepper to taste |
|    crackers | Chopped onions to taste |
| 1/2 c. evaporated milk | |

Drain 1 pint oysters. Mix the corn, cracker crumbs, milk, butter and salt with the oysters. Add the pepper and onions and place in a buttered casserole. Bake at 350 degrees for 1 hour.

*Mrs. J. H. Romero, Kinder, Louisiana*

## CRAB MEAT CASSEROLE

| | |
|---|---|
| 1/4 c. butter | 2 hard-cooked eggs, diced |
| 1/3 c. flour | 1/4 c. chopped green pepper |
| 1 1/3 c. milk | 1 pimento, chopped |
| 1   6 1/2-oz. can crab meat | 1 tsp. salt |
| 2 c. chopped celery | 1/2 c. buttered bread crumbs |
| 1/4 c. chopped almonds | |

Melt the butter in a saucepan, then blend in the flour. Add the milk gradually and cook, stirring constantly, until thick. Add the crab meat, celery, almonds, eggs, green pepper, pimento and salt. Turn into a buttered casserole and top with crumbs. Bake at 350 degrees for about 45 minutes or until browned. 4 servings.

*Jane Parker, Millen, Georgia*

## SHRIMP AND RICE CASSEROLE

| | |
|---|---|
| 2 c. cooked rice | 2 tbsp. onion |
| 2 c. cooked shrimp | 1/2 c. crushed corn flakes |
| 1 can celery soup | 1/3 c. slivered almonds |
| 1/2 c. milk | 2 tbsp. melted butter |

Combine the rice and shrimp in a buttered casserole. Place the soup in a saucepan and stir in the milk over low heat until smooth. Add the soup mixture and the onion to the rice mixture and mix well. Top with the corn flakes, almonds and butter. Bake at 325 degrees for 30 minutes. 8 servings.

*Mrs. F. E. Crawford, Houston, Texas*

## FIESTA DAY SHRIMP POT

| | |
|---|---|
| 1 1/2 lb. fresh shrimp | 1/4 tsp. pepper |
| 1/2 c. olive or salad oil | 1/4 c. lemon juice |
| 3 tbsp. chopped onion | 3/4 c. tomato sauce |
| 1/4 c. chopped green pepper | 1   10-oz. package frozen |
| 1 clove of garlic, minced | succotash, partially thawed |
| 1 1/2 c. converted rice | 1   10-oz. package frozen baby |
| 2 1/2 c. water | okra, partially thawed |
| 1 1/2 tsp. salt | 3/4 c. frozen green beans, |
| 1/2 tsp. oregano | partially thawed |

Clean the shrimp and set aside. Heat the olive oil in a large, deep skillet. Add the onion, green pepper, garlic and rice and cook, stirring constantly, until rice is lightly browned. Add the water, seasonings, lemon juice, tomato sauce and vegetables and blend gently. Cover and cook over low heat for 15 minutes. Uncover and arrange shrimp on top. Cover and cook for 10 minutes longer or until rice is tender and shrimp are pink. Serve from skillet or turn into a casserole. Two 8 or 10-ounce packages frozen, peeled and deveined shrimp may be substituted for fresh shrimp  8-10 servings.

*Photograph for this recipe on page 136.*

## TAMALE-BEAN CASSEROLE

3 slices bacon
1 No. 300 can pork and
  beans
1 No. 300 can chili without
  beans
1 tbsp. mustard

1 tbsp. chopped onion
1 can tamales, drained
1/2 c. grated Cheddar
  cheese
1/2 c. grated Romano cheese

Fry the bacon in a skillet until crisp, then drain and crumble. Combine the beans, chili, mustard, onion and bacon in a bowl. Place half the tamales in an oiled casserole. Spread with half the chili mixture and sprinkle with half the cheeses. Repeat layers. Bake at 350 degrees for 15 minutes. 6 servings.

*Louise Stuart, Monticello, Arkansas*

## LIVER-RICE CASSEROLE

1 lb. sliced beef liver
1/4 c. chopped green pepper
1/2 c. chopped celery
1 med. onion, diced
2 tbsp. fat
1   8-oz. can tomato sauce
1   16-oz. can tomatoes

1 1/2 tsp. salt
1/2 tsp. pepper
1/8 tsp. thyme
3 c. cooked rice
1/2 c. grated Cheddar
  cheese

Cut the liver in 1-inch squares. Cook the liver, green pepper, celery and onion in fat in a skillet until the liver is lightly browned and vegetables are tender, then pour off the fat. Add the remaining ingredients except cheese. Pour into a greased casserole and sprinkle with the cheese. Bake at 350 degrees for 20 to 30 minutes. 4-5 servings.

*Mrs. Virginia Davis, Blountstown, Florida*

## SMOTHERED LIVER AND VEGETABLES

1 lb. sliced beef or pork
  liver
1/4 c. flour
1/4 tsp. salt
1/8 tsp. celery seed
1/8 tsp. thyme
1 1/2 c. cooked rice
1 c. diced cooked carrots

1 c. peeled chopped
  tomatoes
1/4 c. chopped onions
1 tbsp. snipped parsley
4 tbsp. butter
1/4 tsp. crushed basil
  leaves

Cover the liver with boiling water in a shallow dish and let stand for 10 minutes. Drain and wipe dry. Combine the flour, salt, celery seed and thyme, then roll the liver in flour mixture. Place in a shallow, buttered casserole and cover with the rice and carrots. Mix the tomatoes, onions and parsley and spoon over the carrots. Melt the butter but do not brown. Remove from heat and add basil. Let stand for 15 minutes, then spoon evenly over casserole and cover. Bake at 350 degrees for 50 minutes. Uncover and bake for 10 minutes longer or until brown. 4 servings.

*Ruth G. Newman, Galax, Virginia*

## FRANK KABOBS WITH KRAUT

| | |
|---|---|
| 2 med. green peppers | 4 tbsp. butter |
| 1 lb. frankfurters | 1/2 tsp. salt |
| 1 med. cucumber, sliced | 1/8 tsp. pepper |
| 3/4 lb. small white onions, | 4 tbsp. brown sugar |
|    parboiled | 1/2 c. chopped onion |
| 3 1/2 c. undrained sauerkraut | |

Cut 1 1/2 green peppers into 1-inch squares and chop remaining green pepper. Cut the frankfurters into 1 1/2-inch pieces. Alternate frankfurters, cucumber, whole onions and green pepper squares on skewers to make 8 kabobs and place in a shallow pan. Drain the sauerkraut and reserve 1/2 cup liquid. Combine the reserved liquid, 2 tablespoons butter, salt, pepper and 2 tablespoons brown sugar in a small saucepan and heat just until butter is melted. Pour over the kabobs and let stand for about 1 hour. Broil kabobs for 7 minutes on each side or until done. Saute the sauerkraut in a saucepan in remaining butter with chopped onion and chopped green pepper until onion is tender. Stir in remaining brown sugar and place in a shallow baking dish. Place the kabobs on the sauerkraut mixture. Bake at 350 degrees until heated through. One 1-pound can small onions may be substituted for the parboiled onions. 8 servings.

## GRITS SOUFFLE

| | |
|---|---|
| 4 c. milk | 2 tbsp. butter |
| 1 c. quick grits | 2 eggs, separated |
| 2 tbsp. sugar | Salt and pepper to taste |

Pour the milk in a double boiler, then add the grits, sugar and butter and cook for 15 minutes or until thick. Add a small amount of the hot mixture to the beaten egg yolks in a bowl, stirring constantly, then stir back into the hot mixture in the double boiler. Remove from heat and fold in stiffly beaten egg whites. Season with salt and pepper, then pour into a buttered souffle dish and dot with additional butter. Bake at 350 degrees for 30 minutes or until brown and firm. 4 servings.

*Mrs. Ira Waits, Bienville, Louisiana*

## SOUTHWESTERN GRITS DELUXE

| | |
|---|---|
| 1 1/2 c. grits | 2 tsp. savory salt |
| 6 c. boiling water | 2 tsp. salt |
| 1 1/2 sticks butter | Dash of hot sauce |
| 1 lb. grated American cheese | 3 eggs, well beaten |

Cook the grits in boiling water in a saucepan for 15 minutes, stirring frequently. Add remaining ingredients and mix well. Turn into 2 greased casseroles. Bake for 30 minutes at 350 degrees. 12 servings.

*Mrs. Viola Wheless McKinney, Kingsville, Texas*

## BARBECUED RICE

| | |
|---|---|
| 1 stick margarine | 1 c. chicken broth |
| 1 c. chopped celery | 1 tsp. liquid smoke |
| 1 med. onion, chopped | Salt and pepper to taste |
| 2 cans cream of chicken soup | 2 c. cooked rice |
| | 1/4 tsp. garlic salt |

Melt the margarine in a heavy skillet. Add the celery and onion and cook until the celery is clear. Add the soup, broth, liquid smoke, salt and pepper and bring to a boil. Place the soup mixture in a casserole. Add the rice and garlic salt. Bake at 350 degrees for about 45 minutes.

*Mrs. Dick Wilson, Joiner, Arkansas*

## GREEN RICE SUPREME

| | |
|---|---|
| 1 pkg. precooked rice | 2 tsp. garlic salt |
| 1/2 lb. sharp Cheddar cheese | 1/4 c. cooking oil |
| 1 c. chopped onion | 1 c. milk |
| 1 c. chopped green pepper | Salt and pepper to taste |
| 1/2 c. dried parsley flakes | |

Prepare the rice according to package directions, then let stand, covered, for 15 minutes. Grate the cheese and reserve a small amount for topping. Combine the rice, onion, green pepper, parsley, garlic salt, oil, milk, remaining cheese, salt and pepper in a casserole. Bake for 30 minutes at 350 degrees. Remove from the oven and sprinkle with reserved cheese. Return to oven and bake for 10 minutes longer. 12 servings.

*Mrs. W. A. Cox, Olney, Texas*

## SPANISH RICE

| | |
|---|---|
| 6 slices bacon, chopped | 3 c. cooked rice |
| 1/4 c. chopped onion | 1 tsp. salt |
| 1/4 c. chopped green pepper | 1/8 tsp. pepper |
| 2 c. canned tomatoes | 1/4 c. grated cheese (opt.) |

Fry the bacon in a skillet until crisp, then remove and drain. Add the onion and green pepper to the drippings and cook slowly until the onion is soft. Add the tomatoes, rice, salt, pepper and bacon. Place in a greased casserole and sprinkle with grated cheese. Bake at 350 degrees for 30 minutes. 8 servings.

*Mrs. J. C. Howard, McCarley, Mississippi*

## WILD RICE WITH MUSHROOMS

| | |
|---|---|
| 2 c. wild rice | 2 tbsp. flour |
| 1 c. sliced mushrooms | 2 c. light cream |
| 1 c. sliced pitted ripe olives | 2  3-oz. packages cream cheese |
| 6 tbsp. butter | |

Cook the wild rice according to package directions. Saute the mushrooms and olives in 3 tablespoons butter in a saucepan. Melt remaining butter in a saucepan, then blend in the flour. Stir in the cream and cook, stirring constantly, until thickened. Add the cream cheese and stir until melted. Combine the rice, mushroom mixture and the sauce in a buttered casserole. Bake at 375 degrees for 1 hour. 6-8 servings.

*Mrs. Dean Resler, Sterling, Colorado*

## CHEESE CASSEROLE

| | |
|---|---|
| 6 slices day-old bread | 1 1/2 c. milk |
| Butter | 1/4 tsp. salt |
| 1 c. grated cheese | 1 tsp. Worcestershire sauce |
| 2 eggs, beaten | Paprika |

Spread the slices of bread with butter and place half the slices in a large, shallow baking dish. Sprinkle with half the cheese and repeat layers. Combine the eggs, milk, salt and Worcestershire sauce and pour over the cheese. Sprinkle with paprika and place the baking dish in a pan of water. Bake at 350 degrees for 35 minutes or until set. 4 servings.

*Mrs. Glenn Hoggatt, Perryton, Texas*

## DEVILED EGG CASSEROLE

| | |
|---|---|
| 1 doz. hard-cooked eggs | 2 tbsp. flour |
| 1 tsp. mustard | 2 c. milk |
| 1 tsp. minced onion | 3/4 tsp. salt |
| 2 tbsp. mayonnaise | 1/8 tsp. pepper |
| 2 tbsp. pickle relish | 2 c. crushed potato chips |
| 2 tbsp. butter | |

Slice the eggs in half and turn out the yolks into a shallow dish. Mash and mix the yolks with the mustard, onion, mayonnaise and relish. Fill the egg whites with the yolk mixture. Melt the butter in a saucepan, then blend in the flour. Add the milk gradually and cook, stirring constantly, until thickened, then add the salt and pepper. Place half the eggs in a buttered casserole and cover with half the sauce. Sprinkle with half the potato chips and repeat the layers. Bake for 25 minutes at 350 degrees.

*Mrs. Dewey Teal, Cheraw, South Carolina*

## NOODLES ROMANOFF

| | |
|---|---|
| 2   8-oz. packages noodles | 1 bunch green onions, minced |
| 3 c. large curd cottage cheese | 1 pt. sour cream |
| 2 tsp. Worcestershire sauce | 1/2 tsp. hot sauce |
| 2 cloves of garlic, minced | 1 c. grated Parmesan cheese |

Cook the noodles according to package directions and combine with the cottage cheese, Worcestershire sauce, garlic, onions, sour cream and hot sauce in a large bowl. Toss to mix well, then pour in a buttered casserole and sprinkle with the grated cheese. Bake at 350 degrees for 25 minutes. 16-18 servings.

*Anna P. Williams, Hobbs, New Mexico*

## SPAGHETTI CASSEROLE

| | |
|---|---|
| 1 c. milk | 1 tbsp. chopped green pepper |
| 1 c. grated cheese | 1 tbsp. chopped onion |
| 1/4 c. butter | 1 tbsp. parsley |
| 1/2 lb. spaghetti, cooked | 3 eggs, separated |
| 4 tbsp. chopped pimento | |

Scald the milk in a saucepan over medium heat, then add the cheese and butter, stirring until melted. Pour the cheese mixture over the spaghetti in a large bowl and mix well. Combine remaining ingredients except egg whites and add to the spaghetti mixture. Beat the egg whites until stiff and fold into the spaghetti mixture. Turn into a greased casserole. Bake at 325 degrees for 1 hour. 4-6 servings.

*Agnes Smith, McKinney, Kentucky*

## MACARONI AND CHEESE CASSEROLE

| | |
|---|---|
| 1   1-lb. package elbow<br>     macaroni<br>2 tbsp. butter<br>3 tbsp. flour | 2 c. milk<br>Salt and pepper to taste<br>1/2 lb. process cheese, grated<br>3 slices toasted bread |

Cook the macaroni according to package directions, then drain and rinse. Place in a greased casserole. Melt the butter in a saucepan, then blend in the flour. Add the milk gradually and cook, stirring constantly, until thick. Add salt and pepper. Add the cheese and stir until melted. Pour over the macaroni and mix lightly. Cut the bread into small cubes, sprinkle over the macaroni mixture and press in lightly. Bake in 350-degree oven for about 30 minutes.

*Mrs. G. L. Jacobs, King George, Virginia*

## MACARONI-ZUCCHINI CASSEROLE

| | |
|---|---|
| Salt<br>3 qt. boiling water<br>2 c. elbow macaroni<br>4 tbsp. butter or margarine<br>2 tbsp. flour<br>1/8 tsp. white pepper | 2 c. milk<br>1 c. cubed Cheddar cheese<br>1 c. cubed Swiss cheese<br>1 1/2 lb. sliced zucchini,<br>     cooked<br>1/2 c. fine dry bread crumbs |

Add 1 tablespoon salt to the boiling water and add the macaroni gradually so that water continues to boil. Cook, stirring occasionally, until tender, then drain in a colander. Melt 2 tablespoons butter in a saucepan and blend in the flour, 1 teaspoon salt and pepper. Add the milk gradually and cook, stirring constantly, until sauce boils for 1 minute. Reduce heat. Add the cheeses and stir until cheeses melt. Place half the macaroni in a 3-quart casserole and top with half the zucchini and half the sauce. Repeat layers. Melt remaining butter and mix with the bread crumbs. Sprinkle over casserole. Sprinkle with nutmeg, if desired. Bake in 350-degree oven for 30 minutes. 6 servings.

# breads

Cowboys who traveled alone in the Old Southwest went light and fast. But even away from the ranch, they liked to eat right. Some early cowboy took the initiative to satisfy the necessity of speedy travel and the habit of hearty eating — and he invented biscuits that were quick and easy to make as well as delicious to eat. Before bedding down the night of his journey, he'd mix dry ingredients in a sack and fasten the sack onto his saddle. The next day he'd simply put lard in a skillet over the fire, water down his flour mixture, and drop it into the sputtering grease for steaming hot and filling biscuits. Ever since biscuits won their way into cowboys' hearts in this manner, some kind of bread always appears on Southwestern tables at mealtime.

In this section you'll find recipes for favorite Southwestern breads. Some are like the cowboys' simple biscuits, others for muffins, rolls, buns, and coffee cakes. Many have origins outside the region. Corn bread, spoon bread, and hush puppies were introduced to the Southwest by Southern settlers, and tortillas became part of the cookery through neighboring Mexico. These breads found an appreciative welcome in the Southwest, and today regional natives claim them for their own.

You'll call them your own, too, when you try the recipes in the following pages. All are so "Come and get it" good!

## BEAUTIFUL BUTTERMILK BISCUITS

| | |
|---|---|
| 2 c. flour | 1/2 tsp. salt |
| 2 tsp. baking powder | 1 c. buttermilk |
| 1/2 tsp. soda | 1/3 c. salad oil |

Sift dry ingredients together into a bowl, then blend in the buttermilk and oil. Turn out onto a floured board and knead. Pat out and cut with a biscuit cutter. Place on a greased baking sheet. Bake in 450-degree oven until lightly browned.

*Rosalie McClusky, Bartlesville, Oklahoma*

## DELICIOUS BISCUITS

| | |
|---|---|
| 2 c. sifted flour | 1/3 c. shortening |
| 2 tsp. baking powder | 3/4 c. milk |
| 3/4 tsp. salt | |

Sift the flour, baking powder and salt together into a bowl and cut in the shortening until well blended. Add enough milk slowly to make a soft dough. Knead on a lightly floured board, then roll out to 3/4-inch thickness. Cut with a biscuit cutter and place on a greased baking sheet. Bake at 450 degrees for 15 minutes.

*Miss Porfie Valdez, Las Vegas, New Mexico*

## RANCHERO RAISED BISCUITS

| | |
|---|---|
| 2/3 c. dark seedless raisins | 1 pkg. yeast |
| 1 c. scalded milk | 3 tbsp. warm water |
| 2 tbsp. sugar | 1 egg, beaten |
| 3 tbsp. shortening | 2 1/2 c. sifted flour |
| 1 1/2 tsp. salt | Melted butter |
| Yellow cornmeal | |

Combine the raisins, milk, sugar, shortening, salt and 1/2 cup cornmeal in a bowl. Dissolve the yeast in warm water in a warm bowl, then add to the raisin mixture. Add the egg and flour and mix until well blended. Drop by spoonfuls, barely touching, into greased 9-inch round baking pans lightly sprinkled with cornmeal. Brush with melted butter and sprinkle lightly with cornmeal. Let rise in a warm place for about 45 minutes or until doubled in bulk. Bake at 400 degrees for about 20 minutes or until lightly browned. Serve hot with butter and jam or jelly. 1 1/2 dozen small biscuits.

*Photograph for this recipe on page 160.*

## MALTED CEREAL COFFEE CAKE

| | |
|---|---|
| 1 c. sugar | 3 tsp. baking powder |
| 1 c. shortening | 1 tsp. salt |
| 2 eggs, beaten | 1 1/4 c. (packed) brown sugar |
| 1 c. milk | 1 tbsp. cinnamon |
| 1 tsp. vanilla | 1/2 c. margarine |
| Flour | 1 c. malted cereal granules |

Cream the sugar and shortening in a bowl, then stir in the eggs. Mix the milk and vanilla. Sift 3 cups flour, baking powder and salt together and add to creamed mixture alternately with milk mixture. Mix the brown sugar, 3 tablespoons flour, cinnamon, margarine and cereal granules and spread over batter. Bake at 350 degrees for about 25 minutes.

*Mrs. Carl Morris, Hawesville, Kentucky*

## PINEAPPLE YEAST TWIST

| | |
|---|---|
| 1   1-lb. 4 1/2-oz. can crushed pineapple | 1/3 c. soft butter |
| 3 tbsp. warm water | 2 egg yolks |
| 1 1/2 pkg. yeast | 1/4 c. half and half |
| 2 1/2 c. sifted flour | Melted butter |
| 3 tbsp. sugar | 2 c. sifted powdered sugar |
| 1 tsp. salt | Pecan halves |
| | Candied cherries |

Drain the pineapple well, pressing out most of the liquid, and reserve 1/2 cup pineapple and the syrup. Pour the water into a small, warm bowl and sprinkle with yeast. Stir until dissolved. Place the flour, sugar, salt, butter, egg yolks, half and half and remaining pineapple in a large bowl. Add the yeast and beat with an electric mixer or with a spoon for 2 to 3 minutes or until blended. Scrape down bowl and cover. Refrigerate for 3 or 4 hours or overnight. Divide into 4 equal parts. Roll each part on a lightly floured board to a 12-inch rope. Twist 2 ropes together lightly on greased baking sheet. Pinch ends and tuck under to seal. Make another loaf with remaining 2 ropes. Cover with dampened cloth and let rise in a warm place for about 50 minutes or until doubled in bulk. Brush with melted butter. Bake at 375 degrees for about 30 minutes. Remove to wire rack. Blend reserved pineapple with the powdered sugar, adding 1 tablespoon reserved syrup, if needed, to make thick spreading consistency. Spread on top of warm loaves and decorate with pecan halves and cherries.

## PINEAPPLE UPSIDE-DOWN COFFEE CAKE

| | |
|---|---|
| 1/4 c. butter | 1/3 c. instant nonfat dry milk |
| 1/4 c. honey | 3 tsp. baking powder |
| 1  8 1/2-oz. can crushed | 1/2 tsp. salt |
|    pineapple | 1/2 c. sugar |
| 1/4 c. shredded coconut | 1/3 c. shortening |
| 1 c. flour | 1 egg, beaten |
| 3/4 c. cornmeal | |

Melt the butter in an 8 x 8 x 2-inch pan. Add the honey and blend. Drain the pineapple and reserve juice. Spread pineapple over butter mixture, then spread coconut over pineapple. Sift dry ingredients together 3 times into a mixing bowl and cut in the shortening until well blended. Add enough water to reserved pineapple juice to make 1/2 cup liquid, then add the egg. Add to flour mixture and mix well. Pour into prepared pan. Bake at 400 degrees for about 25 minutes. Cool in pan for 5 minutes. Invert over plate and let stand for 1 minute. Remove pan, cut into squares and serve warm.

*Mrs. J. B. Carpenter, Landrum, South Carolina*


## CRISPY HUSH PUPPIES

| | |
|---|---|
| 1/2 c. sifted flour | 1/2 tsp. salt |
| 2 tsp. baking powder | 3/4 c. milk |
| 1 1/2 c. cornmeal | 1 egg, well beaten |
| 1 tbsp. sugar | 1 sm. onion, minced |

Sift dry ingredients together into a bowl, then stir in remaining ingredients. Drop by teaspoonfuls into deep fat at 350 degrees and cook until brown. Drain on absorbent paper.

*Mrs. J. M. Killingsworth, Mayfield, Oklahoma*


## SPANISH CORN BREAD

| | |
|---|---|
| 2 eggs, slightly beaten | 1/2 tsp. soda |
| 1 c. buttermilk | 1 sm. can green chilies |
| 1/4 c. melted butter | 1 sm. can cream-style corn |
| 1 c. cornmeal | 1 c. grated longhorn cheese |
| 1 tsp. salt | 1 sm. onion, grated |
| 1 tsp. baking powder | |

Mix the eggs, buttermilk and butter in a bowl. Add the dry ingredients and mix just until blended. Drain and chop the green chilies, then add to the egg mixture. Add the corn, cheese and onion and mix well. Pour into a greased baking pan. Bake at 400 degrees for 25 minutes.

*Mrs. H. T. Brasell, Portales, New Mexico*

## MEXICAN SPOON BREAD

| | |
|---|---|
| 1 c. cornmeal | 1/2 c. melted shortening |
| 1 tsp. salt | 1 sm. can green chilies |
| 2 eggs, separated | 1 1/2 c. grated cheese |
| 1 No. 303 can cream-style corn | |

Mix the cornmeal and salt in a bowl. Beat the egg yolks well. Stir in the corn and shortening, then stir into the cornmeal mixture. Drain and chop the green chilies and stir into the cornmeal mixture. Stir in the cheese. Beat the egg whites until stiff peaks form and fold into the cornmeal mixture. Place in a greased casserole. Bake at 400 degrees for 45 minutes or until done.

*Mrs. Millie Ellis, Willcox, Arizona*

## SOPAPILLAS

| | |
|---|---|
| 3 c. flour | 1/2 tsp. salt |
| 1 tbsp. baking powder | 1 tbsp. shortening |

Sift the dry ingredients together into a bowl and cut in shortening until mixture resembles fine meal. Add enough water to make a stiff dough and stir until blended. Roll out 1/8 inch thick on a lightly floured board and cut into squares. Fry in deep fat at 350 degrees until puffy and golden brown. Drain on paper towels. Serve with honey, if desired. 6-8 servings.

*Mrs. Florence Walker, Fort Lyon, Colorado*

## TORTILLAS

| | |
|---|---|
| 1 c. milk | 1/2 tsp. salt |
| 3/4 c. cornstarch | 2 eggs, beaten |
| 1/3 c. cornmeal | 2 tbsp. melted butter |

Mix the milk and cornstarch in a bowl until smooth. Add the cornmeal and salt and mix well. Stir in the eggs and butter. Pour 3 tablespoons cornmeal mixture for each tortilla into a hot, greased 6-inch skillet. Cook until brown. Turn and cook until brown. 12 tortillas.

*Mrs. Adelaide Morrow, Baltimore, Maryland*

## INDIAN BREAD

| | |
|---|---|
| 2 c. sifted flour | 1/2 c. shredded sharp American |
| 1/2 tsp. salt | process cheese |
| 2 tbsp. shortening | 1/2 to 2/3 c. water |

Mix the flour and salt in a bowl and cut in shortening. Add the cheese. Stir in enough water to make a soft dough. Knead and pound on a floured surface for 10 to 15 minutes. Cover and let stand for 30 minutes. Roll out very thin and cut in 4-inch circles. Fry in deep, hot fat until puffed and golden brown, turning once. Drain on paper towels and keep warm until served.

*Mrs. Otis Phelps, Pine Bluff, Arkansas*

## RAISED DOUGHNUTS

| | |
|---|---|
| 1 1/4 c. milk, scalded | 3 eggs |
| 1/4 c. shortening | 3/4 c. sugar |
| 1/2 tsp. salt | 1 1/2 tsp. cinnamon |
| 1 pkg. yeast | 1/4 tsp. nutmeg |
| 5 c. sifted flour | 1/8 tsp. mace |

Combine the milk, shortening and salt in a bowl and cool to lukewarm. Add the yeast and let stand for 5 minutes. Stir well. Add 2 1/2 cups flour and beat until smooth. Cover and let rise until bubbly. Add the eggs, sugar and spices and mix well. Add enough remaining flour to make a stiff dough and knead on a floured surface until smooth. Place in a greased bowl and cover. Let rise until doubled in bulk. Roll out on a floured surface 1/2 inch thick and cut with a doughnut cutter. Let rise until doubled in bulk. Fry in deep fat at 375 degrees for 3 minutes, turning once. 3 dozen.

*Willie Gerken, Anadarko, Oklahoma*

## TRENZAS PARA EL TE

| | |
|---|---|
| Milk | 1/2 c. warm water |
| Sugar | 2 pkg. dry yeast |
| 1 tsp. salt | 5 egg yolks, slightly beaten |
| 1/4 c. margarine | 4 1/4 c. (about) unsifted flour |

Scald 1/2 cup milk in a saucepan and stir in 1/2 cup sugar, salt and margarine. Cool to lukewarm. Pour the warm water into a large, warm bowl and sprinkle with yeast. Stir until dissolved. Add the milk mixture, 4 egg yolks and half the flour and beat until smooth. Add enough remaining flour to form a soft dough.

Turn out onto a lightly floured board and knead for 8 to 10 minutes or until smooth and elastic. Cover and let rise in a warm place, free from draft, for about 1 hour or until doubled in bulk. Punch down. Turn out onto a lightly floured board and divide in half. Divide half the dough into 3 equal pieces. Roll each piece into a rope 14 inches long. Place the ropes on a greased baking sheet and braid. Repeat with remaining dough. Blend remaining egg yolk and 1 tablespoon milk and brush on braids. Sprinkle with sugar. Let rise in a warm place, free from draft, for about 45 minutes or until doubled in bulk. Bake at 350 degrees for 30 minutes or until done.

## CARROT BREAD

| | |
|---|---|
| 1/2 c. lukewarm water | 2 c. warm water |
| 5 tbsp. sugar | 1 c. grated carrots |
| 2 pkg. yeast | 1 c. ground raisins |
| 1/2 c. melted shortening | Flour |
| 1 egg, beaten | Butter |
| 2 tsp. salt | |

Mix the lukewarm water, 1 tablespoon sugar and yeast in a bowl and let stand for 5 minutes. Pour the shortening into a large mixing bowl and cool to lukewarm. Add the egg, remaining sugar, salt and warm water and mix. Add yeast mixture, carrots, raisins and 6 cups flour and mix well. Turn onto a floured board and knead in about 4 cups flour. Place in a bowl and let rise for 1 hour. Punch down. Place in 2 greased loaf pans and let rise until doubled in bulk. Bake at 375 degrees for 20 minutes and brush with butter. Reduce temperature to 300 degrees and bake for 25 minutes longer.

*Mrs. W. W. Gallaway, Uvalde, Texas*

## CASSEROLE SESAME BREAD

| | |
|---|---|
| Milk | 1 1/2 c. warm water |
| 4 1/2 tbsp. sugar | 3 eggs, beaten |
| 1 1/2 tbsp. salt | 1/2 c. instant nonfat dry milk |
| 2 tbsp. cooking oil | 6 3/4 c. all-purpose flour |
| 3 pkg. yeast | 1 tbsp. sesame or poppy seed |

Scald 1 1/2 cups milk in a saucepan and stir in sugar, salt and oil. Pour into large bowl and cool to lukewarm. Sprinkle yeast on water in a small bowl and stir until dissolved. Stir the eggs into milk mixture, then stir in the yeast. Add powdered milk and flour and beat until blended. Cover with a towel and let rise for about 40 minutes or until doubled in bulk. Stir down and beat vigorously for 30 seconds. Turn out on a lightly floured board and knead for 4 minutes. Place in a well-greased casserole and brush top with 2 tablespoons milk. Sprinkle with sesame seed. Bake in 400-degree oven for 40 to 50 minutes or until done. Remove from oven and let cool for 5 minutes. Turn out on a rack to cool.

*Mrs. William Jones, Augusta, Georgia*

## DILLY BREAD

| | |
|---|---|
| 1 pkg. dry yeast | 1 tsp. dillseed |
| 1/4 c. warm water | 1 tsp. salt |
| 1 c. cottage cheese | 1/4 tsp. soda |
| 2 tbsp. sugar | 1 egg |
| 1 tbsp. minced onion | 2 1/4 to 2 1/2 c. flour |
| 1 tbsp. melted butter | |

Dissolve the yeast in water. Heat the cottage cheese in a bowl over hot water until lukewarm. Add the sugar, onion, butter, dillseed, salt and soda and mix. Add the egg and yeast and stir well. Add enough flour to make a stiff dough and mix well. Let rise in a warm place for 50 to 60 minutes or until doubled in bulk. Stir down. Turn into 2 small loaf pans and let rise in a warm place for 40 minutes. Bake in a 350-degree oven for about 35 minutes or until golden brown. Remove from pans. Spread additional butter over bread and sprinkle with additional salt.

*Bruce Keener, Jr., Louisville, Tennessee*

## DOUBLE-GOOD BREAD

| | |
|---|---|
| 1/4 c. sugar | 3 tbsp. instant potatoes |
| 1 tbsp. salt | 1 pkg. yeast |
| 1/4 c. butter | 6 c. flour, sifted |
| 2 lge. eggs | 6 tbsp. wheat germ |
| 2 c. water | |

Mix the sugar, salt, butter and eggs in a large bowl. Mix the water with potatoes in a saucepan and heat until warm. Add to egg mixture and mix well. Sprinkle with yeast and mix well. Mix the flour and wheat germ. Add half the flour mixture to yeast mixture and mix well. Add remaining flour mixture and mix. Cover and let rise in a warm place until doubled in bulk. Knead on a floured surface. Cut in half and place in 2 greased bread pans. Cover and let rise almost to tops of pans. Bake at 350 degrees for 30 to 35 minutes or until brown.

*Mrs. James J. Elder, North Miami, Florida*

## ONION CASSEROLE BREAD

| | |
|---|---|
| 1 c. milk, scalded | 3/4 c. warm water |
| 3 tbsp. sugar | 1 env. onion soup mix |
| 1 1/2 tbsp. butter or margarine | 4 c. unsifted flour |
| 1 pkg. dry yeast | |

Mix the milk, sugar and butter in a medium bowl and cool to lukewarm. Dissolve the yeast in the warm water and stir into milk mixture. Add the soup mix and flour and blend for about 2 minutes. Cover bowl and let rise in a warm place, free from draft, for about 45 minutes or until doubled in bulk. Stir down and beat for about 30 seconds. Turn into a greased 1 1/2-quart casserole. Bake at 375 degrees for 1 hour.

*Cindy Lloyd, Pensacola, Florida*

## GINGERBREAD MUFFINS

| | |
|---|---|
| 1 egg, beaten | 1/2 tsp. cloves |
| 3/4 c. sugar | 1/2 tsp. salt |
| 6 tbsp. shortening | 2 1/2 c. flour |
| 3/4 c. molasses | 1/2 tsp. cinnamon |
| 1 c. buttermilk | 1 1/2 tsp. soda |
| 1/2 tsp. ginger | |

Combine the egg, sugar, shortening, molasses and buttermilk in a bowl. Mix remaining ingredients and stir into the egg mixture. Fill greased muffin cups 2/3 full. Bake at 400 degrees for 20 to 25 minutes. 18 muffins.

*Mrs. Ernest H. Dillon, Jet, Oklahoma*

## MACARONI MUFFINS

| | |
|---|---|
| 2 c. cornmeal | 1/2 tsp. soda |
| 2 tsp. baking powder | 1 1/2 c. buttermilk |
| 2 tsp. sugar | 1 egg, beaten |
| 1 tsp. salt | 1 c. chopped cooked macaroni |
| 3 tbsp. vegetable oil | |

Preheat oven to 425 degrees. Sift the cornmeal, baking powder, sugar and salt together into a bowl and stir in the oil. Mix the soda and 1 cup buttermilk and stir into cornmeal mixture. Add remaining buttermilk and egg and stir until mixed. Add the macaroni and stir lightly. Place in hot, greased muffin cups. Bake for 15 minutes or until brown.

*Becky Walker, Dyersburg, Tennessee*

## TWIN MOUNTAIN MUFFINS

| | |
|---|---|
| 1/4 c. shortening | 4 tbsp. baking powder |
| 1/4 c. sugar | 1/2 tsp. salt |
| 1 egg, beaten | 1 c. milk |
| 2 c. flour | |

Cream the shortening and sugar in a bowl, then stir in the egg. Sift dry ingredients together and add to creamed mixture alternately with milk. Fill well-greased muffin tins 1/2 full. Bake at 375 degrees for 20 minutes. 12 muffins.

*Mrs. Bettie McCray, Elizabeth, West Virginia*

## DOUBLE CORN PANCAKES

| | |
|---|---|
| 1 c. packaged pancake mix | 1  1-lb. can cream-style corn |
| 1 c. cornmeal | 1 c. milk |
| 1 tsp. baking powder | 2 tbsp. salad oil |
| 2 eggs, slightly beaten | |

Mix the dry ingredients in a bowl. Combine the eggs, corn, milk and oil. Add to dry ingredients and stir just until moistened. Pour 1/4 cup for each pancake onto a hot, lightly greased griddle or skillet and cook until brown on both sides, turning once. About sixteen 4-inch pancakes.

*Mrs. Paul Lumpkin, Houston, Texas*

## PRUNE POCKET BUNS

| | |
|---|---|
| 1 c. milk | 2 eggs, beaten |
| 1/2 c. sour cream | 4 c. unsifted flour |
| Sugar | 1 1/2 c. chopped cooked |
| 1 tsp. salt | prunes, drained |
| 6 tbsp. margarine | 2/3 c. chopped pecans |
| 1/4 c. warm water | 2/3 c. raisins |
| 1 pkg. yeast | 1 1/2 tsp. cinnamon |

Stir the milk into sour cream in a saucepan gradually and mix until smooth. Scald the milk mixture, then stir in 1/2 cup sugar, salt and margarine. Cool to lukewarm. Pour the warm water into a large, warm bowl. Sprinkle with yeast and stir until dissolved. Stir in the milk mixture, eggs and flour and beat vigorously for 1 minute. Cover and let rise in a warm place, free from draft, for about 1 hour or until doubled in bulk. Combine the prunes, pecans, 2/3 cup sugar, raisins and cinnamon. Stir the yeast mixture down. Spoon 1 tablespoon into each well-greased and lightly floured muffin cup and top each with 1 tablespoon prune mixture. Spoon 1 tablespoon yeast mixture over prune mixture in each muffin cup. Let rise in a warm place, free from draft, for about 1 hour or until doubled in bulk. Bake at 375 degrees for 12 to 15 minutes or until done. One 1-pound 9-ounce jar prunes, drained and chopped, may be substituted for cooked prunes. About 2 1/2 dozen.

## PARKER HOUSE ROLLS

| | |
|---|---|
| 1 c. milk | 1/4 c. sugar |
| 1 pkg. yeast | 4 c. sifted flour |

| | |
|---|---|
| **1 1/2 tbsp. salt** | **4 tbsp. shortening** |
| **1 egg, beaten** | **Melted butter** |

Scald the milk and cool to lukewarm. Add the yeast and sugar and stir until dissolved. Add 1/2 of the flour, salt, egg and shortening and beat thoroughly. Add remaining flour gradually and mix well. Place on a lightly floured board and knead for about 5 minutes or until smooth and elastic. Place in a bowl, cover and let rise until doubled in bulk. Roll out on a floured surface 1/4 inch thick and cut with a biscuit cutter. Crease with the dull side of a knife and brush with melted butter. Fold over and place on a greased cookie sheet. Let rise until doubled in bulk. Bake at 400 degrees for 15 to 20 minutes. 2 dozen.

*Sandra Baldwin, Blount County, Alabama*

## CRUSTY POPPY SEED ROLLS

| | |
|---|---|
| **2 pkg. dry yeast** | **6 1/2 to 7 c. flour** |
| **1 3/4 c. warm water** | **3 egg whites** |
| **4 tsp. sugar** | **Poppy seed** |
| **2 tsp. salt** | **Coarse salt** |
| **2 tbsp. melted shortening** | |

Add the yeast to warm water in a bowl and let stand for 5 minutes. Add the sugar, salt, shortening and 2 cups flour and mix well. Beat 2 egg whites until stiff and stir into dough. Add the remaining flour and mix until dough leaves side of bowl. Let rise until doubled in bulk. Shape into French rolls and place on greased baking sheet. Beat remaining egg white lightly and stir in 1 tablespoon water. Brush over the rolls. Sprinkle with poppy seed and coarse salt and let rise until doubled in bulk. Bake at 425 degrees until brown. 2 dozen.

*Margaret Crawford, Meeker, Colorado*

## BUTTERHORNS

| | |
|---|---|
| **1 pkg. yeast** | **2/3 tsp. salt** |
| **Sugar** | **1/2 c. melted butter** |
| **1 c. milk** | **3 to 3 1/2 c. flour** |
| **3 eggs** | |

Mix the yeast and 1 tablespoon sugar. Add 1/4 cup warm water and stir until dissolved. Scald the milk and cool to lukewarm. Beat the eggs in a bowl until light. Add 1/2 cup sugar, salt, butter and milk and mix well. Add enough flour to make a medium-stiff dough and mix until well blended. Cover and let rise until doubled in bulk. Turn out on a floured board and knead lightly. Divide in half and roll each half to a 12-inch circle. Spread with additional butter and cut each circle into 8 wedges. Roll each wedge from wide end to point and place at least 2 1/2 inches apart on a greased cookie sheet, point side down. Let rise until doubled in bulk. Bake at 350 degrees for 20 minutes.

*Mrs. Edwin Davis, Huntsville, Alabama*

## MEXICAN BREAKFAST ROLLS

| | |
|---|---|
| 7 1/2 to 8 1/2 c. unsifted flour | 1/2 c. milk |
| 1 c. sugar | 3/4 c. margarine |
| 1 1/2 tsp. salt | 2 eggs |
| 1 1/2 tsp. aniseed | 1/4 c. (firmly packed) brown |
| 1 pkg. dry yeast |    sugar |
| 1 1/2 c. water | |

Mix 2 cups flour, sugar, salt, aniseed and undissolved yeast in a large bowl. Combine the water, milk and 1/2 cup margarine in a saucepan and place over low heat until liquids are warm. Margarine does not need to melt. Add to dry ingredients gradually and beat for 2 minutes with electric mixer at medium speed, scraping bowl occasionally. Add eggs and 1 cup flour and beat at high speed for 2 minutes, scraping bowl occasionally. Stir in enough remaining flour to make a soft dough. Turn out onto a lightly floured board and knead for 8 to 10 minutes or until smooth and elastic. Place in a greased bowl, turning to grease top. Cover and let rise in a warm place, free from draft, for about 1 hour or until doubled in bulk. Punch down and turn out onto a lightly floured board. Divide into 48 equal pieces. Shape into balls and place 16 in each of 3 greased 9-inch round or square cake pans. Cover and let rise in a warm place, free from draft, for about 1 hour or until doubled in bulk. Melt remaining margarine and brown sugar in a saucepan over low heat, blending well. Bake the rolls in a 350-degree oven for 25 minutes. Remove from oven and brush with the brown sugar syrup. Return to oven and bake for 5 to 10 minutes longer or until done.

## CHOCOLATE-CINNAMON BUNS

| | |
|---|---|
| 1 pkg. dry yeast | Sugar |
| 3/4 c. warm water | 1 egg |
| 1/4 c. shortening | 1/3 c. cocoa |
| 1 tsp. salt | 2 1/2 c. flour |

| | |
|---|---|
| **1 tsp. soft butter** | **1/4 c. chopped pecans** |
| **1 1/2 tsp. cinnamon** | |

Dissolve the yeast in warm water in a bowl. Add the shortening, salt, 1/2 cup sugar, egg, cocoa and 1 cup flour and beat well. Add enough remaining flour to make a stiff dough and cover. Let rise in a warm place until doubled in bulk. Knead on a well-floured board, then roll out to a 12 x 9-inch rectangle. Combine the butter, cinnamon, 3 tablespoons sugar and pecans and spread over dough. Roll from long side as for jelly roll and cut into 12 slices. Place in a greased 9-inch square pan and let rise until doubled in bulk. Bake at 375 degrees for 25 minutes.

Icing

| | |
|---|---|
| **1/2 c. butter or margarine** | **1 tsp. vanilla** |
| **1 c. (packed) brown sugar** | **1 c. sifted powdered sugar** |
| **1/2 c. evaporated milk** | |

Combine the butter, brown sugar and milk in a saucepan and bring to a boil. Reduce heat and simmer for 5 minutes, stirring constantly. Remove from heat and cool. Add the vanilla and sugar and mix well. Spread over buns.

*Mrs. Fred Carlson, Montrose, Colorado*

## OATMEAL WAFFLES

| | |
|---|---|
| **1 c. whole wheat flour** | **1/2 tsp. salt** |
| **1/2 c. quick-cooking oats** | **2 eggs, beaten** |
| **1/2 c. wheat germ** | **1 1/4 c. milk** |
| **1 tbsp. brown sugar** | **6 tbsp. salad oil** |
| **3 tsp. baking powder** | |

Combine first 6 ingredients in a bowl. Add the eggs, milk and oil and blend well. Bake in hot waffle iron until golden brown. 4 servings.

*Mrs. Robert Hessemer, Tuscon, Arizona*

## ORANGE WAFFLES

| | |
|---|---|
| **1/2 tsp. soda** | **1 tsp. sugar** |
| **1 1/4 c. buttermilk** | **Juice and grated rind of 1** |
| **1 1/4 c. flour** | **orange** |
| **1 1/2 tsp. baking powder** | **2 eggs, separated** |
| **1 tsp. salt** | **1/4 c. melted butter** |

Mix the soda and buttermilk in a bowl. Sift dry ingredients together and stir into the buttermilk mixture. Stir in the orange juice and rind, egg yolks and butter, then fold in stiffly beaten egg whites. Bake in waffle iron until golden brown. 4-6 servings.

*Mrs. L. Murray Noumann, Tulsa, Oklahoma*

# desserts and beverages

Southwesterners are some of the most resourceful people in the country, and when it comes to using available foodstuffs, they just can't be beat. Look what they did with the coffee bean the minute it came to San Antonio. Coffee pots were soon steaming all over the Southwest, and this hot black drink was even declared the regional beverage. Southwesterners were just as quick to make other beverages and many desserts with accessible ingredients, whether imported or native.

For one of their favorite desserts, Southwesterners just walk to the nearest watermelon patch and pick the plumpest, shiniest fruit they can find. Into more complicated desserts go other locally grown fruits and native nuts. In this section you'll find recipes for chilled desserts that use oranges and nuts. Favorite pies and cookies contain cherries and pecans. Cobblers are packed with strawberries.

Strawberries also go into favorite punches. In fact, all fruit drinks are just natural developments of the abundance of regional fruits and Southwestern quickness to make use of them. In early Southwestern Christmas celebrations, fruit punch was served to accompany fruit cake! Southwesterners have also converted tomatoes into cocktails and chocolate into delicious beverages.

You, too, can reap the benefits of Southwestern resourcefulness in the dessert and beverage recipes that follow.

## BUTTERMILK POUND CAKE

| | |
|---|---|
| 3 c. sifted all-purpose flour | 4 eggs |
| 1/2 tsp. soda | 1 tsp. vanilla |
| 1/2 tsp. baking powder | 1 tsp. lemon extract |
| 3/4 tsp. salt | 1 c. buttermilk |
| 1 c. butter | Confectioners' sugar |
| 2 c. sugar | |

Sift the flour, soda, baking powder and salt together twice. Cream the butter with sugar in a bowl until light and fluffy. Add the eggs, one at a time, beating well after each addition, then blend in flavorings. Add the flour mixture alternately with buttermilk, beating until smooth after each addition. Pour into a greased, floured and brown paper-lined 10-inch tube pan. Bake in a 350-degree oven for about 1 hour and 10 minutes or until a cake tester inserted in the center comes out clean. Remove from the pan and cool. Dust with confectioners' sugar.

## COCONUT POUND CAKE

| | |
|---|---|
| 1 c. butter | 1 tsp. baking powder |
| 1/2 c. shortening | 1 tsp. salt |
| 3 c. sugar | 1 c. evaporated milk |
| 6 eggs | 1 tbsp. lemon juice |
| 3 c. sifted flour | 1 can flaked coconut |

Have all ingredients at room temperature. Preheat oven to 200 degrees. Cream the butter, shortening and sugar in a mixing bowl until fluffy. Add the eggs, one at a time, beating well after each addition. Sift dry ingredients together and add to creamed mixture alternately with milk, beginning and ending with dry ingredients. Add the lemon juice and coconut and blend well. Pour into a greased and floured tube pan. Place in oven and increase temperature to 325 degrees. Bake for 1 hour and 20 minutes without opening oven door. Test cake for doneness and bake for about 10 minutes longer, if needed. Frost or serve plain.

*Mrs. William N. Seaford, Mocksville, North Carolina*

## OATMEAL CAKE

| | |
|---|---|
| 1 1/4 c. boiling water | 1 1/3 c. flour |
| 1 c. rolled oats | 1/2 tsp. salt |
| 1/2 c. shortening or butter | 1 tsp. soda |
| 1 c. sugar | 1 tsp. cinnamon |
| 1 c. (packed) brown sugar | 1/2 tsp. vanilla |
| 2 eggs | 1/2 c. chopped nuts |

Pour the boiling water over rolled oats and let stand for 20 minutes. Cream the shortening and sugars in a bowl. Add the eggs and beat well. Add oatmeal mixture and mix. Sift the flour with salt, soda and cinnamon and stir into oatmeal mixture. Add vanilla and nuts and beat until smooth. Pour into a greased and floured oblong pan. Bake at 350 degrees for about 40 minutes.

### Broiler Frosting

| | |
|---|---|
| 6 tbsp. butter | 1/2 tsp. vanilla |
| 1/4 c. cream | 1 c. shredded coconut |
| 1/2 c. (packed) brown sugar | 1 c. chopped nuts |

Mix all ingredients and spread on warm cake. Broil until browned.

*Betty Pustejovsky, Taft, Texas*

## WHITE FRUITCAKE

| | |
|---|---|
| 1 lb. mixed candied fruits | 1 1/2 c. sugar |
| 1 c. white raisins | 2 1/4 c. cake flour |
| 1 c. chopped pitted dates | 1/2 tsp. salt |
| 3 c. mixed nuts | 1 tsp. baking powder |
| 1 c. butter | 1/4 tsp. cinnamon |
| 5 eggs, beaten | 1/4 tsp. allspice |
| 1/2 c. orange juice or milk | 1 tsp. vanilla |
| 1/4 c. light corn syrup | |

Combine fruits and nuts. Cream the butter in a large mixing bowl. Add the eggs, orange juice, corn syrup and sugar and mix well. Sift dry ingredients together and stir in the fruit mixture. Add to butter mixture gradually, then add vanilla. Beat well and pour into waxed paper-lined tube pan. Bake at 250 degrees for 3 hours. One 5-pound cake.

*Mrs. S. L. Winters, Louisville, Kentucky*

## ALMOND BISQUE

1 sm. package lemon gelatin
2 tbsp. sugar
1/4 tsp. salt
1 c. boiling water
1/2 c. cold water

1 c. whipped cream
1 tsp. almond extract
6 toasted crushed macaroons
6 marshmallows, quartered
3 tbsp. chopped candied cherries

Dissolve the gelatin, sugar and salt in boiling water in a bowl. Add cold water and chill until thickened. Whip until frothy. Fold in remaining ingredients and pour into a mold. Chill until firm. 6 servings.

*Mrs. Agnes Hackley, Louisville, Kentucky*

## ORANGE CASHEW ANGEL

1/3 c. sifted all-purpose flour
2/3 c. sugar
1/4 tsp. salt
2 eggs, separated

2 sm. cans evaporated milk
2/3 c. orange juice
1 tbsp. grated orange rind
1/2 c. slivered cashew nuts

Sift the flour, sugar and salt together into a mixing bowl. Beat the egg yolks and add milk, orange juice and grated rind. Blend into flour mixture. Beat egg whites until stiff and fold into flour mixture. Pour into eight 8-ounce custard cups and sprinkle with cashew nuts. Set custard cups in pan of hot water. Bake at 325 degrees for 40 to 45 minutes, then chill. Serve with whipped cream, if desired.

*Mrs. Charles Riemenschneider, Weesatche, Texas*

## RASPBERRY RIPPLE

20 graham crackers, crushed
1/3 c. butter or margarine
1/3 c. sugar
50 marshmallows
1 c. milk

1 1/3 c. whipped cream
1 sm. package raspberry gelatin
1 1/2 c. hot water
1 pkg. frozen raspberries

Combine the cracker crumbs, butter and sugar and press half the mixture in bottom of a large pan. Combine the marshmallows and milk in a saucepan and cook over low heat, stirring constantly, until marshmallows are melted. Cool, then fold in whipped cream. Pour over crumb mixture in pan and chill. Dissolve the gelatin in hot water in a bowl and stir in frozen raspberries. Chill until thickened. Pour over marshmallow mixture and sprinkle with remaining crumb mixture. Refrigerate overnight. 15 servings.

*Mrs. Ermin Borgstrom, Big Cabin, Oklahoma*

## APPLE-CHAMPAGNE COMPOTE

3 Washington State golden
  Delicious apples

1 1/2 c. California champagne
2 c. sliced strawberries

**1 c. powdered sugar**         **Pineapple slices**
**Shredded coconut or nuts**

Pare, core and slice the apples in very thin circles. Place in a bowl and cover with champagne and strawberries. Sprinkle with powdered sugar and chill for 3 hours. Place in clear glass compote dishes and sprinkle with shredded coconut. Top with a pineapple slice.

*Photograph for this recipe below.*

## POMMES MERINGUES

**1 1/4 c. sugar**         **1/4 c. orange juice**
**1 c. water**         **2 egg whites**
**1/8 tsp. salt**         **1/2 tsp. vanilla**
**5 med. golden Delicious apples**

Combine 1 cup sugar, water and salt in a saucepan and bring to boiling point. Pare, quarter and core the apples. Add to the syrup and cover. Bring to boiling point and reduce heat. Simmer for 15 minutes or until apples are tender. Drain the apples and place in a buttered 1-quart casserole. Sprinkle with orange juice. Beat the egg whites until stiff peaks form, adding remaining sugar gradually. Add the vanilla and beat until mixed. Drop from spoon over apples. Bake at 325 degrees for 15 minutes or until brown. Serve warm or cold. Red wine may be substituted for orange juice. 6 servings.

## COFFEE-MARSHMALLOW BROWNIES

| | |
|---|---|
| 1/2 c. shortening | 1 c. sifted self-rising flour |
| 1 c. sugar | 1 c. miniature marshmallows |
| 2 oz. unsweetened chocolate | 3 tbsp. strong coffee |
| 2 eggs, beaten | 1 tsp. vanilla |
| 1 c. broken walnuts | |

Cream the shortening and sugar in a mixing bowl. Melt the chocolate over hot water, then stir into creamed mixture. Add the eggs and mix well. Add remaining ingredients in order listed and pour into well-greased 9 x 9 x 2-inch pan. Bake at 350 degrees for 50 minutes or until done. Cut into squares.

*Mrs. Rachel Cockerham, Lowegap, North Carolina*

## RANGER COOKIES

| | |
|---|---|
| 1 c. shortening | 1 1/4 tsp. soda |
| 1 c. sugar | 1 tsp. baking powder |
| 1 c. (packed) brown sugar | 1/2 tsp. salt |
| 2 eggs | 1 c. chopped pecans |
| 3 c. crushed corn flakes | 1 tsp. vanilla |
| 1 c. oats | |

Cream the shortening and sugars until smooth. Add the eggs, one at a time, beating well after each addition. Stir in the corn flakes and oats. Sift the soda, baking powder and salt together and add, small amount at a time, to the creamed mixture. Stir in the pecans and vanilla. Drop from a teaspoon onto a greased cookie sheet. Bake at 375 degrees for about 10 minutes or until brown. One cup shredded coconut may be substituted for the pecans.

*Mrs. J. R. Camp, Orange, Texas*

## ROLLED ALMOND WAFERS

| | |
|---|---|
| 3/4 c. ground unblanched almonds | 1 tbsp. flour |
| 1/2 c. unsalted soft butter | Dash of salt |
| 1/2 c. sugar | 2 tbsp. heavy cream |

Combine all ingredients in a small, heavy saucepan and heat, stirring, until butter melts. Drop from teaspoon 3 inches apart on greased and floured cookie sheets, having only 6 cookies at a time on a cookie sheet. Bake at 350 degrees for 7 minutes or until edges begin to brown, but centers are still bubbling. Cool for 1 to 2 minutes, then loosen with a thin knife. Wrap each cookie around the handle of a knife or wooden spoon, and place, joined side down, on racks to cool. 3 dozen.

*Mrs. Evangeline Heasley, Corpus Christi, Texas*

## SOUR CREAM-COCONUT WAFERS

| | |
|---|---|
| 3 c. flour | 1/2 tsp. salt |
| 1/2 tsp. baking powder | 1/4 tsp. soda |

3/4 c. butter or margarine
1 c. (packed) brown sugar
2 eggs, beaten
1 1/2 tsp. vanilla

1/4 tsp. orange extract
1/3 c. sour cream
1 c. flaked coconut

Combine first 4 ingredients. Cream the butter and brown sugar in a mixing bowl until light and fluffy. Add eggs and flavorings and beat well. Blend in half the flour mixture. Add sour cream and mix thoroughly. Blend in remaining flour mixture. Add coconut and mix well. Shape into rolls and wrap in waxed paper. Chill overnight. Slice 1/4 inch thick and place on lightly greased baking sheets. Bake at 400 degrees for about 10 minutes. 8 dozen.

*Mrs. Tom C. Nix, Lexington, Kentucky*

## BISCUIT TORTONI

3/4 c. sugar
3/4 c. strong coffee
1 tbsp. butter

3 egg yolks, beaten
25 coconut macaroons
1 pt. whipping cream

Mix the sugar and coffee in a saucepan and cook until mixture spins a thread. Add the butter and cool. Beat in egg yolks. Pour into a refrigerator tray and freeze, stirring occasionally. Roll macaroons into crumbs and line refrigerator tray with crumbs, reserving 3/4 cup. Whip the cream until stiff and beat in frozen mixture slowly. Pour into prepared tray and top with reserved crumbs. Freeze.

*Helen Sergent, Gate City, Virginia*

## PRIZE ICE CREAM

1 c. milk, scalded
2 eggs, slightly beaten
1 tsp. vanilla

Dash of salt
1 c. light corn syrup
1 c. heavy cream, whipped

Mix the milk, eggs and vanilla in the top of a double boiler. Cook over boiling water, stirring, until mixture coats a spoon. Stir in salt and corn syrup and cool. Fold in whipped cream. Turn into a refrigerator tray and freeze until mushy. Place in a bowl and beat until fluffy. Return to refrigerator tray and freeze until firm. 4 servings.

*Mrs. E. E. Evans, Yuma, Arizona*

## PEPPERMINT PIE

1 pkg. dessert topping mix
2 sticks peppermint candy,
  crushed

1 pt. soft vanilla ice cream
1 tsp. peppermint flavoring
1   10-in. graham cracker crust

Prepare the topping mix according to package directions. Combine the candy, ice cream and flavoring and mix well, then fold in the topping mixture. Turn into the crust and freeze for several hours.

*Nina Scanland, Dallas, Texas*

## EASY STRAWBERRY COBBLER

| | |
|---|---|
| 1 stick butter | 1 c. milk |
| 1 c. flour | 3 c. strawberries |
| 2 c. sugar | 1 c. water |
| 3 tsp. baking powder | Cinnamon to taste |
| 1/2 tsp. salt | |

Melt the butter in a 9 x 13-inch baking dish. Mix the flour, 1 cup sugar, baking powder and salt in a bowl and stir in the milk gradually. Pour into the baking dish. Combine the strawberries, water and remaining sugar. Pour the strawberry mixture over the batter and sprinkle with cinnamon. Bake at 350 degrees for 45 minutes or until golden brown. Cut in squares and serve topped with whipped cream or ice cream. 8 servings.

*Mrs. Oliver Bauer, Castell, Texas*

## MINCEMEAT-CHEESE PINWHEELS

| | |
|---|---|
| 2 sm. packages cream cheese | 1/2 tsp. baking powder |
| 1 c. butter or margarine | Pinch of salt |
| 2 eggs, separated | Mincemeat pie filling |
| 2 c. flour | Sugar |

Blend the cream cheese and butter in a bowl. Add egg yolks and mix well. Stir in the flour, baking powder and salt. Roll out on a floured surface to 1/8-inch thickness. Cut into 2 1/2-inch squares and slash corners of squares. Brush with slightly beaten egg whites. Place filling in center and fold every other point to center. Brush again with egg whites and sprinkle with sugar. Place on a cookie sheet. Bake in 375-degree oven for 15 to 20 minutes or until brown. 50 pinwheels.

*Lucille Reid Marker, Robertsdale, Alabama*

## RAISIN-PECAN PIE

| | |
|---|---|
| 1/2 c. butter | 1 c. chopped pecans |
| 1 1/4 c. sugar | 1 tsp. vanilla |
| 3 eggs, separated | 1 unbaked pie shell |
| 1 c. chopped raisins | |

Cream the butter with 1 cup sugar. Add the beaten egg yolks. Beat 1 egg white until stiff and blend into the butter mixture. Add the raisins, pecans and 1/2 teaspoon vanilla and mix well. Turn into the pie shell. Bake at 400 degrees for 20 minutes. Beat the remaining egg whites until soft peaks form, then add remaining sugar gradually, beating until stiff peaks form. Blend in the remaining vanilla. Spread the meringue over top of pie. Reduce temperature to 325 degrees and bake for 15 minutes longer or until browned.

*Mrs. Jack Goforth, Dallas, Texas*

## RED CHERRY PIE

| | |
|---|---|
| 4 c. frozen cherries, thawed | 3/4 c. sugar |
| | 3 tbsp. cornstarch |

**Dash of salt**
**2 tbsp. butter**
**1 drop of almond extract**

**3 drops of red food**
  **coloring**
**Pastry for 2-crust pie**

Drain the cherries and reserve 1/4 cup syrup. Place the cherries and sugar in a saucepan and bring to a boil, stirring frequently. Mix the cornstarch and reserved cherry syrup and stir into cherry mixture. Remove from heat. Add the salt, butter, almond extract and food coloring and mix well. Cool. Line a 10-inch pie plate with pastry and fill with cherry mixture. Top with lattice crust and flute edge. Bake at 450 degrees for 10 minutes. Reduce temperature to 350 degrees and bake for about 45 minutes longer.

*Mrs. Larry Smith, Albany, Georgia*

## FIESTA RAISIN PIE

**2 c. dark seedless raisins**
**1 c. fresh cranberries**
**3/4 c. sugar**
**1/8 tsp. salt**
**1 1/2 tbsp. cornstarch**

**1/2 c. water**
**1  8 3/4-oz. can crushed**
  **pineapple**
**2 tbsp. butter or margarine**
**Pastry for 2-crust pie**

Grind the raisins and cranberries together. Combine the sugar, salt, cornstarch and water in a saucepan and cook, stirring, until mixture begins to clear. Add the undrained pineapple and raisin mixture and cook, stirring, until mixture comes to a boil. Remove from heat and blend in the butter. Line a 9-inch pie pan with pastry, building a high fluted edge. Roll remaining pastry to 7 1/2-inch circle. Prick with a fork and score with a pastry wheel. Place on a baking sheet. Place the raisin mixture in pastry-lined pie pan and place below oven center. Bake at 425 degrees for about 25 minutes. Bake the pastry round for 8 to 10 minutes or until brown. Cool. Place over filling and press lightly. Serve warm or cold. Garnish with whipped cream or ice cream, if desired.

## PEARS A LA CREME

6 fresh California Bartlett
  pears
2 tbsp. lemon juice
1 c. water
1  3 3/4-oz. package instant
  vanilla pudding mix
1 tbsp. brandy

2/3 c. (packed) brown sugar
3 tbsp. flour
1/8 tsp. salt
1/3 c. heavy cream
2 tbsp. butter or margarine
1/4 tsp. vanilla

Peel the pears and core from bottom with a grapefruit knife. Stand upright in a shallow baking pan. Pour the lemon juice and water over the pears and cover with foil. Bake at 400 degrees for 25 minutes. Drain and cool. Prepare pudding according to package directions, beating in brandy after thickened. Chill. Blend the sugar, flour and salt in a saucepan and stir in the cream. Bring to a boil over medium heat, stirring constantly. Cook for 2 minutes, then stir in the butter until melted. Remove from heat and stir in the vanilla. Spoon the pudding into 6 dessert dishes and stand the pears in center. Spoon sauce over pears. Sauce will thicken as it cools. Reheat, if necessary, to spoon over pears. One teaspoon vanilla may be substituted for the brandy. 6 servings.

*Photograph for this recipe on page 174.*

## CHOCOLATE-RICE PUDDING

2/3 c. rice
1 tbsp. melted butter
2 egg yolks, beaten
1 tsp. vanilla

1 c. cream
3 tbsp. cocoa
1 1/2 c. sugar

Cook the rice according to package directions. Mix the butter, egg yolks, vanilla and cream and add to the rice gradually, stirring constantly. Combine the cocoa and sugar and blend thoroughly, then add to the rice mixture. Place in a greased 9-inch square pan. Bake at 350 degrees for about 30 minutes.

Meringue

2 egg whites
1/4 tsp. vanilla

4 tbsp. sugar

Place the egg whites in a small bowl and beat until soft peaks form. Add the vanilla. Add the sugar gradually and beat until stiff peaks form. Spread over the pudding. Bake for about 10 minutes longer or until brown. 6 servings.

*Mrs. Gale Charles, El Reno, Oklahoma*

## DATE PUDDING

1 1/4 c. sifted flour
1/4 tsp. baking powder
1/4 tsp. salt

1 c. chopped pecans
1 pkg. dates, chopped
1 tsp. soda

| | |
|---|---|
| **1 c. boiling water** | **1 c. sugar** |
| **1/4 c. butter or margarine** | **1 egg** |

Preheat oven to 325 degrees. Sift the flour with baking powder and salt. Add the pecans and mix well. Place the dates in a bowl. Add soda and boiling water and let stand. Cream the butter and sugar in a bowl until light, then beat in egg. Add the flour mixture and mix thoroughly. Stir in the date mixture and pour into a greased 9-inch square pan. Bake for 1 hour. Serve warm with hard sauce or whipped cream.

*Mrs. I. B. Randolph, Asheville, North Carolina*

## PIONEER PUDDING

| | |
|---|---|
| **2 c. flour, sifted** | **3/4 c. seedless raisins** |
| **1/2 tsp. salt** | **1 egg, beaten** |
| **1/2 tsp. soda** | **1/2 c. water** |
| **1 c. ground beef suet** | **Caramel Sauce** |

Sift the flour, salt and soda together into a large bowl. Add the suet and raisins, stirring to coat well. Add the egg and water and mix well. Form into a loaf and wrap in aluminum foil. Pour water to a level of 2 inches in a kettle, then place the loaf on a rack and cover the kettle. Steam for 2 hours. Serve with Caramel Sauce.

### Caramel Sauce

| | |
|---|---|
| **Sugar** | **1/4 c. cornstarch** |
| **1 tsp. butter** | |

Pour 1/4 cup sugar in a heavy pan and cook until melted and brown, stirring constantly. Add the butter and 1/2 cup water, stirring until the butter is melted. Combine the cornstarch and 1/2 cup sugar in a bowl, then stir in 1 1/2 cups water. Add to the sugar mixture in the pan and bring to a boil. Cook until thick. Serve with the pudding. 8 servings.

*Mrs. Gertrude O'Steen, Waco, Texas*

## FRENCH CHOCOLATE

| | |
|---|---|
| **2 1/2   1-oz. squares unsweetened chocolate** | **1/2 tsp. salt** |
| **1/2 c. water** | **1/2 c. heavy cream, whipped** |
| **2/3 c. sugar** | **1 qt. hot milk** |

Combine the chocolate and water in a saucepan and cook over low heat, stirring, until the chocolate melts. Add the sugar and salt and bring to a boil. Reduce heat and simmer for 4 minutes. Cool to room temperature, then fold in whipped cream. Place 1 heaping tablespoon chocolate mixture in each cup and fill with hot milk. Stir and serve.

*Floy Williams, Albuquerque, New Mexico*

## RANCH COFFEE PUNCH

| | |
|---|---|
| 1/4 c. sugar | 5 c. milk |
| 1/3 c. instant coffee | 1 pt. vanilla ice cream |
| Dash of salt | Whipped cream |
| 1 tsp. vanilla | Nutmeg |

Combine the sugar, coffee, salt, vanilla and milk in a large bowl and stir until the sugar is dissolved. Chill. Spoon the ice cream into a punch bowl and pour the coffee mixture over the ice cream. Top with dollops of whipped cream and sprinkle with nutmeg. Serve in punch cups. 12 servings.

*Mrs. Deats Headlee, Denton, Texas*

## HOLIDAY EGGNOG

| | |
|---|---|
| 12 eggs, separated | 1 qt. milk |
| 1 1/2 c. sugar | 1 qt. bourbon |
| 1/4 tsp. salt | 1 c. rum |
| 1 qt. heavy cream, whipped | Nutmeg |

Place the egg yolks in a large bowl and beat until lemon colored. Add 1 cup sugar and the salt and beat until light. Beat the egg whites until stiff peaks form, adding remaining sugar gradually. Fold into the egg yolk mixture, then fold in the whipped cream. Add the milk, bourbon and rum, stirring carefully. Pour into a large container and chill. Let mellow for at least 1 week before serving. Place in a punch bowl. Ladle into small cups and sprinkle with nutmeg. 30 servings.

*Eva Bowden, Houston, Texas*

## CHAMPAGNE PUNCH BOWL

| | |
|---|---|
| 2  7-oz. bottles club soda | 2 c. sauterne |
| 1 fifth champagne | 1 c. cognac |
| 1 1/2 lb. seedless green grapes | 2 tbsp. sugar |
| | 6 strawberries, washed |

Chill the club soda and the champagne. Wash and dry the grapes and place on a small tray, then freeze. Combine the sauterne, cognac and sugar and stir until the sugar is dissolved. Chill for several hours, then pour into a punch bowl and stir in the soda. Add the grapes and strawberries. Stir the champagne into punch just before serving. Sixteen 4-ounce servings.

*Mrs. Henrietta S. Cobb, Birmingham, Alabama*

## CRANBERRY PUNCH

| | |
|---|---|
| 1  1-pt. bottle cranberry juice | 1  46-oz. can pineapple juice |
| 1 1/2 c. sugar | 1  1-qt. bottle ginger ale |
| 1  12-oz. can apricot nectar | Drop of red food coloring |

Pour the cranberry juice into a saucepan and add the sugar. Cook and stir until the sugar is dissolved. Remove from heat and add the nectar and pineapple juice. Add the ginger ale and food coloring just before serving. Pour over a block of ice in a punch bowl. 20 servings.

*Mrs. Walter R. Irwin, Amarillo, Texas*

## PINEAPPLE FRAPPE

1   1-lb. 4-oz. can crushed
   pineapple

1 c. canned pineapple juice
16 ice cubes

Whirl all ingredients in electric blender at high speed until smooth. 6 servings.

*Photograph for this recipe below.*

## PINEAPPLE MELON BATIDAS

1 sm. cantaloupe
1   1-lb. 4-oz. can crushed
   pineapple

12 ice cubes
Chilled sparkling water

Peel and seed the cantaloupe and cut into chunks. Whirl the cantaloupe, pineapple and ice cubes in electric blender at high speed until smooth. Fill serving glasses 2/3 full. Add sparkling water and stir. 6 servings.

## DAIQUIRI PUNCH

3 sm. cans frozen limeade
2 c. pineapple juice
2 c. water

3 bottles lemon-lime
carbonated beverage
2 c. vodka

Mix all ingredients in a large metal container. Freeze, stirring occasionally, until ice crystals have formed around edge. Place in a punch bowl and serve in punch cups. 12 servings.

*Bettye Mires, San Antonio, Texas*

## MINT PARTY PUNCH

3 qt. unsweetened pineapple
juice
Juice of 8 lemons
Juice of 8 oranges
Juice of 3 limes
2 c. sugar

1 c. mint leaves (opt.)
4 qt. ginger ale
4 qt. carbonated water
2 c. quartered Bing
cherries (opt.)

Combine the fruit juices, sugar and mint leaves in a large bowl and mix thoroughly. Chill, then strain. Add the ginger ale, carbonated water and cherries just before serving. Pour over a large cake of ice in a punch bowl. Garnish with thin slices of lemon and lime. 35 servings.

*Mrs. C. W. Zander, Riesel, Texas*

## STRAWBERRY DELIGHT PUNCH

1 qt. ginger ale
1 1/4 c. pineapple juice
Juice of 3 lemons

1/2 c. orange juice
1 pkg. frozen strawberries
1 pt. vanilla ice cream

Chill the ginger ale and juices. Thaw and mash the strawberries. Place in a punch bowl and add half the ice cream. Mix well, then stir in ginger ale and fruit juices. Garnish the punch with remaining ice cream. 15 servings.

*Eleanor Melichar, Maryland, Oklahoma*

## TOMATO COCKTAIL

1 bushel ripe tomatoes
3 lge. bunches celery,
finely chopped
3 hot peppers

2 lge. onions, finely
chopped
1 c. sugar
1/4 c. salt

Combine the tomatoes, celery, peppers and onions in a large kettle and cook until soft. Strain through a colander and then through a sieve. Add the sugar and salt to juice in a large kettle and bring to a boil. Cook for 8 minutes, then pour into hot sterilized jars and seal. Serve cold. 16 quarts.

*Mrs. Eunice Bishop, Florence, Colorado*